If you engage in travel, you will arrive.

—Ibn Arabi (1165–1240)

Bill Viola

Reasons for Knocking at an Empty House

Writings 1973–1994

Edited by Robert Violette in collaboration with the author

Introduction by Jean-Christophe Ammann

The MIT Press

Anthony d'Offay Gallery London

Second Printing, 1998

Text © 1995 Bill Viola and Anthony d'Offay Gallery
"Violence and Beauty" © 1993 Jean Christophe Ammann

First published in the United States in 1995 by
The MIT Press, Cambridge, Massachusetts,
in association with the Anthony d'Offay Gallery, London

All rights reserved. No part of this book may be reproduced
in any form or by any electronic or mechanical means (including
photocopying, recording, or information storage and retrieval) without
permission in writing from the publisher.

Designed by Peter B. Willberg
Typeset by ACC Computing
Printed and bound in Italy by Grafiche Milani

Frontispiece: Bill Viola on location in New York during production of
Sodium Vapor (including Constellations and Oracle), 1979, videotape,
color, stereo sound, 15:14 minutes. Photo: Kira Perov.

Cover: Bill Viola in *What Is Not and That Which Is* (detail), 1992, video/
sound installation. Edition 1: Centro Cultural Arte Contemporaneo,
Mexico City. Photo: Kira Perov.

Library of Congress Cataloging-in-Publication Data

Viola, Bill, 1951–
    Reasons for knocking at an empty house: writings 1973–1994 /
Bill Viola; edited by Robert Violette in collaboration with the author;
introduction by Jean-Christophe Ammann.

    p.   cm.
    Includes chronology, bibliographical references and index.
ISBN 0-262-72025-6 (pb: acid-free paper)
    1. Viola, Bill, 1951–   —Philosophy. 2. Viola, Bill,
1951–   —Themes, motives. 1. Violette, Robert. II. Title.
N6537.V56A35   1995   95-14426
700.92—dc20   CIP

Contents

Preface

Bill Viola has said "Everything I have ever published, or created as an artist, has come from these books." He was referring to the collection of notebooks that for the last 25 years he has used to record and develop his ideas for videotapes and installations. In addition to the conceptual and technical explorations that are the basis of his work, these books also contain comments on contemporary culture and the state of video art, observations from travels abroad, and countless commentaries and transcriptions from books on subjects as varied as religion and history, perception and memory, landscape and philosophy. This publication brings together, for the first time, previously unpublished notebook entries and project proposals, as well as published essays, interviews, and statements.

The installations and videotapes we have chosen to reproduce in this book are accompanied by descriptions written by Viola, or by complementary notebook entries and drawings. This juxtaposition of texts and images has been made in close collaboration with the artist in order to draw out relationships that exist between his works and writings, or to emphasize particular themes. The contents are carefully built up to give a sense of the artist's progress of ideas over time.

We would like to express our grateful thanks to Bill Viola for his unfailing commitment to the project, for allowing us unprecedented access to his archives, and for his good humor and patience at a time when he was simultaneously preparing to represent the United States at the 46th Venice Biennale. We are also deeply grateful to Kira Perov, the artist's wife, for her tireless editorial collaboration and fine photographs.

We would like to thank Jean-Christophe Ammann for his insightful introduction to Viola's work; Peter B. Willberg for his design; Jim Cohan and Anthony d'Offay for their support and guidance; and also Dianna Pescar, Martin Friedman, Michael Nash, Otto Neumaier, Alexander Pühringer, Jörg Zutter, Irena Hoare, Amanda Sharrad, Raymond Bellour, Russell Ferguson, Stephen Edwards, Sue Malin, Andrew Hunter, André Iten, and Valérie Leuba.

Robert Violette

Acknowledgements

With the many interpreters, communicators, and "middlemen" operating in contemporary art and culture, it is unfortunately a rare opportunity for an artist to be able to speak to the public directly about their work and ideas in their own words. This book is such an opportunity, and I sincerely thank the Anthony d'Offay Gallery, Anthony and Anne, Jim Cohan, and especially Robert Violette, for their commitment and support for this project. I thank Robert Violette for his many long hours and tireless devotion to the highest standards of quality in this book, both physical and conceptual, and for his personal sensitivity and professional objectivity in reviewing the material from the notebooks, which no one previously has been given access to.

I want to thank Kira Perov for her insight, too many late nights, and dedication to insuring that this book, as with everything she does, would be the best possible object of her efforts and the most accurate reflection of the work and ideas we both share and care deeply about. Her photographic eye is on these pages, her concerned hand has touched every detail, and her heart, love, and guiding spirit is the major part of the life we share together with our work and family.

I also want to thank all of the editors, publishers, and interviewers who first gave the opportunity to write and to publish the texts in this book.

And finally, I want to thank all of my teachers, past, present, and future, for their guidance, knowledge, and inspiration. They are present in every word, and make me feel that everything I do or write is not really "mine" in the most positive and affirming way. It is my hope that the words and images in this book may keep the wheel turning and perhaps may inspire others as I have been inspired.

Bill Viola
Long Beach, California, 1995

Illustrations

I Do Not Know What It Is I Am Like, 1986, videotape.

Violence and Beauty *Jean-Christophe Ammann*

Within the framework of Bill Viola's video installations the large picture projection is a necessity. They are not enlarged pictures. They are sequences of images, conceived on a large scale, which are all, in different and sometimes brutal ways, aimed at the body of the viewer.

In the videotape *Chott el-Djerid (A Portrait in Light and Heat)*, 1979, the beauty of landscape, water, light, and color is so unbearable that one wants to scream. The beauty arises not from the interplay of the elements, but from the conceptual "logic," which irresistibly draws the viewer into a cosmos in which he recognizes himself again. The beauty that fascinates and enthralls us is not an end in itself. We immerse ourselves in the beauty without losing ourselves in it. We recognize it and are at the same time absorbed in it. We are not afraid of it, out of fear of ourselves. The images plumb our profoundest motives. The *fata morgana* of a person dying of thirst turns into images that are seen as if under water. Throwing a stone into a hole in the ice is like jumping into a mirror.

The scream I have just spoken of, this expression of the body in the face of an overwhelming emotion, this archaic scream of a girl in the empty concourse of the Union Railroad Station in Los Angeles, occurs in *Anthem*, 1983, in response, as it were, to the escalator that moves rhythmically, smoothly, and with the utmost elegance. This scream is violence, as Jean Genêt defines it: "Violence and life are virtually synonymous. The sprouting corn breaking through the icy soil, the sparrow's beak piercing the shell of the egg, the impregnation of a woman, the birth of a child—all testify to violence."[1] The girl's scream goes right through us, repeating itself and constantly starting afresh. The scream is the will to live.

Death is omnipresent, but not as a theme. Once, in *Hatsu Yume (First Dream)*, 1981, a spotlight aimed fiercely at the viewer

---

1. Jean Genêt, "Violence et brutalité," *Le Monde*, 2 September 1977. The detailed article on the title page relates to the Red Army Faction (RAF) and conditions prevailing in Germany at the time, and to the conflict of state, society, and opposition.

from a trawler on a nocturnal fishing expedition repeats the movements of dying squids. The constant presence of death gives Bill Viola's work its transcendency. Death is always transition and transformation.

In *Angel's Gate*, 1989, when a tenement block is blown up or a candle is blown out, when a fruit falls from a branch or a slaughtered deer is exploited, when a hand seeks a purchase under water or a child painfully moves to the surface, when a child is born or the bars of a gate dissolve in light—these are images of transition, of a violent breakthrough to life. Jean Genêt distinguishes between violence and brutality: so too in Bill Viola's work violence is present only as a constitutive part of beauty and death as transition. There is a masterly treatment of the theme in his *I Do Not Know What It Is I Am Like*, 1986. He marvels at what nature has produced. He marvels as a child marvels, but at the same time he condenses this wonderment in a highly complex structure of associations. The film lasts for an hour and a half, and the viewer himself never emerges from his wonderment. Bill Viola's art consists in showing us bison as mountains or shifting dunes, the eyes of exotic birds as the "origin of life" (Courbet), somewhere between *nature morte* and *tableau vivant*. The snail-shell in a little boat, hung with jewelry, looks like a Dutch still-life; some time later the snail creeps out of its shell, leaving the boat and the field of vision. Yet what is dead? What is alive? *Nature morte/nature vivante?* Insects eat their way into an animal carcass reduced to no more than a head. Before our eyes, people in a trance state let their cheeks, lips, arms, and backs be pierced by small metal rods; in order to overcome death they walk across a red-hot carpet of ash. A chick breaks out of its eggshell in order to escape death and, lying on its back, kicks itself into life. Late at night an elephant's trunk seizes the artist's inspiring teacup and enters his studio, as in a dream—menacing, real, soothing. The camera moves under water. The fish becomes a bird in the form of a helicopter. The flight leads from the Fiji Islands to the far north of Canada. The fish is carried like a metal insignium through mountain valleys and forests. The helicopter—which one never sees during the flight—lands in a clearing. The fish, deposited in the clearing, turns out to be a real fish. Instantly insects and birds fall upon it. Before long it merges with the forest floor. The videotape begins with drops of water. The water has been dripping for millions of years, forming stalactite caves. Forms appear as in an opened body—bloody, veined, slippery. Creeping insects feed on the precious liquid.

Bill Viola does not simulate anything. Through the telephoto lens the images begin to dissolve, to fluctuate, to break up into a sea of colors, then become suddenly precise; they plunge into the water and are reflected in the water, in the eyes of the animals; they become painting, art history, a document, pitiless reality, dream and reality. What is shown is never an end in itself: it is as though history, determined by fate, were bound to come to an end, yet this never happens, because everything repeatedly starts all over again. Death is transition. A perpetual beginning and ending, violence and beauty. In Bill Viola's cyclic thinking there is no place for brutality, because it is a deformation of violence.

Bill Viola's work deals with life, with survival, with the will to live, and hence also with death. The birth of his son and the death of his mother in *The Passing*, 1991, are not to be understood sentimentally in accordance with the familiar pattern by which feelings are represented. They are part of a comprehensive vision of emergence and evanescence. Pain and joy are not discrete or mutually independent sensations. They are occurrences that are transcended in a concept of transition, at once keen and congruent.

To this extent it was only a short step to transferring the pictorial sensuality of the images into a dimension in which bodily sensation is directly addressed in spatial terms. I well remember the shock I felt on seeing *Room for St. John of the Cross*, 1983, at the Museum of Modern Art in New York. In the middle of the room I saw a small square stone house with a single window, surrounded by great fissured mountain chains, deep ravines, and menacing clouds. In this house was a simple table, on which stood a water carafe, a glass, and a monitor. The image, color, resembled a still. It showed a high plateau with stony soil and few trees. If one put one's head through the small window, the noise of the storm abruptly abated and one suddenly noticed that the leaves were moving gently, almost imperceptibly, in the wind.

In the course of nine months of imprisonment and torture, St. John of the Cross (1542–1591) had transformed the raging of his soul and his faith into a grandiose poetry that is still valid today. That day I could look at nothing else. I forgot the much advertised Frank Stella exhibition just one floor below. I returned to my hotel through the streets of New York, which seemed for all the world like deep ravines in a mountain range, carrying in my heart the trembling treeleaves on that bleak and lofty plateau.

That was the start of my friendship with Bill Viola. In 1988, long after it had been decided that he was to create a room for the Museum of Modern Art in Frankfurt am Main, I saw *The Sleep of Reason*, 1988, in Pittsburgh during the Carnegie International exhibition. In a high, brightly-lit room a bouquet of flowers and a monitor stood on an antique chest. The black-and-white image showed the face of a sleeping man, sometimes a sleeping woman. Dreams furrowed the sleeping faces like the blowing wind. Unexpectedly the light went out and the image disappeared from the monitor. Enormous images appeared on the walls, accompanied by corresponding noises: burning forests, fleeing animals, people under water trying to orient themselves and moving upwards, houses collapsing. Suddenly the light came back on, and the faces of the sleepers reappeared on the monitor. It was at once clear to me how we carry death within us, day after day, and how strongly our existence is affected by fear—not of something specific, but fear pure and simple. No matter how frightening and literally breathtaking these images are, they are also comforting. Perhaps because of their remoteness from everyday experience and their over-whelming beauty. Perhaps also because they reconcile us with our-selves. An artist comes along and tells us that we are not superhuman, not heroes, that man was not invented by television, by "Dynasty" or "Dallas." Reconciliation with ourselves—catharsis—is not intimidating: rather, it mobilizes forces that are truly our own, not clichés foisted upon us.

It may happen that one enters *The Stopping Mind*, 1991, at the Frankfurt Museum of Modern Art, in a moment of quiet. On four enormous and related screens one sees images frozen in movement, their beauty reminiscent of abstract paintings or galactic constellations. However, they may also be images of the kind that are glimpsed only for a fraction of a second and have long since disappeared by the time one is aware of them, as though still attached to the retina. Then suddenly one is terrified as the whole room begins to move and one hears deafening noises. One imagines that one is in the middle of an earthquake, that one's neck is being twisted round. One plunges into a swaying tulip-field, rushes through a room, knocking over a table and glasses.

Just as suddenly quiet returns: one finds oneself facing images frozen in motion and accordingly blurred. Then suddenly the room is in motion again, swaying, jerking, cracking, bursting.

In the center of the room one hears, over an invisible parabolic loudspeaker, the voice of the artist whispering directly into one's ear:

"... there is nothing but black. There is nothing but silence. I can feel my body. I am lying in a dark space. I can feel my body lying here. I am awake. I feel my breathing, in and out, quiet and regular. I can feel my breathing. I move my body. I slowly roll over and look up. I see nothing. There is nothing. There is no light. There is no darkness. There is no volume. There is no distance. There is no sound. There is no silence. There is the sensation of space, but there is no image. There is the sensation of my body with its extension and the weight pressing down. I can feel my body pressing down. And there is this silent voice ringing in the darkness. A voice ringing in the blackness. I bring my hand up to my face. I move my hand but there is nothing. I move my hand back and forth and I feel the slight movement of air across my cheek. The air moving across my cheek but I see nothing. Nothing in the blackness. My body does not move. I lie completely still. I don't move. I don't move my body, not even to swallow. Slowly I become aware of the loss of sensation in my limbs. The loss of sensation of my body. I don't know how long I have been lying like this. I don't know how long I've been lying here. Lying in the silence. I imagine the black space. I imagine the silence. The darkness of no image. The silence of no sound. I imagine my body. I imagine my body in this dark space. The space is like a large black cloud of soft cotton, silent and weightless. A soft black mass slowly pressing in around my body. I can feel it slowly pressing in around my body. Pressing in around me. Everything is closing down. Closing down around my body. It's closing down around me until only a small opening remains. A small opening around my face. Only a small opening around my face remains. Outside of this—the oblivion of nothing. The oblivion of nothing. Outside of this there is only darkness. There is only blackness. There is nothing. I am like a body under water breathing through the small opening of a straw. A body under water breathing. Breathing through a small opening. Finally, I let that go. I let it go. I feel myself submerge. Submerging into the blackness. Letting go. Sinking down into the black mass. Submerging into the void. The senseless and weightless void. The great comfort of the senseless and weightless void, where ..."

The voice speaks of the "darkness of no image. The silence of no sound," and around this voice, which invades the body of the listener and viewer, the images rage and whir. Images that we know from our earliest memories—water, fire, caves, canyons between buildings, nocturnal apparitions aimed directly at bodily sensation, leaping at the body, just like the voice. (The noises were recorded at the time of filming, then electronically amplified and edited.)

The connection with *Room for St. John of the Cross* is becoming evident. The voice has replaced the bare cell of the visionary. Let us understand precisely what has happened here. It is not a question of artistic overweening, but of intensifying the physical presence of the work, of linking word and image. Ultimately the house, the table, and the monitor in *Room for St. John of the Cross* are representative, narrative elements. In *The Stopping Mind* the artist, using his own voice, could consistently only relate his own bodily experience to a variety of his pictorial experiences and thereby create a link between dream, imagination, and reality. This is not intended as an evaluation. But in *The Stopping Mind* Bill Viola has taken another decisive step.

Since the work was conceived from the beginning as a permanent video installation, it seems to me appropriate to consider the aspect of permanence. The images, stored on four video laser discs and projected by four video projectors, stop and start synchronically according to a principle of chance, which is so arranged that the duration of the still image is in inverse proportion to the moving image; the still image only rarely lasts for as long as 30 seconds. This proportion arises simply from the circumstance of receptive bearability. At the end of each sequence of images the chance stopping and starting is automatically reprogrammed, so that for years it will be possible to see constantly changing still images, similar and different. This component is important, not least because, by using this time structure, Bill Viola for the first time introduces the generative principles of order and disorder—necessity and chance—the principles that determine our daily life, like seeking and finding.

"I am like a body under water, breathing through the small opening of a straw. A body under water breathing. Breathing through a small opening. Finally, I let that go. I let it go. I feel myself submerge. Submerging into the blackness. Letting go. Sinking down into the black mass. Submerging into the void. The senseless and weightless void. . . ." This last part of the text for *The Stopping Mind* is the theme for *The Arc of Ascent*, 1992, the work he created for "documenta 9." How often we wake from anxiety dreams, desperately fighting for breath and afraid of suffocating. The three video images—projected immediately above one another, 23 feet high and 10 feet wide—of a clothed male body under water radiate extraordinary comfort. There are sounds of water gurgling and flowing. Only gradually do the outlines of the body take shape. It never occurs to one to think that one is looking at a corpse. The constant fluctuation of the water models the body and its clothing in extreme slow motion and reveals its dimensions, and when it suddenly whizzes upwards in the second part—the reverse of diving—the water begins to darken from below. In a long sequence the darkness rises. It is as though dusk were slowly passing over into night, as though a raised horizon were covered with storm clouds. The darkness is not black: it pulsates, gurgles porously and is shot through with colors. One cannot but recall pictures by Clyfford Still, and suddenly one becomes aware that here we have an artist painting a grandiose picture by means of video projection.

Whatever video may be, Bill Viola has given the medium its dignity, just as painters once promoted perspective or others—one thinks of Seurat—conferred autonomy on color.

Excursus

Violence: In a New York City street we see a man. He loads his gun, takes aim and fires into the air. Smoke emerges from the barrel. The report is clear and close. The man walks on, comes towards us and fires again. The report becomes dull and recedes. Again he walks on and fires again. The report becomes muffled, as if coming from a great distance. The last shot sounds like a distant echo from an indeterminable direction.

The man approaches us, but we never see him clearly. As he approaches, the sense of his action becomes alien as a form of consciousness. The absurd refutes itself in a reverse movement of image, action, and noise (*Truth Through Mass Individuation*, 1976).

In *Anthem* the girl's scream, electronically modified, "underscores" the whole tape. It is a frightful scream, now like a lowing, now like a roar, now like a howl, now like a muffled, prolonged, death-rattle, first rising, then fading. But it is only at the end of the tape that the scream can be seen to be uttered by the girl, when her hitherto silent mouth opens and we hear the long drawn-out sounds that struck terror into the viewer's ear and embody both the violence and the beauty of life.

Proportion, balance (beauty)

The erotic animal-like movements of the oil-well hydraulics in *Anthem*: calm, steady, unhurried, persevering without quickening. In *Chott el-Djerid*: the man walking, sinking, staggering, wading in the snow. In *Hatsu Yume*: the boulder with piled-up stones. It appears immense, perhaps 10 feet high. Clouds scud across the sky above it. People struggle against the storm. They stride past the boulder on their way to the top—small figures by comparison. Only later, seeing it beside a little girl, do we realize that it is perhaps no more than two feet high.

In *Chott el-Djerid* and *I Do Not Know What It Is I Am Like*: the architecture in the landscape, as though nature had *conceived* houses, tombs of marabouts, small mosques, as though the groups of trees on hilltops had created the huge shape of the bison in their own image.

The sensual tubes of light projected by moving cars at night: not a mega-city impression, not an aesthetic end in itself, but an immediate image of the flow of life, like the long snake in *Anthem*, winding its way up the tree-trunk and disappearing into a hole in a branch.

Transition

The throwing of a stone into the water and the immersion of the camera in *Chott el-Djerid*. The dive in *The Reflecting Pool*, 1977–79, which does not take place because, in a fairly long sequence, the diver dissolves into mid-dive into the picture and into nature (the forest) and at some later point, as if by chance, leaves the pool. The skeleton of the fish in *I Do Not Know What It Is I Am Like*, disintegrating in the soil of the forest. In *Anthem* the enormous growth removed by surgeons from a woman's body, which has been opened up with a motor saw but will go on living, as the beating heart proves. In the same videotape the painful eye operation that helps a patient regain his sight. What an animal's eyes mean for its survival is shown in *I Do Not Know What It Is I Am Like*: eyes that move with lightning speed, their pupils dilating and contracting, eyes that turn inwards, as though listening, and suddenly strike without warning, eyes that cannot be distracted, that are tensely attentive, obdurate, statuesque. And again in *Anthem*: the bodies of the sunbathers, the beach games, the beating heart in a sun-tanned chest. This is how *Anthem* ends.

Translated from the German by David McLintock

"FRANKLY, DESPITE the GLIB TRANSLITERATIVE CLARITY
OF the ORIENTALISTS, WE CANNOT HOPE to UNDERSTAND
the GREATER PART of the 'TAWASIN'. The ILLUSION
OF UNDERSTANDING THUS GOES WITH the
ORIENTALISTS. FOR EXAMPLE: 'FANA' MEANS
'A STATE OF ANNIHILATION'. SO IT IS EXPLAINED.
BUT WHAT IS <u>FANA</u>? THIS IS NOT A LINGUISTIC
OR EPISTEMOLOGICAL PROBLEM."

MUQADDEM 'ABD AI-QADIR as-SUFI

Introduction The <u>TAWASIN</u>

"IF the ONLY TOOL YOU HAVE IS A HAMMER,
YOU TEND to TREAT EVERYTHING AS IF IT
WERE A NAIL."

ABRAHAM MASLOW

" THERE ARE THREE WAYS OF PERCEPTION.
ONE WAY OF PERCEPTION BELONGS to the SURFACE
OF the MIND; THAT IS THOUGHT. THOUGHT
MANIFESTS To OUR MIND WITH A DEFINITE FORM,
LINE AND COLOUR.
        THE NEXT WAY OF PERCEPTION IS FEELING.
IT IS FELT BY QUITE ANOTHER PART OF the HEART;
IT IS FELT BY the DEPTH OF the HEART, NOT BY
the SURFACE. AND THEREFORE the MORE the HEART
QUALITY IS WAKENED IN A PERSON, the MORE
HE PERCEIVES the FEELINGS OF OTHERS. THAT
PERSON IS SENSITIVE, BECAUSE to HIM the

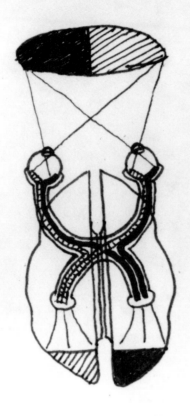

THOUGHTS AND FEELINGS OF OTHERS ARE CLEAR. THE
PERSON WHO LIVES ON THE SURFACE DOES NOT PERCEIVE
FEELINGS CLEARLY. ALSO, THERE IS A DIFFERENCE BETWEEN
THE EVOLUTION OF THE TWO, OF THE ONE WHO LIVES ON
THE SURFACE OF THE HEART AND THE OTHER WHO LIVES
IN THE DEPTH; IN OTHER WORDS OF THE ONE LIVING
IN HIS MIND AND THE OTHER LIVING IN THE HEART.

BUT THERE IS A THIRD WAY OF PERCEPTION, WHICH
IS NOT EVEN BY FEELING, WHICH MAY BE CALLED A
SPIRITUAL LANGUAGE. THIS FEELING COMES FROM THE
DEEPEST DEPTH OF THE HEART. IT IS THE VOICE
OF THE SPIRIT. IT DOES NOT BELONG TO THE

(CONTINUED AFTER NEXT PAGE)

... LANTERN, IT BELONGS to the LIGHT; BUT IN the LANTERN IT BECOMES MORE DISTINCT AND CLEAR. AND THIS PERCEPTION MAY BE CALLED INTUITION, THERE IS NO BETTER NAME FOR IT. IN ORDER to STUDY LIFE FULLY THESE THREE PERCEPTIONS MUST BE DEVELOPED. THEN ALONE ONE IS ABLE to STUDY LIFE FULLY; AND IT IS BY STUDYING IT FULLY THAT ONE IS ABLE to FORM A JUDGMENT UPON IT. "

KHAN — COSMIC LANGUAGE

"THE WORLD IS SEEN AS A MANIFESTATION OF FORMS COMPOSED OF SEPARATE TRANSITORY ELEMENTS, FORMS WHICH ARE THEMSELVES TRANSITORY TRANSIENT AND HENCE ILLUSORY. ALL PHENOMENA ARE ONLY STATES OF MOMENTARY EXISTENCE IN A STREAM OF CONTINUOUS ARISING AND DECAY. THE WORLD THAT APPEARS to OUR EYES CAN BE SEEN WITH THE INNER EYE OF CLAIRVOYANCY IN ALL ITS CAUSAL RELATIONSHIPS; IT CAN BE SURVEYED BY THE INNER EYE IN ITS PAST, PRESENT, AND FUTURE STAGES. THE IDENTITY OF THE VOID AND THE MANIFEST, REPEATEDLY EMPHASIZED IN THE LITERATURE OF "PERFECT WISDOM WHICH HAS ATTAINED THE OTHER SHORE," ENABLES THE ARTIST to SEE THE WORLD OF PHENOMENA AS A VISION, AS A STATE YET to BE REALIZED, IN WHICH FORM AND COLOR ARE EXCHANGED AT WILL IN

ACCORDANCE WITH THE INTENSITY OF CONTEMPLATION.
THE VALUE OF THE COLORS IS RELATIVE AND ADJUSTS
ITSELF TO THE ASPECT OF THE MOMENT AND NOT TO
EXTERNAL REALITY. SIMILARLY, MEDITATIONS ON
REMOTE LANDS OF THE BUDDHAS AND THE CELESTIAL
REALMS OF THE BODHISATTVAS OPEN UP TO THE
ARTIST A VISIONARY WORLD OF DIVINE SPHERES
TO BE EXPERIENCED IN A SUPER-SENSUAL WAY,
SPHERES WHICH HE THEN TRIES TO DEPICT IN
TRANSPARENT COLOURS."

DETLEF INGO LAUF
TIBETAN SACRED ART

" ... THE TRUTH IS YOURSELF, BUT NOT YOUR
MERE BODILY SELF,
YOUR REAL SELF IS HIGHER THAN 'YOU'
AND 'ME'.
THIS VISIBLE 'YOU' WHICH YOU FANCY to be YOURSELF
IS LIMITED IN PLACE, THE REAL 'YOU' IS NOT
LIMITED.
WHY, O PEARL, LINGER YOU TREMBLING IN
YOUR SHELL?
ESTEEM NOT YOURSELF MERE SUGAR-CANE, BUT
REAL SUGAR.
THIS OUTWARD 'YOU' IS FOREIGN TO YOUR
REAL 'YOU';
CLING TO YOUR REAL SELF, QUIT THIS
DUAL SELF.
YOUR LAST SELF ATTAINS TO YOUR FIRST (REAL)
SELF ONLY THROUGH YOUR ATTENDING EARNESTLY
TO THAT UNION. YOUR REAL SELF LIES HID
BENEATH YOUR OUTWARD SELF, FOR ———

VIGIL - BURNING of the OIL LAMP,
          WAITING FOR SOMETHING
          to RETURN.

UNFILLED - the MIDNIGHT SESSIONS

IT IS A SPIRITUAL PHENOMENON to BE
IN AN ACCIDENT OR to GET KILLED.
[VIDEOTAPE - 5 HOUR ACCIDENT FRAME]

III.   PREFACE to VIDEOTAPES

The IDEA OF SPIRITUALISM is CHIEFLY the
IDEA OF HIGHER MIND — BEYOND GENIUS
OR ANY OTHER CATEGORY OF THOUGHT SO
CULTURALLY DEFINED: The HUMAN MIND
IS CAPABLE OF REACHING INCREDIBLE LEVELS
OF A HIGHER KNOWLEDGE, WHICH SOME
CALL UNION WITH GOD. IN ANY EVENT,
THESE LEVELS ARE NOT CULTURALLY
DETERMINED, BUT ARE TO VARYING DEGREES
UNIVERSAL, COMMON to PEOPLES ALL OVER
the WORLD. IT IS THROUGH THIS CHANNEL,
the PSYCHOLOGICAL METHOD, that THE FOLLOWING
IMAGES ATTEMPT AN APPROACH to the
BEAUTY AND DEPTH of the HUMAN MIND.

"I AM the SERVANT OF HIM WHO LOOKS
        INTO HIMSELF."
                                    Jalal-al Din RUMI

Information 1973

Information is the manifestation of an aberrant electronic nonsignal passing through the video switcher in a normal color TV studio, and being retrieved at various points along its path. It is the result of a technical mistake made while working in the studio late one night, when the output of a videotape recorder was accidentally routed through the studio switcher and back into its own input. When the record button was pressed, the machine tried to record itself. The resulting electronic perturbations affected everything else in the studio: color appeared where there was no color signal, there was sound where there was no audio connected, and every button punched on the video switcher created a different effect. After this error was discovered and traced back, it became possible to sit at the switcher as if it were a musical instrument and learn to "play" this nonsignal. Once the basic parameters were understood, a second videotape recorder was used to record the result. *Information* is that tape.

—1973

Previous page: *Information*, 1973, videotape

IMAGE BANK -   TWO BANKS OF SIX MONITORS STAND FACING EACH OTHER.
THE TWO CENTER MONITORS IN EACH BANK FORM THE
FOCAL POINT OF THE PIECE. IN BANK #1 (PHOTO 4),
THE CENTRAL POINT **IS** THE CONVERGENCE OF THE UP AND
DOWN ESCALATORS. IN BANK #2 (PHOTO 5), THE FOCUS
IS THE VIEWER'S OWN IMAGE CASCADING INTO AND OUT
OF ITSELF VIA TWO AUTOMATIC SCANNING CAMERAS.
THE THEMES OF CONVERGING AND DIVERGING MOTION
ARE INTEGRATED INTO THE ENTIRE MATRIX BY FOUR
OTHER STATIONARY CAMERAS.

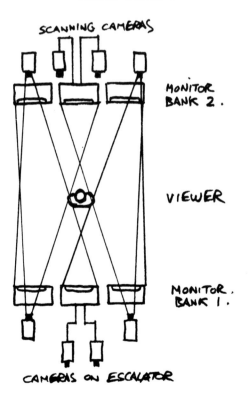

SCANNING CAMERAS

MONITOR
BANK 2.

VIEWER

MONITOR.
BANK 1.

CAMERAS ON ESCALATOR

IMAGE BANK WAS SET UP JANUARY 7, 1974 THROUGH FEBRUARY 1, 1974
AT LINCOLN FIRST BANK, ROCHESTER N.Y.

Late one night, I was working with a magnifying glass and a single spotlight in my studio. I noticed that I could make some interesting luminous figures by focusing the light onto the wall with the lens. Suddenly, for no particular reason, I decided to put my head in place of the wall and focus those light patterns into my eye. At first I was disappointed. "Nothing" happened. Expecting some kind of dazzling display, all I saw was the room with the spotlight in it, undergoing slight degrees of distortion as I moved the lens. Then, like a shock wave, I realized that the image I saw of the room was *the same* as those light patterns I saw on the wall. In the latter case, the surface of my retina had been substituted for the surface of the wall, and those luminous forms had been interpreted by the organizing matrix of rods and cones in my eye, and then by my brain, as "the room with the spotlight in it." The light was the same in both cases, it just was decoded differently. I realized then that the visual world exists in all places in all directions at once; where we intercept this array of reflected light determines our "own point of view." There is literally a world within every grain of sand, within every reflection on every object.

—Note, Florence, Italy, 1975

The finished tape itself lies somewhere between the time and place of the moment of recording and my own mental image or projection of the outcome at that time. Standing there with a camera and recorder, I was fascinated by the fact that the playback reality of those recorded moments was to be found more in the space through the lens of the camera, on the surface of the vidicon tube, than out in the space where I was standing, hearing, smelling, watching, touching. For me, the focus of those moments (when the recorder was going) was on that magic surface, and my conscious concentration was aimed there, inside the camera. I realized that it offered the only way out of the scene I was in, through a little aperture and off into another place that would exist beyond the present time and place.

I also knew that access to this "chute" would allow me to do things I could only *think* of doing normally—such as traveling back with a bell-ring at the speed of sound, or controlling the course of the sun through the sky. Recording something, I feel, is not so much capturing an existing thing as it is creating a new one. I want to have more of an input in this process of creation than simply to determine where to point the camera. An active position enables me to exceed my own physical limitations and manifest my imaginings, which then serves more to really transform myself than just to change the images existing within the confines of the monitor screen. Each time a tape is finished it is like the release of a long-held breath, and with it, naturally, is signaled the need for another.

—Note on *Red Tape*, videotape, 1975

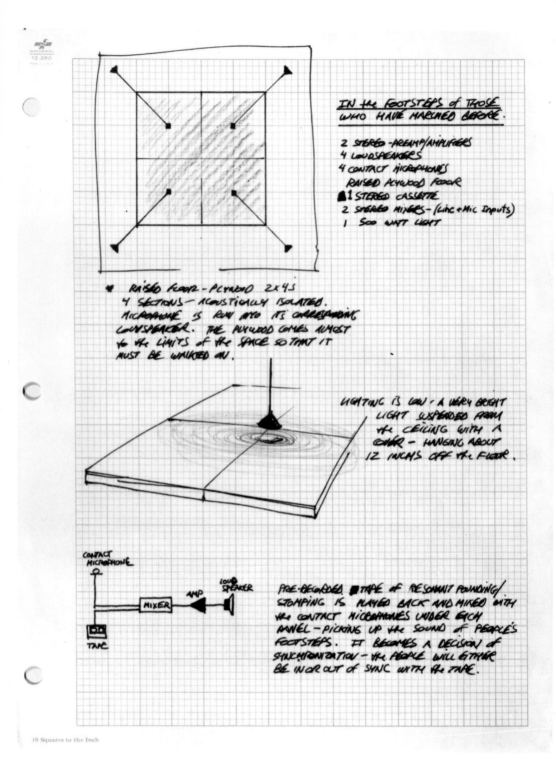

IN the FOOTSTEPS of THOSE
WHO HAVE MARCHED BEFORE.

2 STEREO - PREAMP/AMPLIFIERS
4 LOUDSPEAKERS
4 CONTACT MICROPHONES
  RAISED PLYWOOD FLOOR
1 STEREO CASSETTE
2 STEREO MIXERS - (Line + Mic Inputs)
1 500 WATT LIGHT

* RAISED FLOOR - PLYWOOD 2X4s
4 SECTIONS - ACOUSTICALLY ISOLATED.
MICROPHONE IS RUN INTO ITS CORRESPONDING
LOUDSPEAKER. THE PLYWOOD COMES ALMOST
to the LIMITS of the SPACE SO THAT IT
MUST BE WALKED ON.

LIGHTING IS LOW - A VERY BRIGHT
LIGHT SUSPENDED FROM
the CEILING WITH A
COVER - HANGING ABOUT
12 INCHS OFF the FLOOR.

CONTACT
MICROPHONE

MIXER   AMP   LOUD
              SPEAKER

TAPE

PRE-RECORDED TAPE of RESONANT POUNDING/
STOMPING IS PLAYED BACK AND MIXED WITH
the CONTACT MICROPHONES UNDER EACH
PANEL - PICKING UP the SOUND of PEOPLE'S
FOOTSTEPS. IT BECOMES A DECISION of
SYNCHRONIZATION - the PEOPLE WILL EITHER
BE IN OR OUT of SYNC WITH the TAPE.

This page and opposite: drawings for sound installations, *In the Footsteps of Those Who Have Marched Before*, 1973, and *The Mysterious Virtue*, 1973

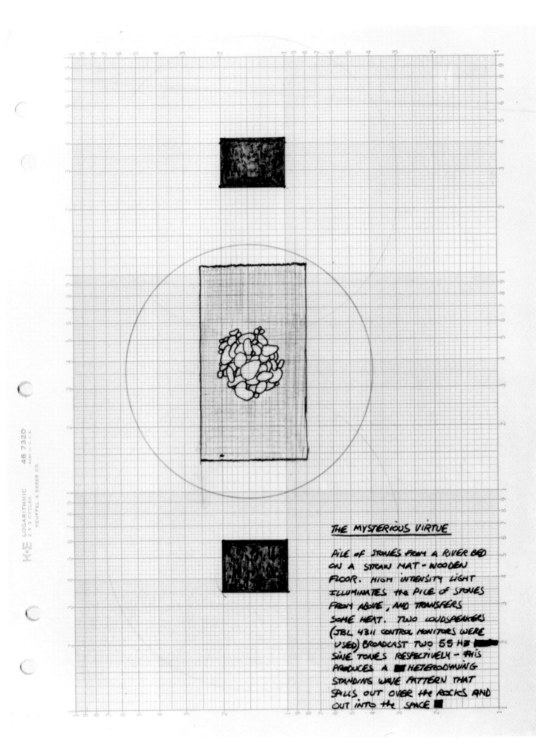

THE MYSTERIOUS VIRTUE

PILE OF STONES FROM A RIVER BED
ON A STRAW MAT - WOODEN
FLOOR. HIGH INTENSITY LIGHT
ILLUMINATES the PILE OF STONES
FROM ABOVE, AND TRANSFERS
SOME HEAT. TWO LOUDSPEAKERS
(JBL 4311 CONTROL MONITORS WERE
USED) BROADCAST TWO 55 HZ ▬
SINE TONES RESPECTIVELY - THIS
PRODUCES A ▬ HETERODYNING
STANDING WAVE PATTERN THAT
SPILLS OUT OVER the ROCKS AND
OUT INTO the SPACE ▬

Following pages: drawings for sound installations, *Broadcast Spirit Release*, 1973, and
Hallway Nodes, 1973   35

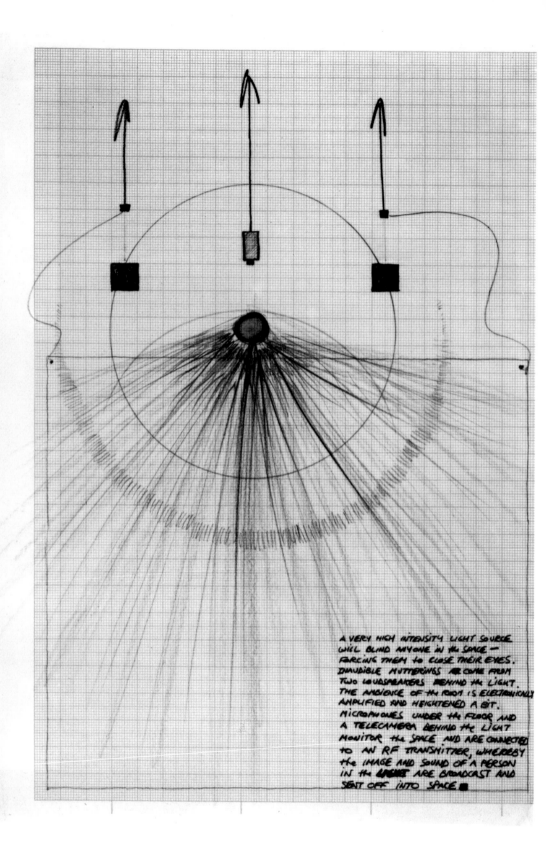

A VERY HIGH INTENSITY LIGHT SOURCE
WILL BLIND ANYONE IN THE SPACE —
FORCING THEM TO CLOSE THEIR EYES.
INAUDIBLE MUTTERINGS ARE COME FROM
TWO LOUDSPEAKERS BEHIND THE LIGHT.
THE AMBIENCE OF THE ROOM IS ELECTRONICALLY
AMPLIFIED AND HEIGHTENED A BIT.
MICROPHONES UNDER THE FLOOR AND
A TELECAMERA BEHIND THE LIGHT
MONITOR THE SPACE AND ARE CONNECTED
TO AN RF TRANSMITTER, WHEREBY
THE IMAGE AND SOUND OF A PERSON
IN THE SPACE ARE BROADCAST AND
SENT OFF INTO SPACE ▪

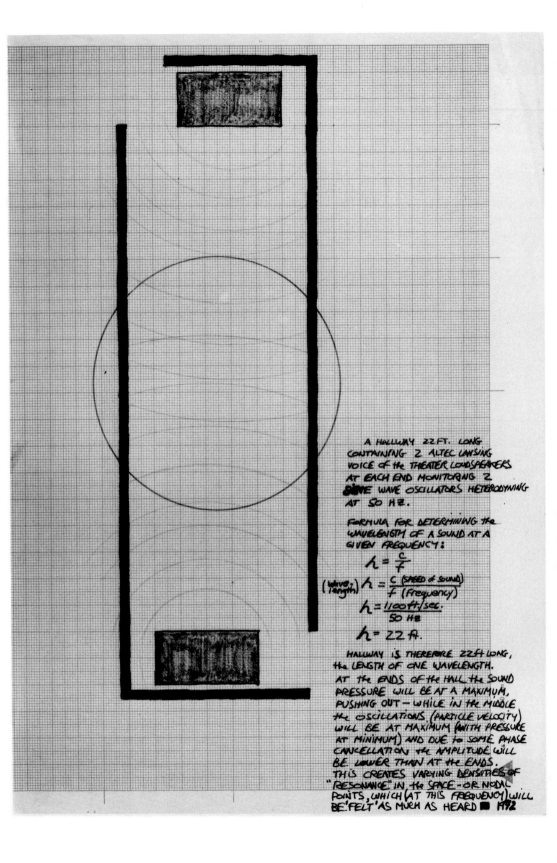

A HALLWAY 22 FT. LONG
CONTAINING 2 ALTEC LANSING
VOICE of the THEATER LOUDSPEAKERS
AT EACH END MONITORING 2
SINE WAVE OSCILLATORS HETERODYNING
AT 50 HZ.

FORMULA FOR DETERMINING the
WAVELENGTH OF A SOUND AT A
GIVEN FREQUENCY:

$$\lambda = \frac{C}{F}$$

$(\text{wave length}) \quad \lambda = \frac{C \text{ (SPEED of SOUND)}}{F \text{ (frequency)}}$

$$\lambda = \frac{1100 \text{ ft/sec.}}{50 \text{ Hz}}$$

$$\lambda = 22 \text{ ft.}$$

HALLWAY IS THEREFORE 22 ft LONG,
the LENGTH OF ONE WAVELENGTH.
AT the ENDS OF the HALL the SOUND
PRESSURE WILL BE AT A MAXIMUM,
PUSHING OUT — WHILE IN the MIDDLE
the OSCILLATIONS (PARTICLE VELOCITY)
WILL BE AT MAXIMUM (WITH PRESSURE
AT MINIMUM) AND DUE to SOME PHASE
CANCELLATION the AMPLITUDE WILL
BE LOWER THAN AT the ENDS.
THIS CREATES VARYING DENSITIES OF
"RESONANCE" IN the SPACE - OR NODAL
POINTS, WHICH (AT THIS FREQUENCY) WILL
BE "FELT" AS MUCH AS HEARD ■ 1972

Il Vapore 1975

First installation using the video system configuration devised for the videotape *Olfaction* (1974).

The system for the installation is executed in two stages. First, after the space is set up and the iron pot, mat, camera, and lights, etc., are all set in their fixed positions, a videotape was made of myself kneeling before the pot, pouring water from a separate bucket into it with my mouth. A microphone was placed close to pick up water sounds. This process was slow and deliberate, lasting one hour, and occurred as a solitary performance, the space locked and closed to the public.

Next, eucalyptus leaves were put into the pot and the water brought to a boil from a small camping stove previously placed underneath. The one-hour videotape was rewound, and played back, the audio being monitored directly on a small speaker under the video monitor. The video was sent into an SEG [special effects generator] and mixed (50% dissolve) with the signal from the live camera. Since the camera and the objects have never moved, the taped space and the live space line up exactly in the mixed image on the monitor. The only thing to have changed, myself pouring water into the pot, could be seen and heard in the monitor's space, but in the actual room, no person was there sitting in front of the steaming pot.

Stage two—the audience is let in. The installation begins. Eucalyptus vapors have filled the space with a strong menthol smell. Persons can see themselves on the monitor live, in the background behind the pot, and, simultaneously, the figure of a person filling the pot with water is also visible and audible co-existing with them in the same space. Past and present tense co-exist equally.

The following verse from the poetry of Jallaludin Rumi (1207–1273) has inspired this piece:

> Though water be enclosed in a
> reservoir
> Yet air will absorb it, for it is its
> supporter;
> It sets it free and bears it to its
> source,
> Little by little, so that you see not
> the process.
> In like manner, this breath of ours
> by degrees
> Steals away our souls from the
> prison house of earth.

On the monitor screen in the photo the seated figure is barely visible as he pours water from his mouth into the iron pot.

—Unpublished description, 1975

"If the doors to perception were cleansed, then everything would appear to man as it is—infinite."

—William Blake (1757–1827)

The spectrum of electromagnetic energy vibrations that make up the universe at large far exceeds the narrow band-width, or "window," open to us through our sensory receptors. As philosophers through the ages have stated, the human senses can thus be considered "limiters" to the total amount of energy bombarding our beings, preventing the individual from being overwhelmed by the tremendous volume of information existing at each and every instant. Imagination is our key to the doorway of perception. The television medium, when coupled with the human mind, can offer us sight beyond the range of our everyday consciousness, but only if it is our desire, both as viewers and as creators, to want to do so.

—Note, 1979

I was walking home one rainy evening in New York City and I had
to stop briefly to wipe the raindrops off my eyeglasses. As I held my
glasses up to clean them, a car drove by and I instantly noticed the
image of its headlights passing through all the tiny raindrops clinging
to the surface of my lenses. I looked closer. Another car went by.
I could clearly see within each droplet a perfect little image of the
street with the lights and the cars passing by. I cleaned off my glasses
and put them on so I could see. I looked around and saw that the water
drops on the hood of a parked car were also imaging the street scene.
I realized, in fact, that every drop of water, even the falling rain, was
doing the same. Seeing the drop images on the lenses of my glasses
helped me to realize that these images were not reflections, but were
optical images. Each waterdrop was functioning as a tiny wide-angle
lens to image the world around. Exhilarated, I raced back to my studio,
got out my video camera and began to experiment with magnifying the
image in the waterdrop

—Note, 1976

He Weeps for You 1976

One of the foundations of ancient philosophy is the concept of the correspondence between the microcosm and the macrocosm, or the belief that everything on the higher order, or scale, of existence reflects and is contained in the manifestation and operation of the lower orders. This has been expressed in religious thought as the symbolic correspondence of the divine (the heavens) and the mundane (the earth), and also finds representation in the theories of contemporary physics that describe how each particle of matter in space contains information about the state of the entire universe.

The ensemble of elements in *He Weeps for You* evokes a "tuned space," where not only is everything locked into a single rhythmical cadence, but a dynamic interactive system is created where all elements (the water drop, the video image, the sound, the viewer, and the room) function together in a reflexive and unified way as a larger instrument.

The traditional philosophy of the microcosm/macrocosm has been profoundly expressed in the Islamic mystical tradition of Sufism. The Persian poet Jallaludin Rumi (1207–1273) developed these concepts with subtle variation in the course of his life's work. In *The Masnavi* he wrote:

> With every moment a world is born and dies,
>> And know that for you, with every moment come death and
>> renewal.

—Note, 1976

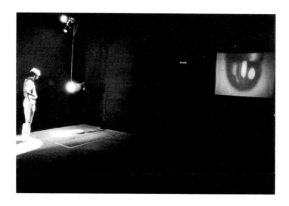

Know the world is a mirror from head to foot,
In every atom are a hundred blazing suns.
If you cleave the heart of one drop of water,
A hundred pure oceans emerge from it.
If you examine closely each grain of sand,
A thousand atoms may be seen in it.
In its members a gnat is like an elephant.
In its qualities a drop of rain is like the Nile.
The heart of a barley-corn equals a hundred harvests,
A world dwells in the heart of a millet seed.
In the wing of a gnat is the ocean of life.
In the pupil of the eye a heaven:
What though the grain of the heart be small
It is a station of the Lord of both worlds to dwell therein.

—Mahmud Shabistari (13th century), *Gulshan-i-rāz*
transcribed in notebook, December 1, 1977

He Weeps for You, 1976, video/sound installation   43

Migration 1976

A slow, continuous journey through changes in scale, punctuated by the sounding of a gong, the piece concerns the nature of the detail of an image. In visual terms, this is known as "acuity" and is related to the number of photoreceptors in a given surface area of the retina. In television terms, detail is referred to as "resolution," and is a measure of the number of picture elements in a given horizontal or vertical direction of the video frame. Reality, unlike the image on the retina or on the television tube, is infinitely resolvable: "resolution" and "acuity" are properties only of images. The piece evolves into an exploration of the optical properties of a drop of water, revealing in it an image of the individual and a suggestion of the transient nature of the world he or she possesses within.

—1976

Every part of a space contains knowledge of every other.

—Note, July 6, 1975

THE MOUNTAIN (cont'd)

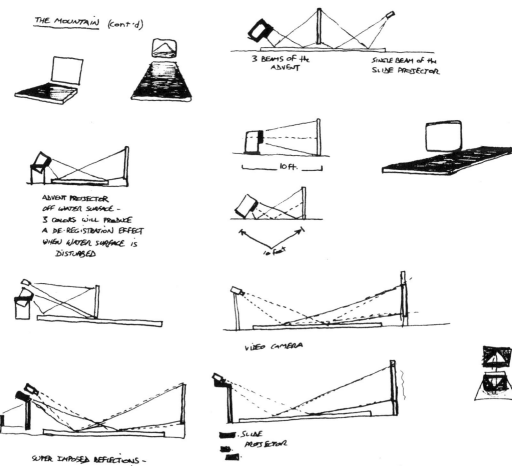

3 BEAMS of the ADVENT

SINGLE BEAM of the SLIDE PROJECTOR

10 ft.

10 feet

ADVENT PROJECTOR OFF WATER SURFACE — 3 COLORS WILL PRODUCE A DE-REGISTRATION EFFECT WHEN WATER SURFACE IS DISTURBED

VIDEO CAMERA

SUPER IMPOSED REFLECTIONS — VIDEO CAMERA AND SLIDE PROJECTOR

.SLIDE PROJECTOR

THE PROJECTED IMAGE, LYING AT THE END OF A LONG TROUGH

THE MOUNTAIN AS IMAGE.
THE IMAGE OF the MOUNTAIN MUST BE SOLID AND UNMOVING. YET, the SLIGHTEST SHIFTING IN the SPACE CAN CAUSE the WHOLE THING to UNRAVEL DRASTICALLY.

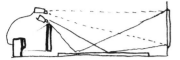

MOUNTAIN

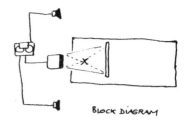

BLOCK DIAGRAM

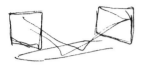

TAPE OF MOUNTAIN ON SCREEN WITH
RIPPLES. PLACED IN FRONT OF A
STILL POND.

THE (DESTRUCTION) UNRAVELING OF AN IMAGE...
ALL THAT IS SOLID, UNCHANGING, FIRM (the
MOUNTAIN/the IMAGE) DISINTEGRATES AT A
FEATHER'S TOUCH AND PROVES TO BE EXTREMELY
FRAGILE AND DELICATE.

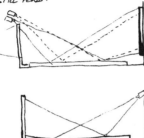

Song for the MOUNTAIN

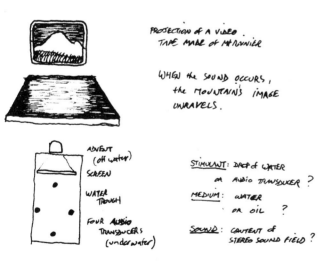

PROJECTION OF A VIDEO.
TAPE MADE OF Mt RAINIER

WHEN the SOUND OCCURS,
the MOUNTAIN'S IMAGE
UNRAVELS.

ADVENT
(off water)
SCREEN

WATER
TROUGH

FOUR AUDIO
TRANSDUCERS
(underwater)

STIMULANT: DROP OF WATER
or AUDIO TRANSDUCER ?

MEDIUM: WATER
or OIL ?

SOUND: CONTENT of
STEREO SOUND FIELD ?

Drawings for *Moving Stillness (Mt. Rainier)*, 1979, video/sound installation   47

Street Music

On Sunday, September 26, 1976, at 8 a.m., I fired a rifle into the air several times on the corner of Cedar and Nassau streets in the Wall Street district of New York.

The shots were recorded on several stereo audiotape recorders with various miking configurations. The tapes are intended to be played back both at normal speed and at slower speeds to reveal sound echo patterns and reverberation in the deserted streets.

—Note, 1976

The Space Between the Teeth 1976

The structure of *The Space Between the Teeth* is modeled on the acoustic phenomenon and psychological dynamics of a person screaming at the top of his lungs at the end of a long, dark, industrial corridor. Computer editing techniques were used to orchestrate mathematically precise relationships between sound and image, and to create the temporal figure/ground reversal seen in the second half of the tape.

—1976

The Space Between the Teeth, 1976, videotape   51

```
camera    breaks from the eye

camera    as   nose
camera    as   ear
camera    as   hand
camera    as   insect
camera    as   consciousness.

camera    as   microscope
camera    as   telescope
```

—Note, 1980

Landscape can exist as a reflection on the inner walls of the mind, or as a projection of the inner state without. Flat open vast space lends itself to a clearer monitoring of the subjective inner world. Contemporary urban spaces talk to you, incessantly—signs call out, to try to grab you, programmed general consensus signals determine where and when you walk, the intersecting spheres of psychic perceptive space of others in too close proximity creates confusion and imbalance. The "stillness" of a sleeping apartment building of 150 families is not "stillness" at all. Removing all cues, from the outside, the voices of the inner state become louder, clearer.

—Note, 1979

Chott el-Djerid (A Portrait in Light and Heat) 1979

I want to go to a place that seems like it's at the end of the world.
A vantage point from which one can stand and peer out into the void—
the world beyond—what would be above the surface to the fish. Where
all becomes strange and unfamiliar. There is nothing to lean on. No
references. It is said the mind plays "tricks." Standing there, a place
where, after a long arduous journey, you realize you can go no further.
Each time you advance towards it, it recedes further. You have reached
the edge. All you can do is stand there and peer out into the void,
watching. Standing there, you strain to look further, to see beyond,
strain to make out familiar shapes and forms. You finally realize that
the void is yourself. It is like some huge mirror for your mind. Clear
and uncluttered, it is the opposite of our urban distractive spaces. Out
here, the unbound mind can run free. Imagination reigns. Space
becomes a projection screen. Inside becomes outside. You can see what
you are.

  I want to travel to this place and stand and watch with my camera.
Watch the days pass, watch the light change, listen to the landscape.
It is a harsh place. It is difficult to reach. It feels like it's at the
end of the world. It is the edge.

—Note, April 29, 1979

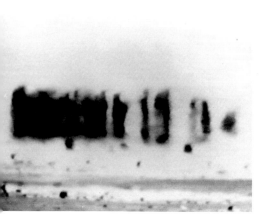

Chott el-Djerid is the name of a vast, dry salt lake in the Tunisian Sahara Desert, where mirages are most likely to form in the midday sun. Here the intense desert heat manipulates, bends, and distorts the light rays to such an extent that one actually sees things that are not there. Trees and sand dunes float off the ground, the edges of mountains and buildings ripple and vibrate, color and form blend into one shimmering dance. The desert mirages are set against images of the bleak winter prairies of Illinois and Saskatchewan, Canada, some of them recorded in a snowstorm. The opposite climactic conditions induce a similar aura of uncertainty, disorientation, and unfamiliarity.

Through special telephoto lenses adapted for video, the camera confronts the final barrier of the limits of the image. At what point does the breakdown of normal conditions, or the lack of adequate visual information, cause us to re-evaluate our perceptions of reality and realize that we are looking at something out of the ordinary—a transformation of the physical into the psychological? If one believes that hallucinations are the manifestation of some chemical or biological imbalance in the brain, then mirages and desert heat distortions can be considered hallucinations of the landscape. It was like physically being inside someone else's dream.

—1979

Chott el-Djerid (A Portrait in Light and Heat), 1979, videotape   55

A large oak tree standing alone in an
open field was spotlit by a high-
powered searchlight beam positioned a
quarter of a mile away. The searchlight was turned on in the late afternoon. As the daylight faded, the beam
gradually became visible and the tree
glowed with luminous intensity into
the night. A negative shadow of its
dark form was cast out across the valley, visible for several miles. The moon
was also seen at times coming through
the clouds behind the tree. The beam
was turned off several hours after the
sun had set.

—*The Tree of Life*, 1977

Ancestral lines cannot be broken. Without them there is no childhood. Without them there can be no right dreams. The river flows, it is continually changing, continually moving, yet it is always a river. Now, before, after. As such, so is the line from you to your ancestors, for outside the physical there is an unbroken thread. It cannot be seen, yet can be felt. You may call it a *déjà-vu*, an unconscious sense of familiarity about a certain place or circumstance. You may call it a certain yearning for certain foods, for certain experiences, for a certain type of person. You may call it your "nature." For what is nature but the execution of some master plan? The embodiment of some intelligence too broad or whole to be conceived of as one. And just as science discovers more about the apparent existence of a purpose or consciousness in all things, so too will they realize that what you call your likes and dislikes, attractions and repulsions, your personality expressed in your like things, is nothing more than the expression of this same thread of intelligence. And this intelligence is the wisdom of your ancestors, the wisdom of age beyond the limits of the corporeal, accumulating down through the generations. They are not so far off the track, those scientist people, when they probe into the tiny world of the unseen for this thread, yet their insistence on the use of the metaphors of the physical world will prevent them from ever really touching it.

—Note, February 19, 1977
[upon return from the Solomon Islands]

The Porcupine and the Car

Once, a friend of mine gave me a shopping bag full of used audio cassette tapes that he had retrieved from the garbage at his office. Thrilled at the prospect of unlimited free recording time, I got an idea to set up a tape recorder right in the center of activity in my house, the kitchen, and to try and record everything that went on. My idea was to have an ongoing, almost continuous, record of all sonic activity in that space. When played back, it would create a sort of stream-of-consciousness parallel world to the present, but displaced in time. I kept the recorder loaded with tapes all the time I was at home, which then being my summer vacation was practically all the time. By the end of the week, when I had accumulated well over 24 hours of tape, I suddenly realized a distressing thought. I would need 24 hours, exactly the time it took to record, to play all this stuff back. Furthermore, if I kept this up, say, for a year, I would have to stop after six months to begin playing back, and if I got really ambitious and made it my life's work, I would have to stop my life when it was only half over to sit down and listen to all the material for the rest of my life, plus a little additional time for rewinding all the cassettes. It was a horrible thought, so I took down my tape recorder and immediately stopped the project.

There is another way to look at the functioning of human sensory systems, at the perception of the world and our particular place in it. The common conception is to compare our sense organs with windows, to consider them as openings through which we peer out into the world at large. The twentieth-century philosopher Henri Bergson suggested, however, that the human senses should be regarded as *limiters* to the total amount of energy that bombards our beings, preventing the individual from being overwhelmed by the sheer volume of information that exists at each and every instant. A glance at a scientific chart showing the spectrum of electromagnetic energy vibration that makes

First published in *Image Forum* (Tokyo), vol. 2, no. 3 (January 1981), 46–55.

up the universe, and the narrow slit, or bandwidth, in that scale corresponding to the small range of these vibrations to which our sensory receptors are sensitive, and it would seem that this is indeed the case. As the poet William Blake wrote in 1793, "If the doors to perception were cleansed, then everything would appear to man as it is—infinite."

Information is in a way the opposite of garbage, although in our contemporary commercialized world they may at times appear identical. Both are products of man-made processes, and, with the exception of a few crazy artists now, and some archaeologists far in the future, we can generally say that garbage loses value over time, while information seems to be the process of something gaining value over time. As a rule, information is something to preserve, garbage is something to be destroyed. However, both can be looked on as a kind of waste product, a physical burden, and for contemporary society both are among the most pressing problems of the day. An ancient Sufi saying states that a heavy load of broken pottery and a heavy load of books is the same for the donkey. A recent magazine advertisement for Xerox photocopy machines offers their product as a salvation for today's office staff rapidly sinking under the weight of the ever-mounting information deluge.

Consider for a moment the total number of books, magazine and newspaper articles, radio and television programs, records, videotapes, and films produced in one week alone, and it becomes clear that the major task of today is not information production, but information management (in other words, not information storage but information retrieval; this is precisely what Xerox was selling in their magazine advertisement). In this light, the main problem for artists using video these days lies in deciding what *not* to record. Making a videotape, therefore, might not be so much the creation or building up of some thing, but more like the cutting or carving away of everything else until only a specific thing remains. A similar concept can be seen in Indian classical music and how it differs in approach from Western classical music. Among their many divergencies, two are pertinent here: Indian music places great emphasis on free inspirational playing, or improvisation, and also on its use of the drone. Of the two, the latter is significant because it represents a very different musical (and cultural) philosophy. Western music builds things up, piles notes on top of notes, forms on top of forms, in the way that one would construct a building, until at last the piece is complete. Its base is silence, all the music proceeds from this point. Indian music begins from sound; all the notes and possible notes to be played in a piece are present in the form of the tambura, before the main musicians even start playing. The tambura is a drone instrument, usually of four or five strings, that, due to the particular construction of its bridge, amplifies the overtone or harmonic series of the individual notes in each tuned string. This series of overtone notes describes the scale that the musicians are playing. It produces the familiar complex buzzing or ringing sound that has become for many foreigners "that Indian-music sound." Therefore, when the main musicians play, they are pulling notes out of this already ongoing sound field, the drone. There is no silence. The musicians say that this concept relates to the Hindu philosophy of the cosmic sound or vibration, "Om," which is ever present, going on without beginning or end, everywhere within the universe, and everything proceeds from it.

Contemporary physics, which has been expanding its investigations into the cosmos to include a range in scale (from the micro to macro) that is staggering to the imagination, complains of a problem related to coping with this enormous barrage of information. At Princeton's Institute for Advanced Study, the physicist Freeman Dyson recently declared, "The main problem in particle physics today is to find a problem. That's where the really hard work is." When one is starting out in video, however, even before setting out to find a problem, the hard work at first is to understand the technology, acquire the technical experience and knowledge, and develop craft and technique. This has proved to be a lot more difficult than expected, since at the outset video is so deceptively easy to work with (as will be further discussed). The entire first wave of what is called video art, a period of roughly 13 years from 1963 to 1976 but concentrated in the early seventies, was taken up with just this process. Most of the early video work was devoted to finding "the unique characteristics of the medium." This is without a doubt very important knowledge to acquire, but now, however, most young artists in the eighties should recognize that this is work they need to do privately, to discover on their own. As artistic statements these have already been publicly made.

Some "purist" artists today insist on working in this way, saying that their efforts must be only "video" in nature. Unfortunately they often end up closing themselves off to a great deal of potentially valuable work done in other fields, notably film. Furthermore, since the technology of video is still undergoing rapid change, it is sometimes difficult to tell exactly what its unique characteristics are. (The exact form of, and precise editing on, the frame is one of the traits that the early video purists said was specific to film, yet the facility is now taken for granted by most videomakers using automated electronic video editing systems.) These artists are correct, however, in maintaining that video ought to be taken for what it is, not for what it is like. Looking at the technical development of both video and film, we immediately notice a profound difference: as film has evolved basically out of photography (a film is a succession of discrete photographs), video has emerged from audio technology. A video camera is closer to a microphone in operation than it is to a film camera; video images are recorded on magnetic tape in a tape recorder. Thus we find that video is closer in relationship to sound, or music, than it is to the visual media of film and photography. (This will be the topic of another essay.)

One of the most fascinating aspects of video's technical evolution, and the one that makes it most different from film, is that the video image existed for many years before a way was developed to record it. In other words, it is live, simultaneous with experience. Taping or recording is not an integral part of the system. Film is not film unless it is filming (recording). Video, however, is "videoing" all the time, continually in motion, putting out 30 frames, or images, a second. (In Europe this is 25 frames, due to differences in AC power cycles.) Television existed, as radio did, as live broadcast for about 10 years before the videotape recorder was developed to record it. Video's roots in the live, not recorded, is the underlying characteristic of the medium. Somehow, in a way no one has really been able to explain, time becomes more precious when dealing with video. One's first instinct is to tape everything, but soon this initially easy exercise gives way to a realization that it is a very difficult medium. The slack in video art activity in the late 1970s is testimony to this fact.

When one makes a videotape, one is interfering with an ongoing process, the scanning of the camera. The image one sees on the monitor screen is not really an image at all, but the precise and extremely rapid tracing of a glowing phosphor dot. Due to persistence of human vision, and a slight lag in the phosphor glow, one sees a complete image which is really nothing more than a moving point of light. Robert Arns, writing in *Arts Canada* magazine seven years ago, described film and video as illusion-producing media: both give the illusion of experience in light and sound, but the nature of their illusions is quite different. In film, Arns says, the basic illusion is of movement, produced by the succession of still images flashing on the screen. In video, stillness is the basic illusion: a still image does not exist because the video signal is in constant motion scanning across the screen.

The subsequent evolution of video from the early days has been aimed at increasing control over this continually moving system; in other words, improving control over time. After videotape recorders were invented, the next obstacle was the editing of the tape (control of pre-recorded time), a huge problem as most new owners of home video recorders are discovering (home units can record and play back only; they have no editing facility). At first editing was done physically, by splicing the tape, an unwieldy, awkward, and technically disastrous process. Later, electronic editing was introduced where the desired signal was recorded on another VTR (videotape recorder), posing some new problems but still the system in use today. A remarkable fact is that it was not until 1974, when computer controlled editing systems were introduced in the United States, that the video producer had precise and accurate access to specific individual frames of video for editing. Most filmmakers still find this hard to believe. In this light, it is easy to see why most video artists have been slow in developing a control and sense of time. Editing equipment remains the most difficult and expensive to obtain, so in this area many artists simply lack experience. Most of the early tapes of Bruce Nauman (one of the first video artists) are 60 minutes long, the length of a reel of half-inch tape.

A common complaint of the super-8 home movie makers has been that the restriction of the three-minute cartridge causes every cut to be shortened; so that maintaining continuity becomes a problem. Many home movies look like Sergei Eisenstein's montage technique films. Home video users, on the other hand, find there is a tendency just to load a one-hour cassette and shoot away continuously. In this case, the continuity of the long shot becomes the problem.

The mass replication aspect of video images is an important factor for artists, because the manual skill of accurate rendering, held in the West since the Renaissance to be a corner-stone of the artist's craft, is now no longer an issue. We have been witnessing its decline since the arrival of photography in the nineteenth century. There are nevertheless many people today who still think that an artist is someone who draws realistically; indeed, the training given in many art schools seems to agree with this perception. Gradually, however, more people are realizing that the twentieth-century artist is not necessarily someone who draws well, but someone who thinks well.

As we move faster and faster into the age of electronic communication, the technology seems to be evolving increasingly realistic methods of rendering the real world. The often-cited act of taking the image, or representation, of the thing to be the thing itself seems to have become a particularly contemporary phenomenon. We rely more and more on electronic data as a surrogate for direct social interaction. No one has ever confused a portrait painting, or even an early black-and-white photograph, with the person it depicted. However, when telephones were first installed and people could speak directly over long distances but not face to face, the English slang word "phoney" came into use. Fearful that the new device could be used to deceive, people used "phoney" to describe someone or something that wasn't real or true. The genuine "hyper-realist" artists of today are not the painters of the school of the same name, but the commercial film and television producers; for it is they who deal with something that has become almost more real than real: a person's image.

Reflecting on this trend of the recording media becoming more and more realistic, one can easily say that their ultimate goal is perhaps to become invisible, to become completely transparent, to become indistinguishable from what they record (i.e., to achieve the highest "fidelity"). Looking to the future, most people in the field would say that film and television are steering themselves towards some kind of life-size, three-dimensional, holographic, audio-visual projection, almost indistinguishable from a real scene. Farther far-out futurists speak of a medium-less medium, electrical stimulation directly to the brain to evoke sequences of mental sensations virtually identical with perceived external reality. Of course, this is all still a long way off, and if energy prices keep going up we will all have to burn our home video recorders as firewood long before.

Today, various distortions (differences between the recorded object and the actual object caused by the physical characteristics of the recording media) are listed by manufacturers, along with weight, size, etc., as specifications describing their products. An important one for tape recorders is the signal-to-noise ratio (S/N), which is basically a measurement of the difference in level between the signal (the thing recorded) and the level of internal noise (in audio heard as hiss) inherent in the electronic circuits of the tape machine itself. Quality of equipment and, therefore, price are determined by the lowest amounts of distortion (or deviation from reality) present in the system.

One of the most interesting aspects of the recording media is how they tell us so much about the way we perceive the world. Experimental psychologists were among the first to realize that recording media have provided us with surrogate sensory perceptual systems, in some ways similar, in some ways different, from our own, but nonetheless with a specific set of characteristics that we can hold up and compare against ourselves. This has proved invaluable in laboratory experiments on perception. One might think that the distortions described above are the sole property of electronic systems, but this does not seem to be the case. John Cage, the contemporary composer, often tells the story of an experience he had inside the anechoic chamber at MIT in Boston. An anechoic chamber is a completely soundproof room, designed so that no sound is reflected from its walls; sound travels out from a source but does not bounce back. Cage was let inside this soundless space and left alone for a short time. When he emerged, he asked the engineer why, if the room was silent, had he heard two sounds. He described them to the engineer, who said that the high one was his nervous system in operation, and that the low one was his blood in circulation. Human "signal-to-noise" ratio.

Experiences such as these give us a very different view of what we call information. In fact, as some have suggested, information may be to a large extent the projection of our internal structure and biophysical order onto the external world. Dr. John Lilly, pioneer researcher in communication with dolphins, conducted some extremely interesting experiments on himself after his initial dolphin research. The major breakthrough in this work was Lilly's decision to use himself as subject, a reversal of the dominant role of the scientist as outside observer. In so doing, he immediately entered the domain of the subjective. Lilly's work involved immersing himself in a sensory deprivation environment even more extreme than the one Cage found himself in. This was a tank of salt-water heated to the same temperature as the human bloodstream. There was no light, no sound; the buoyancy of the salt-water reduced the effects of gravity and minimized the sense of touch. Lilly, mostly submerged with only his face above water to breathe, found it difficult to sense the difference between his inside and outside. (It all seems remarkably like a womb.) Floating in this state of nothingness, he even discovered that he could relax his muscles enough to urinate without thinking about it. The water in the tank was constantly filtered and recirculated, so that he could remain inside for hours without interruption.

It is hard to imagine what this experience can be like. One's first thought is that it must be like nothing, or similar perhaps to when one goes to sleep, or stares at a blank wall or into a dark room. Lilly found, however, that it was not like this at all. Instead, he saw things, he heard things, and his experience was almost as full and cluttered as his everyday life. Lilly believed these phenomena to be hallucinations and for a while tried to invent ways to quell them. But then he realized a startling thought: if there is no outside stimulation, the mind seems to make up things to perceive that appear to come from the outside. So perhaps he actually saw the patterns of his own mind, the projections of his own brain in the process of thinking. He was looking at an audio-visual display of the neurological circuits at work in his brain.

This phenomenon has been known in various forms throughout the ages. People have always spoken of the "rabbit" or the "man" in the moon, and cloud formations have been a popular form of image visualization. In Western science, theories of visual perception have proceeded from the emission theory (i.e., that the eye sends out rays or particles which strike objects in the external world and enable perception) to the current reception model (that the retina is a surface that senses the reception of light rays as photons coming in to strike it from the outside). The experimental psychologist Rorschach has immortalized his name in connection with this process by his famous ink-blot test, in which a random ink-blot is made on a piece of paper and subjects are asked to report what they see in its abstract shapes. Artists have known for a long time that the most interesting connections in things involve areas of low, or ambiguous, information, so-called "gaps" in recognition. This is the time of involvement, of participation by the viewer, in a work of art. The process of learning itself demands that initially one must be confronted with something one does not understand. René Magritte wrote, "People who look for symbolic meanings fail to grasp the inherent poetry and mystery of the image. No doubt they sense this mystery, but they wish to get rid of it. They are afraid. By asking 'What does this mean?', they express a wish that everything be understandable. But if one does not reject the mystery, one has quite a different response. One asks other things."

This view is exactly opposite to the one that a student of communication receives at university, yet it is the very basis of communication. Modern masters of information, such as the CIA and many politicians, know full well that real power lies in what is *not* said, in what is *not* spoken, and survival depends on making statements that are as multi-faceted and ambiguous as permissible. Disclosing information, "communication" as most people know it, can mean sure disaster as far as these people are concerned. Yet the broadcast media, the students of media, and many video artists continue to operate under the old models, creating more and more boring works.

One of the most distressing changes taking place is in the area of children's toys. (It has become such a big business, infected with the same ignorant greed as everything else.) Toys are becoming more and

more "advanced," loaded down with gadgets, gimmicks, buzzers, flashing lights, and anything else manufacturers can think of to throw in.
Children are being robbed of their imaginations at a younger and
younger age. A block of wood can be anything from a boat to a
spaceship; it can change instantly into any form desired, and it does not
run on batteries. Observing how many people are being raised by this
culture, is hardly surprising when they come to a video art show they
are utterly confused and ask questions such as "What is this?" "Why
is this art?" and the familiar "What does this mean?"

Information storage and retrieval are other words for information
encoding and decoding. Humans seem to possess built-in decoders
which insist on deciphering or searching for meaning in (making sense
out of) everything, including, as in Lilly's case, nothing. Science has
been attempting to decode nature for thousands of years with still no
end in sight. Nature, herself the grand code, has consistently awed
scientists with her apparently intrinsic sense of purpose (teleology, as it
is called), supreme harmony, and interrelationships of parts and systems. It is indeed mysterious and beautiful that nature seems fully
aware and conscious of herself. Thorns on plants seem to acknowledge
the existence of hungry vegetarians; many flowers could not live apart
from bees any more than bees could live without them. The list is
endless. If one wants to make a jigsaw puzzle, one must first start with
a complete image, and then cut it up and hand the pieces to someone
saying "Here, put this together." The participant, working backwards
into the system, has the point of view that he or she is creating this
image bit by bit, building it up from nothing piece by piece until all
the parts fit together into one whole.

The act of encoding information is the act of arranging elements
into a pattern, putting intelligence, purpose, or intent into something.
The act of decoding (retrieval) is to extract that organization out of the
pattern, sensing the intent or intelligence behind the organization of
that pattern. People are essentially doing this when they are watching
films and videotapes. Even for artists who claim that they are not at
all interested in content or information, this phenomenon still occurs.
Unfortunately, for many video artists, this skill of building intelligence
into their pieces is not really advanced in comparison with some of the

natural systems, or even with the work of great artists and directors in other media. So much of video art is simply an underestimation of the level of visual literacy, or decoding ability, of the audience.

One of the most exciting, and frustrating, aspects of video technology is that it is changing all the time. The hardware is in a contsant state of transformation and so-called improvement. Two important recent developments are greatly affecting the area of work that has come to be called video art. First is video games; in this current craze we find an interesting phenomenon which concerns the information encoding and decoding processes just described. Video games represent the first widespread implementation of those amazing interactive computer graphic display devices we were told about ten years ago. In function, at least superficially, they fulfill a dream of interactive visual art envisioned originally by the pioneering artists/engineers who developed the first video synthesizers. Quite a few of these individuals, Stephen Beck and Bill Etra among them, are currently designing video games and interactive devices for large Californian electronics firms. As personal users gain more experience with these interactive machines, we can see a new group of champions emerging. Watching one of these video games "champions" in action, it becomes apparent that they are decoding the computer program that someone has designed for the machine. They approach the program from the opposite direction, reconstructing it bit by bit until they have memorized most of the patterns and branches (possible patterns) encoded into the machine. They know, for example, that if they shoot the last man in the top row right, a certain sequence will be triggered and appear on the screen, or that after exactly 14 shots a bonus spaceship will appear and travel across from left to right. Then, when they have finally deciphered most of it, the play becomes mechanical and boring, so they simply move on to a different game. It would be entertaining to arrange a meeting between the users and the game's original programmer. If asked, some of these expert players could perhaps write out most of the original program, although not exactly in the same technical language in which it was written.

The second recent arrival on the video scene, the home video recorder, has enabled far more artists to work in the medium by spreading low-cost equipment around. It has also eliminated a belief that plagued the early days of video as it did early photography: that someone could be considered a "video artist" simply because they had got hold of the equipment at a stage when it was still scarce. Certainly the initial energy and excitement of the video scene 10 years ago could support a lot of this "just tape everything" kind of work, but it carried on far longer than necessary. The medium is becoming more pedestrian and less mystical and glamorous, striking a blow to the power-point of many so-called artists. With this development, however, the potential for individual creative expression is becoming greater.

These two recent developments represent the first shift in consciousness for the average person away from considering their television as something that brings them news, sports, and entertainment programs. This is just the beginning. Experimental systems are already in operation where the TV screen becomes a data terminal, bringing not only news, sports, and entertainment programs, but also teletype newswire services, stock-market reports, all the information in the public library stored frame by frame, information monitoring of home heating and electrical systems, and even bank account statements. This is all "video," and all vastly different from "I Love Lucy" or "Bonanza," and the addition of a personal microprocessor and video disc to this system quickly multiplies the possibilities. John Baldessari, one of the early video artists from California, once said that video is "like a pencil. Art is just one of the things you can do with it." Today video seems closer in analogy to paper, a huge blank sheet upon which any number of vastly different things can take place. Art *is* just one of the things you can do with it.

Video as a pencil. Video as paper. The tools and our metaphors for them are continually changing, but one thing remains more or less the same: the person using these tools. This will probably never change. Most people today do not know the creative possibilities of a pencil and paper any more than a person 100 years from now will know what to do with a digital color video camera. Attending the countless conferences, demonstrations, and video expos can only convince one that the technology is far ahead of the people using it. The limits are more in the user than in the tools. If technology were frozen right now, it would take years for us to catch up with and use the technology at our disposal and to realize its fullest potential. The manufacturers, avidly promoting fashion, consumerism, and market competition, subvert our desire to understand by releasing a steady stream of new models, new designs, and generally orchestrating obsolescence. For some reason, many video artists have also fallen prey to this propaganda of high fashion and mystique in advanced technology: "If only I had this new camera, this latest VTR, then I would really make good video art."

Technology always seems to lead us away from ourselves. Rumi, the Persian Sufi poet and mystic, wrote in 1273, "New organs of perception come into being as a result of necessity—therefore, increase your necessity so that you may increase your perception." The real work of the contemporary video artist, then, after acquiring the necessary technical skills, is in the development and understanding of the self. This is where the really hard work is. The level of use of the tools is a direct reflection of the level of the user. Chopsticks can either be a simple eating utensil or a deadly weapon, depending on who uses them.

Last summer, while shooting video on Mt. Rainier in Washington State, I had a very instructive experience. We were coming down a winding mountain road late one night, when we encountered a large porcupine crossing the road. Fortunately, I spotted him in enough time to stop the car a short distance from where he was standing. We watched him in the bright lights of the car, standing there petrified at this terrifying "close encounter of the third kind." Then, he started to do a strange thing. He began to turn around and around in his place, his sharp quills rising off his body, and emitting a kind of hissing sound. He didn't run away. I realized this dance was actually a move of self-defense. I cut the high-beam headlights of the car to normal, but he continued to move around more furiously. I then cut the lights further to the parking beams, and when he still continued turning around I finally had to kill the lights completely and turn off the engine so as not to give him a heart attack. We watched him in the dim moonlight as he stopped his dance and finally moved off the road. I realized at that time that he was probably walking proudly away thinking how he really gave it to that big, blinding, noisy thing that came lumbering after him out of the night. I'm sure he was inflated with confidence, so pleased with himself that he had won, and certainly would have quite a story to tell when he got home.

Ancient of Days 1979–81

I CAN STILL SEE THIS SLOW MOTION ▮▮▮ WORK —
SLOWING DOWN the CITY to STILLNESS.

I SAW A RELATIONSHIP BETWEEN the BAMBOO CLOSE UPS
AND the ROOF TILES, AND HOW THESE COULD BE
RELATED to the SLOW MOTION SECTIONS.

IN the SLOW MOTION SECTIONS I WANT ▮▮▮ the
PIECE to BE CONSTRUCTED FRAME BY FRAME —
LIKE A BUILDING IS MADE BRICK BY BRICK.
THERE WILL BE NO EXCESS FRAMES.

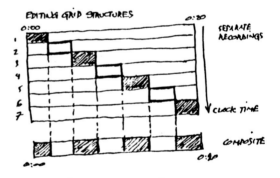

PRESERVING REAL TIME of INDIVIDUAL RECORDED SEGMENTS

DECIDE the DIFFERENCE BETWEEN CAMERA PANNING AND PHYSICAL ARM SWINGING.

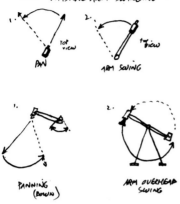

1. PAN (top view)
2. ARM SWING (top view)

1. PANNING (DOWN)
2. ARM OVERHEAD SWING

TRY A DUPLICATION of the 57TH ST. TILT DOWN BUT WITH A ROCKING CAMERA SWING INSTEAD.

CAMERA MOTIONS LINKED to the CARDINAL DIRECTIONS:

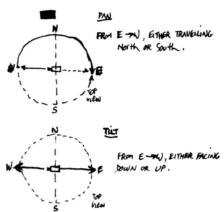

PAN

FROM E → W, EITHER TRAVELLING NORTH OR SOUTH.

N
W — E
S
TOP VIEW

TILT

FROM E → W, EITHER FACING DOWN OR UP.

N
W — E
S
TOP VIEW

LAWN SUNDIAL (for suburbia)

MARKINGS ON LAWN OF A HUGE SUNDIAL CLOCK BUILT ON the CAMERA PIVOT STRUCTURE. TAKE CAREFUL TIME MEASUREMENTS DURING the DAY AND SWING the CAMERA to the MARKED AREAS ON the CIRCUMFERENCE PERTAINING to the TIME of DAY AND ANGLE of the SUN.

OVERALL RHYTHMS IN 'ANCIENT of DAYS':

CMX COMPUTER CONTROLS the RATE of DISSOLVES BETWEEN RECORDED SAMPLES, OR the RESOLUTION of the TIME LAPSE (MAXIMUM TEMPORAL RESOLUTION WOULD BE 1 SAMPLE/FRAME, OR TYPICAL TIME LAPSE FILM TECHNIQUE. VIDEO SAMPLE RATE IS VARIABLE, DUE MAINLY to the TECH. DIFFICULTY + TEDIUM of EDITING EXTRACTING (EDITING) ONE FRAME of VIDEO FROM EACH SAMPLE, AND INVOLVES EXTENDED FRAME GROUPS MAKING UP EACH SAMPLE SEGMENT.
IN "ANCIENT of DAYS" the SAMPLE RATE (ie. RATE of DISSOLVES or EDITS) ACTUALLY BECOMES the CLOCK for the PIECE. THIS RHYTHM IS GRADUALLY INCREASED IN EACH SEGMENT, STARTING FROM

(CONT'D →)

THE ANCIENT of DAYS

	Camera Motion	Space
1. MODEL CITIES : TOWER. 500mm NIKKOR LENS VISIONS OF A TOWER AND SMALL BUILDINGS ... VIEW LOOKING S.E. THE LENS CREATES THAT SLIGHTLY BLURRED MINIATURE CITIES LOOK. IT IS A DISTANT VISION of TIME IN A DISTANT LAND.	STILL	PERSPECTIVAL
2. 57TH ST. TILT : THE VIEW DOWN 57TH ST. LOOKING EAST AT DAWN, WEST AT SUNSET, A SLOW CCTV SCAN of the STREET ENDING UP UPSIDE DOWN IN the WEST for the SUNSET.	TILT	ISOMORPHIC 
3. SCHENECTADY PAN : STARTING FROM WITHIN A COFFEE SHOP (ie. CLOSE UPS of PEOPLE) CAMERA BEGINS SWINGING OUT ONTO the CENTER of TOWN (the entire town is doing it!).	PAN	
4. QUEENS ZOOM : A FRANTIC COMPRESSED TRUCK DOWN A BUSY AVENUE IN QUEENS. (wheelchair dolly)	DOLLY	

<u>COSMOLOGICAL CYCLES</u> ("The Ancient of Days")

the FIRST. STILL TIME LAPSE (TOWER) WHICH PROCEEDS VERY
SLOWLY WITH ONLY A MINIMAL AMOUNT OF DISSOLVE
SEGMENT, to the FRANTIC "QUEEN'S ZOOM" WHICH SPEEDS
THROUGH QUEEN'S at the PACE of A 2-4 FRAME SAMPLE
RATE. ~~BECAUSE~~ BEFORE IT EACH PIECE HAD BEEN
SPEEDING UP SLIGHTLY WITH ITS SAMPLE RATE, BUT
BECAUSE the PANS WILL BE CONTINUOUS WHILE the
DOLLY IS SPATIALLY DISPARATE, DRASTIC CHANGES
ARE ONLY REALLY NOTICED IN the ~~SEU~~ QUEEN'S ZOOM
SECTION. IT BEGINS IN the RATE of the ONE
BEFORE IT, BUT RAPIDLY STARTS SPEEDING UP.

~~EACH PIECE~~
THE FOLLOWING PIECE AFTER THIS IS the PIPE MATRIX,
WITH AN EVEN FASTER SAMPLE RATE THAN THE
QUEENS ZOOM. HOWEVER IT SHOULD BE NOTED
HERE THAT A SHIFT UP IN the FREQUENCY of the
SAMPLE RATE DOES NOT NECESSARILY MEAN AN
INCREASE IN APPARENT MOTION ON the SCREEN.
IF THERE IS A STATIC CAMERA SEQUENCE WHERE
the POINT of VIEW DOES NOT DRASTICALLY CHANGE
DURING the RECORDING, THEN ■ A HIGHER SAMPLE
RATE WILL ONLY SERVE to INCREASE the RESOLUTION
of the TIME LAPSE PROCESS. THIS SHOULD BE
UTILIZED IN "the ANCIENT of DAYS" to CREATE
A VISUAL PEAK or CLIMAX at the FOURTH SECTION
YET the ~~RHYTHM~~ OVERALL RHYTHM (the CLOCK SAMPLE
RATE) KEEPS ON INCREASING for EACH SEGMENT.

<u>TEMPORAL PIVOTAL POINT</u> : CAN ACTUALLY BE A CITY
MONUMENT SOMEWHERE. EVERYTHING MOVING TO the LEFT
SIDE of IT WILL BE IN FORWARD MOTION AND
EVERYTHING MOVING TO the RIGHT of IT WILL BE
IN FORWARD MOTION

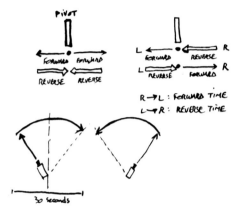

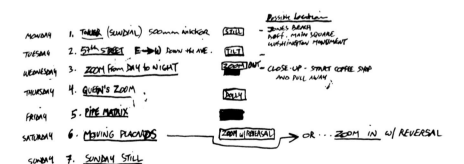

<u>OTHER TECHNIQUES</u>:
    <u>SIMULTANEOUS</u> - MULTI-CAMERA RECORD
    <u>SCANNING ROCK</u> - L→R, R→L PIVOTING w/ TIME REVERSAL

TECH. NOTE

Cosmological Cycles and Temporal Symmetry

1. Scanning: video prefers the scanner as opposed to the telescopic motor-drive due to its inability to record frame by frame. Film would adapt quite readily to the telescope motor-drive as a means of producing camera movement through compressed time. In this instance, the motion of the camera and the time passed would be proportionally equivalent, all occurs within one sweep of the scene. Video method involves multiple passes, or scanning of the scene, and thus requires a compounding of samples to form the final composite image. The duration of each sample is the duration of the final result (while with the filmic it is a percentage of the final) and the number of samples determines the fidelity or resolution and scale of the final composite image.

Techniques:

Scanning + electronic zoom—a CCTV [closed-circuit television] scanner is used to produce within a single sequence a time-lapse landscape pan and zoom.

Automated (repeatable) camera zooming and panning allows for camera motion to be introduced during time-lapse sequences.

Programmed zoom allows for soft wipe effects to be used within the frame, timed to the zoom, so different parts of the image are occurring in different times.

Temporal symmetry—a zoom in can be combined with a zoom out reversed to produce one long zoom in which time reverses itself in the course

A pan L→R can be combined with a pan R→L reversed to produce one long pan in which time reverses itself in the course.

—Note, 1979

Section 4. of *The Ancient of Days*

> Death is non-movement
> Stillness is life
> Stillness is death
> Stillness is the root of all life
> Death is the root of all life.

Section 3. (57th St.) ends with night. It ends upside-down.
Section 4. must be a movement into death—into non-movement.
Beginning in night it emerges into the day.
Beginning with movement, it ends in stillness.
Beginning swiftly it proceeds from slowness to stillness.
It moves from *in* to *out*. (time lapse zoom)

—Note, 1980

Breaking out of the landscape ... Breaking out of the logical shot order ... Breaking out of the sweeping pans...

Reality is not logical, our perception of it is not logical, our conception of it *is*. Reality is open-ended, our mental set imposes structure, order, connections.

—Note, 1980

I want to look so close at things that their intensity burns through your retina and onto the surface of your mind. The video camera is well suited to looking closely at things, elevating the commonplace to higher levels of awareness. I want each image to be the first image, to shine with the intensity of its own first-born being.

—Note, 1980

No beginning/No end/No direction/No duration
     Video as mind
—Note, 1980

Reading Rilke's life through his poetry has allowed me to discover what my Japan piece will be—

I am about to ask an object a question and then listen.

"When a question is posed ceremoniously,
    the universe responds."

This sense of seeing—or seeing the sense of an object—is what I have been after. I have sensed in *Chott* and some of *Reflecting Pool* that intense unrelenting camera vision can be compared to concentrated vision which heralds a shift in consciousness. . . . The object doesn't change, you do. This is what is behind the Buddhism brought from India to China to Japan—this is exactly what the *suiboku-ga* painters were doing. They painted rocks, grasses, a heron—yet these things shone with a light that penetrated far deeper than their pictorial form or even their concepts conveyed by the viewer's words.
This is pure seeing.

—Note, 1980

There are image symbols which can barely be articulated.
They belong to the domain of the visual memory.
Committing them to words rapes their secrets.
Working only from the intangible puts great
pressure on the thought forms.
To remember only.
To forget, erase.
To learn, rearrange.
Can't pick it up. Can't hold it.
Can't see it all at once.
Video haiku. A set pattern of frames.

—Note, 1981

Hatsu Yume (First Dream) 1981

I was thinking about light and its relation to water and to life, and also its opposite—darkness or the night and death. I thought about how we have built entire cities of artificial light as refuge from the dark.

Video treats light like water—it becomes a fluid on the video tube. Water supports the fish like light supports man. Land is the death of the fish. Darkness is the death of man.

—1981

Hatsu Yume (First Dream), 1981, videotape

Following page: printout (detail) of computer editing instructions to assemble frames
of the videotape *Hatsu Yume (First Dream)*, 1981   81

EDT	REL	MODE	TYP P S	T	P-VTR IN	P-VTR OUT	R-VTR IN	R-VTR OUT
BLOCK 001								
062	BLK	V	C		00:00:00:00	00:00:00:00	06:38:29	00:06:38:29
062	001	V	D	01:15	20:06:09:04	20:06:08:16	00:06:38:29	00:06:58:29
	DM-003							
	SUN FADE							
063	001	V	C		20:06:08:17	20:06:08:17	00:06:58:28	00:06:58:28
	DM-003							
063	BLK	V	D	01:03	00:00:00:00	00:00:01:04	00:06:58:28	00:07:00:04
	JAPAN PART 1	ROUGH SEAS in: 00:07:00:04						
064	BLK	VA1A2	C		00:00:00:00	00:00:00:00	00:07:00:04	00:07:00:04
064	001	VA1A2	D	08:00	18:51:32:16	18:51:32:16	00:07:00:04	00:07:17:04
	DM+000							
065	001	VA1A2	C		18:51:30:02	18:51:30:02	00:07:17:04	00:07:25:04
	DM+000							
066	001	VA1A2	C		18:51:22:00	18:51:22:00	00:07:25:04	00:07:31:19
	DM+000							
067	001	VA1A2	C		18:51:13:13	18:51:13:13	00:07:31:19	00:07:37:19
	DM+000							
068	001	VA1A2	C		18:51:07:05	18:51:07:05	00:07:37:19	00:07:42:19
	DM+000					(BLK) AUDIO	00:07:00:04 – 00:07:42:19	
069	001	VA1A2	C		18:50:58:13	18:50:58:13	00:07:42:19	00:07:53:04
	MDM+000							
069		MX	1111032300000000000000000000000000000000000000000000000000000000					
069			D322EF1F000000000000000000000000000000000000000000000000000000000					
070	001	VA1A2	C		18:51:03:00	18:51:03:08	00:07:53:04	00:08:00:06
	DM+004							
071	001	VA1A2	C		18:51:07:04	18:51:07:10	00:08:00:06	00:08:05:21
	DM+004							
072	001	VA1A2	C		18:51:13:13	18:51:13:21	00:08:05:21	00:08:12:26
	DM+004							
073	001	VA1A2	C		18:51:15:28	18:51:16:10	00:08:12:26	00:08:21:11
	DM+005							
074	001	VA1A2	C		18:51:21:05	18:51:21:21	00:08:21:11	00:08:32:01
	DM+005							
	P1=R9A P2=R5A							
075	001	V	C		18:49:38:23	18:49:39:29	00:08:32:01	00:08:44:01
	DM+010							
075	002	V	D	12:00	11:29:27:17	11:29:39:17	00:08:44:01	00:08:56:01
①	R VTR OUT IS	BEGIN WAVE MIST in: 00:07:42:19						
076	BLK	A1A2	C		00:00:00:00	00:00:00:00	00:07:42:19	00:07:42:19
076	001	A1A2	D	40:00	18:46:37:13	18:46:42:11	00:07:42:19	00:08:32:01
	DM+010							
077	001	A1A2	C		18:41:42:11	18:41:43:17	00:08:32:01	00:08:44:01
	DM+010							
077	002	A1A2	D	12:00	11:29:27:17	11:29:39:17	00:08:44:01	00:08:56:01
①	OSORESAN MT MIST	RVTR=MASTER1 P1=SM1 P2=R5A						
078	002	V	C		11:29:39:17	11:29:39:17	00:08:56:01	00:08:56:01
078	001	V	D	04:00	00:22:09:17	00:23:44:27	00:08:56:01	00:09:43:22
	DM+200							
①	AOMORI MT MIST	+1600 RVTR=MASTER1 P1=SM2						
079	001	V	C		01:22:10:06	01:23:23:12	00:09:43:22	00:10:20:09
	DM+200							
	RVTR=MASTER1 P2=9A MANUAL RAISE AUDIO							
080	002	A1A2	C		19:33:16:16	19:33:25:20	00:09:43:22	00:10:20:09
	DM+025							

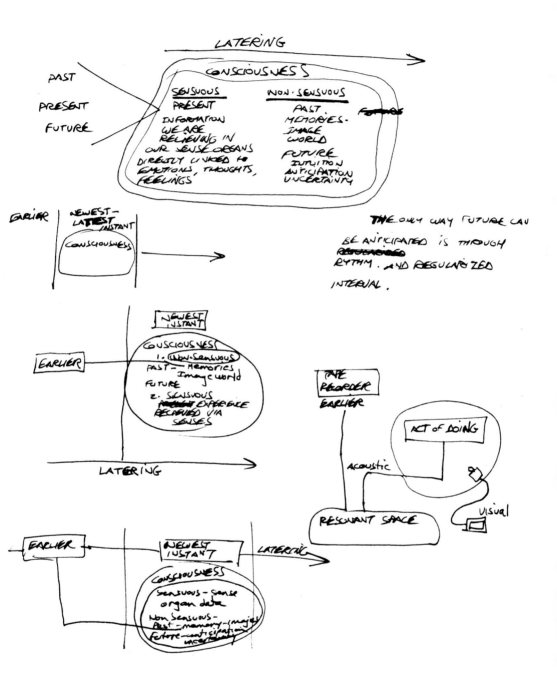

LATERING

CONSCIOUSNESS

SENSUOUS
PRESENT

INFORMATION
WE ARE
RECIEVING IN
OUR SENSE ORGANS
DIRECTLY LINKED to
EMOTIONS, THOUGHTS,
FEELINGS

NON-SENSUOUS
PAST.
MEMORIES.
IMAGE
WORLD

FUTURE
INTUITION
ANTICIPATION
UNCERTAINTY

PAST

PRESENT

FUTURE

EARLIER

NEWEST-
LATEST
INSTANT

CONSCIOUSNESS

THE ONLY WAY FUTURE CAN
BE ANTICIPATED IS THROUGH
RYTHM. AND REGULARIZED
INTERVAL.

NEWEST
INSTANT

EARLIER

CONSCIOUSNESS
1. Non-Sensuous
PAST — Memories
FUTURE Image world
2. SENSUOUS
PRESENT EXPERIENCE
RECIEVED VIA
SENSES

LATERING

TAPE
RECORDER

EARLIER

ACT OF DOING

ACOUSTIC

VISUAL

RESONANT SPACE

EARLIER

NEWEST
INSTANT

LATERING

CONSCIOUSNESS

Sensuous — Sense
organ data

Non Sensuous —
PAST — memory — image
future — anticipation
uncertainty

Raw energy—pure unconscious / expression is always possible—/ it is the catalyst—it is different / when you are older—(H. Yume) / You can let go—you should let go—/ Non-thinking. Child's mind / from an adult is not child's mind—/ it is not adult's mind either.

—Note, January 1984

The nature of images:

My interest in the various image systems of the cultures of the world involves a search for the image that is not an image. This is why I am not interested in "realistic" rendering. Sacred art seems very close because of its symbolic nature. Its intrinsic interwoven meaning on other planes makes it more "conceptual." I am interested not so much in the image whose source lies in the phenomenal world, but rather the image as artifact, or result, or imprint, or even wholly determined by some inner realization. It *is* the image of that inner state and as such must be considered completely accurate and realistic. This is an approach to images from an entirely opposite direction—from within rather than without. Therefore "eye" images are not important and can be misleading. This line of directions involves discussions of basic human perceptual mechanisms, thought processes, physiology, techno- logical surrogate systems, and psychophysics. Perhaps one of the most difficult tasks of the contemporary artist is not to become swamped by the number of techno-tools capable of precision rendering of the visible world (photo, film, video) and to create with these systems the "pure" images of the symbolic. It is much more of a feat than the hand-crafted arts. Images that are not images implies a use of images in ways other than the reproduction for appreciation of the visual physical world. Mandalas are an example of this, having specific function which determines their appearance. Here, too, enters another aspect of some "images that are not images," which involves the "reading" of images or a particular process of observation designed to extract certain information encoded in their forms. This gets into "other ways of seeing," an area not yet adequately explored. Sometimes, images can be the after-results, or a kind of debris, or a certain process which is culminated in the act of making, beyond which the image does not have much use except as artifact. The Zen Ga technique of painting pure circles is an example of this. Computers today can represent this layering of information, or symbolic character of images. The satellite data scans are interesting not because of the technical feats of extreme resolution and close-ups, which most people assume is achieved by some kind of zooming, but rather that all the information (detail) evidenced in the extreme close-up already and always existed in the long shot. There is no zooming involved; like physical realty, all the fineness of resolution is always there, we just determine the appropriate scan ratio for our display. This is quite different to zooming a lens. (Compare this potential to the data branching possibilities inherent in the videodisc/microprocessor systems currently in development.)

—Note, June 1981

Vegetable Memory 1978–80

Tsukiji Fish Market

Brutal afterlife.

There is no afterlife for the soul, only cold, ugly physical death. The body is only physical material, there is no spiritual stuff. When we die we cease to exist, our body just decays and rots, breaking down as other physical materials do.

In the end, hell is where we all shall go, except here "hell" is the non-existence of the afterlife, the world beyond. Our "hell" is our non-belief. We are doomed to be tormented in eternity by the hideous demons of the other side. They will poke us, drown us, number us, classify us, and systematically hack us to pieces. Their language we do not understand. They are the demons of unbelief. We will rot and be destroyed by their hand because we do not believe in the other choice. The spiritual liberation of the soul through death—death is birth. If we do not believe in spiritual afterlife then our bodies *will* rot away into material nothingness. We will cease to exist. This is hell . . . the brutal afterlife.

—Note, 1980

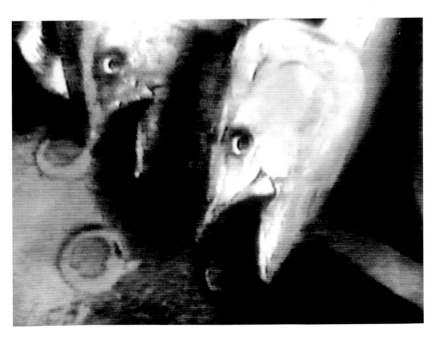

Vegetable Memory, 1978–80, videotape

Sight Unseen: Enlightened Squirrels and Fatal Experiments

I spent an entire day once, from dawn to dusk, sitting in the topmost branches of a tall tree. At times, I got so tired and pained that I thought I might fall out. Birds came by, some landing only a few feet away. If I was absolutely still they wouldn't notice. Two squirrels came running up from below, jumping around. Then, one of them froze, staring right up at me. He hopped onto another branch to get a better view. He just stood there, silent and still, looking. I think he was trying to figure out what I was. For the squirrel, a person is one of those large noisy animals that walk along on the ground. You never find them sitting up in trees. After a long time, he suddenly jumped and ran away down the tree. He knew. I saw him *know*—it was a flash, like those best ideas that come to you late at night.

I thought about those old tests they used in experimental psychology. An image is held in front of you, and it looks like absolutely nothing recognizable (except, maybe, a 1950s abstract painting). Then, all at once, you see—it is a grainy, black-and-white photograph of a cow turned sideways. After that, no matter how you orient the picture, you can never not see the cow. The "threshold of information" has been reached.

Accidents put people in a strange place. Initiation rites and age-old spiritual training ordeals (fire walking, days of continuous dancing, circumcision rituals, holy torture, etc.) are all controlled, staged accidents, ancient technologies designed to bring the organism to a life-threatening crisis state. Survivors of a car crash speak of a time which seems suspended. They watch themselves in slow motion spinning off the road. Police find it difficult to piece together the actual span of events from the witnesses' conflicting descriptions.

Accidents occur faster than the speed of thought; in fact, they demonstrate to us that we *have* a speed of thought—a finite point beyond which events unfold too quickly for us to translate them from input impressions to inner words. This is the time of instinct, when we

First published in *Video 80*, no.4 (Spring/Summer 1982), 31–33.

jerk our hand back from the flame without having to say "This is a flame, it is hot, it is burning my hand." Normally, we operate in the other place. We equate thinking with verbalizing, the voice inside our head becomes "us," constantly chattering away. When things shift either faster or slower outside of this "window," our spokesman becomes confused. Things like temporal elasticity result.

Accidents know no time. Their nature is to happen when not expected. Their time is right *now*, right at *this* moment. Anytime. William Burroughs once commented that he felt he was a miserable writer. "If I really knew how to write," he said, "I could write something that someone would read and it would kill them."

When a colony of ants dies, it dies ant by ant, yet in the space of one day an entire colony of two million ants may perish. When human beings die, they die cell by cell, with some cells functioning long after the others are down. Fingernails continue to grow for a week after death. When people are in car accidents and are wiped out instantly, it is said that a brain by the side of the road may take up to a full three minutes to cease functioning. It takes time for the word to get around. This phenomenon seems somehow related to ideas of relativistic time. The present (here, the realization of death) occurs at different times in different parts of the organism. In "natural causes," the brain goes first—it realizes that the end is in sight and terminates, sending out the word. If we compare man-made techno-systems to the organism, then the "brains" of this organization are living in the "future," and the rest of us to some degree in the past. When World War II ended, soldiers on remote islands in the Pacific were found to be still fighting months, or sometimes years, later. One of the ways animistic tribal cultures know that the spirit world, or afterlife, exists is that when a person dies, that person's memory image in another's mind does not abruptly disappear—thought forms continue to exist within all of those who knew them long after they are gone—for months, even years, and sometimes "forever."

Leto's Watch

Once, when staying in a remote village in the Solomon Islands in the South Pacific, I met a man named Leto, the second-in-command to the chief, and the only person in the village (and perhaps the entire coast) to possess a watch. The first thing Leto wanted to do was to show me his watch. He was so proud. I never found myself close enough to him to admire it in person, but, during the various ceremonial gatherings, he kept holding it up to show me whenever he'd catch my eye. I saw him winding it quite frequently, and holding it up to his ear to hear the ticking. Finally, on the next to last day of my stay, Leto came up to me early in the morning to show me his watch. He thrust it in my face, and I immediately noticed it was severely cracked. Still, the second hand was moving and the watch obviously working. Lastly, I noticed the time—it read half past three. I myself didn't carry a watch the whole time I was in the islands, but from the sun I judged the time to be about nine o'clock in the morning. Leto just stood there beaming smiles at me, and I smiled back. I realized he was his own time zone, and it really didn't matter. If anyone asked him the time (which not too many did), he'd just say "three-thirty," and that was that. If they asked him again the same time the next morning, it would be three-thirty again. I'm still wondering if later someone else from the village didn't get a watch as well, and if so, would that pose any problems at all, or would they both agree to synchronize themselves to the "Leto Time Standard" to avoid discrepancies. Or maybe the watch is just considered a piece of moving jewelry or ornamentation.

I remember when I was young how I used to marvel that the birds knew to wake up one hour later when the clocks were set ahead for daylight saving time. "The sun is setting one hour later today," my father would tell me.

Over a century ago, photography gave us a technology unrivaled in its accuracy in perceiving the true moment, yet few photographers (the most outstanding being Henri Cartier-Bresson) have made this their work and gone beyond the obvious stop-action trademarks of the medium. As cameras have proliferated, the chances have increased that someone would be on hand with one during the time of an accident. One old *Life* magazine series shows a racing car crash in successive stages. It reveals the crowd being mostly unaware the accident was occurring at the time the shutter was snapped. The last few frames show people beginning to turn their heads. Life as moving spheres of awareness.

We continually perceive afterimages. The photosensitive cells on our retinas have a decay time enabling us to view discrete flashes of still pictures as movement. The phosphors on a TV screen also have a decay time, further helping us to see a single point of light moving in a highly ordered repeating pattern as a human face. We carry around the six-month-old image of a friend not seen since fresh in our minds, regardless of the recent changes they or we have been going through. The entire concept of simultaneously linking and sensing a multitude of different points separated by vast distances on earth *at the same instant* has only recently been made a physical possibility in the electronic age, yet it still remains an alien idea to most of us who do not possess special powers. News has always traveled slowly, like the story of the lion with the longest tail in the world who bites the end of it just before going to sleep so that he'll wake up on time in the morning.

Places are pieced together in our minds and become "solid" and "real" structures only after we have been continually moving through them, accumulating "points of view." If an upright rod or flexible slender object is made to spin fast enough, one will perceive it as a solid. It becomes a "virtual volume." Staring into an electric fan in the window on a hot summer day will also reveal a stationary form or translucent solid. When the fan was turned off, I used to love waiting for that magical moment, watching closely until that one instant when my eye could finally catch a single blade and follow it going round until it came to stillness. It was always just one moment.

One of the many remarkable discoveries of Edward O. Wilson, in his studies of insect societies,[1] is the account of how termites constructing tiny arches as the basic building block of their complex nest architecture. When researchers isolated a single termite in a dish with some natural material, nothing happened. With two, there was more

1. Edward O. Wilson, *The Insect Societies* (Cambridge, Massachusetts: Harvard University Press, 1971).

activity, pushing tiny clods of earth around but nothing more. Finally, when there were more together, the seemingly random activity of moving stuff around came together, some sort of quorum or threshold of information was reached, and after a while the first tiny, perfect arch was completed. Each individual termite does not contain a brain large enough to think of things like building arches.

We usually don't think of the idea that knowledge exists between each and every person, waiting to be released by some trigger mechanism, rather than just "out there" somewhere. The idea that it comes from within ourselves seems to go against the whole concept behind public education and our schools. One also thinks of the notion that ideas are "in the air;" how, for example, two scientists, working in isolation in two different parts of the globe, can come up with the same discovery at about the same time. In science, duplication is a confirmation of the truth; in modern art, unfortunately, we immediately look for plagiarism. If we consider "discovery" not to be a process of creation but simply the realization of something that has already exisited, something old and not new, then our perception on these matters drastically shifts.

At one time, the act of perception was considered as creation. The eyes were said to out beams or rays which struck objects, thus making them visible. Vision as transmission. Viewing the images in clouds, reading the tea leaves and coffee stains in cups, seeing the man or the rabbit or whatever in the moon, were common ways to "read" nature. Life as Rorschach test. Meaning had a different meaning.

When you walk down the street, or drive down the freeway, the moon always follows with you. When a group of strangers standing on the corner in front of you look up at the moon, each sees his own moon. "The light of the moon covers the earth, yet it can be contained in a single bowl of water."[2] When the astronauts were coming back from the moon, one of them pointed the TV camera out the window and transmitted a live image of the round earth which appeared simultaneously on millions of TV screens throughout the world.

2. Dogen Zenji (1200–1253), *Shobogenzo*, trans. Kosen Nishiyama and John Stevens (Tokyo: Nakayama Shobo, 1975).

The notion of ideas existing in a space is an old one. Learning and knowledge have long been linked with physical activity and spatial movement. Baby ducks who are carried around in a basket after their mother never learn imprinting. Only the ones who have been allowed to stumble and struggle walking behind learn to recognize her. We are reminded of the teachers in elementary school who yell at their students to sit still and stop fidgeting while solving difficult math problems. In the ages before writing became common, a good memory was essential, and mnemonics, the art of memory, was perfected. One would memorize a long speech by first walking through an actual space, such as a large temple, over and over, learning the path. Later, one placed all of the key points in the speech at different places in the mental image of the temple, and to recall it all, one simply took an imaginary walk along the familiar path, passing all the pre-positioned points in order.[3] Here we have one of the first recording technologies being developed, and just as with the most recent state-of-the-art systems, such as one-inch high-band videotape, there is the concept of mapping time onto a single linear path. Today, we still talk of a "memory lane."

The editing structure of Hollywood films is based on this idea of space. Listening to a film editor talk is like speaking with a sculptor. What is called the grammar of editing is basically the ordering of shifts in camera point of view, which build up a mental image, or virtual volume, of the scene in the viewer's mind. Editors talk of having the viewer "know where they are." There are long shots ("establishing" or "cover" shots), medium shots, close-ups, cut-aways (hands, drinking glasses, views out the window), which are shot separately and all put together like building blocks—in most traditional situations it is usually a spatial process. (Monocular views such as Michael Snow's *Wavelength* and other works by experimental filmmakers break this down.)

Think of how you experience events in a dream or memory. We call it "the mind's eye." Usually, in recalling a scene or describing a dream, we do so from a mysterious, detached, third point of view.

3. Frances Yates, *The Art of Memory* (Chicago: University of Chicago Press, 1966); and A.R. Luria, *The Mind of the Mnemonist* (New York: Basic Books, 1968).

We "see" the scene, and *ourselves within it*, from some other position, quite often off to the side and slightly above all the activity. This is the original camera angle. It existed long before there was even such a thing as a camera. It is the point of view that goes wandering at night, that can fly above the mountains and walk through walls, returning safely by morning. The notion that the camera is some surrogate eye, a metaphor for vision, is not enough. It only grossly resembles the mechanics of the eye, and certainly not normal human stereoscopic vision with integration to brain. In function, it acts more like something akin to what we call consciousness, or human attention. Perhaps the mating of the video system with the computer currently underway will yield a closer approximation to true human "vision."

Once I spent a dark afternoon depressed in a sleazy Manhattan cafeteria, drowning (or amplifying) my sorrows in black coffees. After this grim affair, I trudged out onto the street only to be met by a wild-eyed disheveled character yelling at everyone who was crossing the street towards him. As I got close enough, I could hear what he was saying. He would point at passers-by, staring them in the eye, and yell "Yes, but do you know what you *really* look like?" He was obviously tuned into that other place where all our daily mind's-eyes converge. It was not what my self-image needed that day; in fact, it made me more depressed to know that I even had a self-image. Not quite the original face.

The Fatal Experiment

Weird things always happen in studios late at night. While I was at Syracuse University, the only time I could do my own work in the studio was the middle of the night, the graveyard shift from midnight to dawn. Sometimes, fatigue would set in and the janitor would come in to find me at six o'clock slumped over the controls with the monitors softly hissing away in snow. One night, I was having color shifting problems with one of the monitors, so I went to the closet and pulled out the degausser. A degausser is a strong electromagnet in the shape of a large flat donut, used to neutralize any magnetic buildup on the TV screen (and occasionally erase tapes in the vicinity if one is not careful). That night I got the idea that it might be interesting to see what would happen if I placed the degausser around my head and turned it on. The brain works on some electro-chemical process, I reasoned, and therefore the degausser should be capable of some consciousness altering effects. I raised the magnet and put my head inside. Then I thought, "No, here I am, alone. What if something weird happens? What if I become immobilized? What if my central nervous system starts going haywire? Will they find me slumped on the floor like an overcooked french fry?" And then, the most horrific thought of all, "What if my consciousness is permanently altered? What if the pulses in my brain's neurons are scrambled into an entirely new pattern? How would I know that a change had taken place? Would I remember who I was?" I waited a long, long time, magnet in hand. Finally, and I've never understood why, I decided to do it. I pressed the switch, and the degausser made that familiar buzzing sound. I thought that for a moment I felt extremely light-headed, but that could have been my imagination. I turned it off. Nothing happened. I looked around the room, still the same. I rushed off to the bathroom and looked in the mirror. Everything looked OK, no weird permanently frozen facial contortions. I walked back to the studio, and soon began feeling the tiredness of the hour. I had forgotten what I wanted to do there anyway. I went back home and went to sleep. Everything has been normal ever since.

96   *Reasons for Knocking at an Empty House*, 1983, videotape

Reasons for Knocking at an Empty House 1983

"Reasons for knocking..."—Effect of psychological states on the recording. Sleep deprivation is used as an element in the piece. ... Feeling of claustrophobia. All shot indoors, no outside except for window visions.

—Note, 1979

Existence for existence' sake.
Beyond waiting.
There is nothing to wait for except to live in the next moment.
Just living. Isolating time. The effects of duration. Boredom. Fatigue. Disorientation. Upset cycles. The psychology of isolation and sleep deprivation here is presented in two ways: first, the extreme wide angle cover shot of the room which never changes. A fixed frame. A constant container, both prison and security. Only the motion of the figure and his physical manipulations are visible as change. It becomes a claustrophobic viewing situation. Second—the common hallucinatory properties of sound in these situations is presented by lavalier miking— bringing the audio up close to the person in the room, oftentimes in relation to the visual image, way out of proportion and in opposition to a normal auditory situation. In situations without sleep, even the ticking of a clock can seem deafening.

—Note, 1980

Will There be Condominiums in Data Space?

Possibly the most startling thing about our individual existence is that it is continuous. It is an unbroken thread—we have been living this same moment ever since we were conceived. It is memory, and to some extent sleep, that gives us the impression of a life of discrete parts, periods, or sections, of certain times or "highlights." Hollywood movies and the media, of course, reinforce this perception.

If things are perceived as discrete parts or elements, they can be rearranged. Gaps become most interesting as places of shadow, open to projection. Memory can be regarded as a filter (as are the five senses)— it is a device implanted for our survival. The curse of the mnemonist is the flood of images that are constantly replaying in his brain. He may be able to demonstrate extraordinary feats of recall, but the rest of the banal and the mundane is playing back in there too, endlessly. The

Fig.1 Tibetan Buddhist monks from Ladakh making a sand mandala.

First published in *Video 80*, no.5 (Fall 1982), 36–41. Also published in *Communications*, eds. Raymond Bellour and Anne-Marie Dugnet, no.48 (1988), 61–74.

result can be lack of sleep, psychosis, and even willful death, driving some to seek professional psychiatric help (and thus become history on the pages of medical journals and books).[1] This reincarnates one of the curses of early video art—"record everything," the saturation-bombing approach to life which made so many early video shows so boring and impossible to sit through. Life without editing, it seems, is just not that interesting.

It is only very recently that the ability to forget has become a prized skill. In the age of "information overload," we have reached a critical mass that has accelerated the perfection of recording technologies, an evolution that leads back to ancient times. Artificial memory systems have been around for centuries. The early Greeks had their walks through temple,[2] and successive cultures have refined and developed so-called "mnemo-technics"—Thomas Aquinas described an elaborate memory scheme of projecting images and ideas on places (fig.2); in 1482 Jacobus Publicius wrote of using the spheres of the universe as a memory system (fig.2); Giulio Camillo created a "Memory Theater" in Italy in the early 1500s; and Giordano Bruno diagrammed his system of artificial memory in his work *Shadows*, published in 1582. Frances Yates describes this entire remarkable area in her brilliant book *The Art of Memory* (University of Chicago Press, 1966).

When I was in Japan in 1981, I visited a festival of the dead at one of the most sacred places in the country, Osoresan Mountain. There I saw blind female shamen called *itako* calling back the spirits of the dead for inquiring relatives, a centuries-old practice. Until that time I had felt that the large Japanese electronics companies were way ahead in the development of communications technology. After witnessing the *itako*, however, I realized they were way behind. Right in their own backyard were people who, without the aid of wires or hardware of any sort, have been for ages regularly communicating through time and

1. A.R. Luria, *The Mind of the Mnemonist* (New York: Basic Books, 1968).
2. The Greeks perfected a system of memory that used the mental imprinting of any objects or key points to be remembered onto specific locations along a pathway previously memorized from an actual temple. To recall the points in their proper order, one simply had to take the walk through the temple in one's mind, observing the contents left at each location along the way.

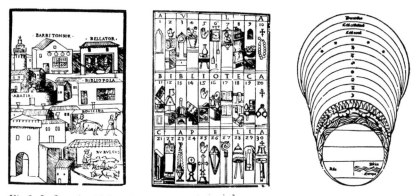

Fig.2 Left and middle: Abbey memory system, and images to be used in the Abbey memory system. From Jahannes Rombach, Congestorium Artificiose Memorie, Venice, 1533. *Right: The Spheres of the Universe as a Memory System, from Jacobus Publicus,* Oratoriae artis epitome, *1482.*

space with ancestors long gone. An interesting place at the temple site (which was perched in the surreal landscape of an extinct volcanic crater) was a special walk for the visiting pilgrims to take along a prescribed trail. The way led from the temple through a volcanic wasteland of rockpiles and smoking fissures to the shores of a crater lake. It was called "the walk through Hell." The path through the landscape and the points along it all had special significance. The *itako*, to call up the dead, took this "walk through Hell" in their minds, bringing the spirits in along the familiar path, and when they were through, sent them back the same way.

The interesting thing about idea spaces and memory systems is that they presuppose the existence of some sort of place, either real or graphic, which has its own structure and architecture. There is always a whole space, which already exists *in its entirety*, onto which ideas and images can be mapped, using only that portion of the space needed.

In addition to the familiar model of pre-recorded time unfolding along a linear path (as evidenced by many things from our writing system to the thread of magnetic tape playing in a videotape recorder), there is another parallel to be linked with modern technology. "Data space" is a term we hear in connection with computers. Information must be entered into a computer's memory to create a set of parameters, defining some sort of ground, or field, where future calculations and binary events will occur. In three-dimensional computer graphics, this field exists as an imaginary but real chunk of space, a conceptual geometry, theoretically infinite, within which various forms may be created, manipulated, extended, and destroyed. The graphics display screen becomes that mysterious third point of view looking in on this space (we often call it our "mind's eye"), which can be moved about and relocated from any angle at will. The catch is that the space must exist in the computer first, so that there is a reference system within which to locate the various coordinates of points and lines called into being by the operator. In our brain, constantly flickering pulses of neuron firings create a steady-state field onto which disturbances and perturbations are registered as percepts and thought forms. This is the notion that something is already "on" before you approach it, like the universe, or like a video camera which always needs to be "video-ing" even if there is only a blank raster ("nothing") to see. Turn it off, and it's not video anymore.

When I had my first experience with computer videotape editing in 1976, one demand this new way of working impressed upon me has remained significant. It is the idea of holism. I saw then that my piece was actually finished and in existence *before* it was executed on the VTRs. Digital computers and software technologies are holistic; they think in terms of whole structures. Wordprocessors allow one to write out, correct, and rearrange the *whole* letter before typing it. Data space is fluid and temporal, hardcopy is for real—an object is born and becomes fixed in time. Chiseling in stone may be the ultimate hard copy.

When I edited a tape with the computer, for the first time in my life I saw that my video piece had a "score," a structure, a pattern that could be written out on paper. We view video and film in the present tense—we "see" one frame at a time passing before us in this moment. We don't see what is before it and what is after it—we only see the narrow slit of "now." Later, when the lights come on, it's gone. The pattern does exist, of course, but only in our memory. Notation systems have been around since the beginning of history, since what we call history *is* notation of events in time, i.e., historical "records." With speech we have graphic writing systems; with music we have the score. They are both symbolic coded systems for the recording and later playback of information events in time. Poetry has always had a level that video or film cannot approach (at least not yet): the existence of the words on paper (how the poem looks, how the words are placed on the page, the gaps, the spacing, etc.). The whole poem is there before us, and, starting at the top of the page, we can see the end before we actually get there.

Our cultural concept of education and knowledge is based upon the idea of building something up from a ground, from zero, and starting piece by piece to put things together, to construct edifices. It is additive. If we approach this process from the other direction, considering it to be backwards, or subtractive, all sorts of things start to happen. Scientists always marvel at nature, at how it seems to be some grand code, with a built-in sense of purpose. Discoveries are made which reveal that more and more things are related, connected. Everything appears to be aware of itself and everything else, all fitting into an interlocking whole. We quite literally carve out our own realities. If you want to make a jigsaw puzzle, you must first start with the whole image, and *then* cut it up. The observer, working backwards into the system, has the point of view that he or she is building things up, putting it together piece by piece. The prophet Mohamed has said, "All knowledge is but a single point—it is the ignorant who have multiplied it."

The Whole is the Sum of Its Parts

A friend of mine is an ethnomusicologist who spent several years studying the gamelan music of Central Java. He was trained in Western music in the States, and spent many years working on his own compositions and performing with other musicians. One of the most frustrating things about his studies in Java, he told me, was trying to work on specific parts of songs with the gamelan musicians. Once they were at a rehearsal, and after running through a piece, he asked them to play only a section from the middle so that he could make sure he got all the notes right. This proved to be an impossible request. After a lot of hemming and hawing, excuses, and several false starts, he realized that the group just could not do it. They insisted on playing the entire piece over again, from beginning to end. In Java, the music was learned by rote, from many years of observation and imitation, not from written notation. The idea of taking a small part out of context, or playing just a few bars, simply did not exist. The music was learned and conceived as a whole in the minds of the musicians.

Giulio Paolini, the contemporary Italian artist, made a little-known but far-reaching videotape in the mid-seventies. It was his first and only tape. Working at an experimental video studio in Florence in the cradle of Western art, he, like many other European artists who visited the art/tapes/22 studio, had his first encounter with video. Instead of simply re-translating into video what he had already been doing before, as most other artists had done, Paolini intuitively recognized the great power underlying the recording media. He took the slides of all his work, most of the pieces he had ever made, and recorded them one at a time on each frame of video. Playing back this tape, the viewer sees 15 years of Paolini's art, his life's work, go by in less than a minute. Poof! It's gone.

It is slowly becoming clear that structuralism, currently out of fashion in the fashion-conscious, ever shifting spotlight of the art world, must be reconsidered. It is vital. However, this new structuralism is not the same as the often over-intellectualized, didactic, structuralism-for-structuralism's-sake that took center stage in the art scene over a decade ago (most visibly through the work of experimental filmmakers). In retrospect, however, the core ideas being expressed then certainly remain important, and perhaps could only have emerged in the way they did given that particular place and moment in cultural time. Furthermore, the anti-content messages that have been espoused in various fields of art in the twentieth century also continue to merit attention. We have all been made aware that, since the Renaissance, Western eyes have been drawn to the visual, to the surface appearance of the world. "Realism" came to mean how something appeared to the eye alone. Looking at the Gothic art before it, along with Asian and so-called Primitive or Tribal Art, it is clear that something fundamental is missing. However, from our viewpoint today, it is also clear that pure structuralism alone is no answer either.

> "Decadent art is simply an art which is no longer felt or energized, but merely denotes, in which there exists no longer any real correspondence between the formal and pictorial elements, its meaning, as it were, negated by the weakness or incongruity of the pictorial element; but it is often ... *far less* conventional than are the primitive or classic stages of the same sequence. True art, pure art, never enters into competition with the unattainable perfection of the world."[3]
>
> —A.K. Coomaraswamy

Structure, or form, has always been the basis of the original pictorial art of both Europe and the East, but the Middle Ages were the last time when both Europe and Asia met on common artistic ground.

> "In Western art, the picture is generally conceived as seen in a frame or through a window, and so brought towards the spectator; but the Oriental image really exists only in our mind and heart and thence is projected or reflected into space."

> "The Indian, or Far Eastern icon, carved or painted, is neither a memory image nor an idealization, but a visual symbolism, ideal in the mathematical sense. ... Where European art naturally depicts a moment of time, an arrested action, or an effect of light, Oriental art represents a continuous condition. In traditional European terms, we should express this by saying that modern European art endeavors to represent things as they are in themselves, Asiatic and Christian art to represent things more nearly as they are in God, or nearer their source."
>
> —A.K. Coomaraswamy

3. A.K. Coomaraswamy, *The Transformation of Nature in Art* (New York: Dover Publications, 1956). (Reprint of the original Harvard University Press edition, Boston, 1934.)

The idea of art as a kind of diagram has for the most part not made it down from the Middle Ages into modern European consciousness. The Renaissance was the turning point, and the subsequent history of Western art can be viewed as the progressive distancing of the arts away from the sacred and towards the profane. The original structural aspect of art, and the idea of a "data space" *was* preserved through the Renaissance, however, in the continued relation between the image and architecture. Painting became an architectural, spatial form, which the viewer experienced by physically walking through it. The older concept of an idea and an image architecture, a memory "place" like the mnemonic temples of the Greeks, is carried through in the great European cathedrals and palaces, as is the relation between memory, spatial movement, and the storage (recording) of ideas.

Something extraordinary is occurring today, in the 1980s, which ties together all these threads. The computer is merging with video. The potential offspring of this marriage is only beginning to be realized. Leaping directly into the farther future for a moment, we can see the seeds of what some have described as the ultimate recording technology: total spatial storage, with the viewer wandering through some three-dimensional, possibly life-sized field of prerecorded or simulated scenes and events evolving in time. At present, the interactive video discs currently on the market have already begun to address some of these possibilities. Making a program for interactive video disc involves the ordering and structuring (i.e., editing) of much more information than will actually be seen by an individual when he or she sits down to play the program. All possible pathways, or branches, that a viewer ("participant" is a better word) may take through the material must already exist at some place on the disc. Entire pre-recorded sections of video may never be encountered by a given observer.

Soon, the way we approach making films and videotapes will drastically change. The notion of a "master" edit and "original" footage will disappear. Editing will become the writing of a software program that will tell the computer how to arrange (i.e., shot order, cuts, dissolves, wipes, etc.) the information on the disc, playing it back in the specified sequence in real time or allowing the viewer to intervene. Nothing needs to be physically "cut" or re-recorded at all. Playback speed, the cardinal 30 frames a second, will become intelligently variable and thus malleable, becoming, as in electronic music practice, merely one fundamental frequency among many which can be modulated, shifted up or down, superimposed, or interrupted according to the parameters of electronic wave theory. Different sections can be assigned to play back at specific speeds or reversed; and individual frames can be held still on the screen for predetermined durations. Other sections can be repeated over and over. Different priorities rule how and in what order one lays material down on the "master" (disc). New talents and skills are needed in making programs—this is not editing as we know it. It was Nikola Tesla, the original uncredited inventor of the radio, who called it "transmission of intelligence." He saw something there that others didn't. After all these years, video is finally getting "intelligence," the eye is being reattached to the brain. As with everything else, however, we will find that the limitations emerging lie more with the abilities and imaginations of the producers and users, rather than in the tools themselves.

As in the figure/ground shifts described in Gestalt psychology, we are in the process of a shift away from the temporal, piece-by-piece approach of *constructing* a program (symbolized by the camera and its monocular, narrow, tunnel-of-vision, single point of view), and towards a spatial, total-field approach of *carving out* potentially multiple programs (symbolized by the computer and its holistic software models, data spaces, and infinite points of view). We are proceeding from models of the eye and ear to models of thought processes and conceptual structures in the brain. "Conceptual Art" will take on a new meaning.

As we take the first steps into data space, we discover that there have been many previous occupants. Artists have been there before. Giulio Camillo's Memory Theater (which he actually constructed in wood, calling it a "constructed body and soul") is one example. Dante's *Divine Comedy* is another. Fascinating relationships between ancient and modern technologies become evident. A simple example can be found

Fig.3 Left: Two deities and yantra diagrams of the same two deities. From a Nepalese illustrated manuscript, c.1760. Right: Ground plan of a temple.

in the Indian Tantric doctrine of the three traditional expressions of the deity: the anthropomorphic, or visual, image; the yantra, or geometric "energy" diagram (fig. 3); and the mantra, or sonic representation through chanting and music. It is interesting to note that these are all considered to be equal—simply outward expressions of the same underlying thing. In form, this is not unlike the nature of electronic systems: the same electronic signal can be an image if fed into a video monitor, an energy diagram if fed into an oscilloscope, and a sequence of sounds if fed into an audio system.

Today, there are visual diagrams of data structures already being used to describe the patterns of information on the computer video disc. The most common one is called "branching," a term borrowed from computer science (fig.4). In this system, the viewer proceeds from top to bottom in time, and may either play the disc uninterrrupted (arrow), or stop at predetermined branching points along the way and go off into related material at other areas on the disc for further study (like a form of "visual footnoting"). Examples of this system go something like—in a program on the desert, the viewer can stop at a point where plants are mentioned, and branch off to more detailed material on the various flora of the valley floor, etc. Although it is clear how this can enhance our current educational system, freeing students from boring and incompetent teachers so they can proceed at their own pace through

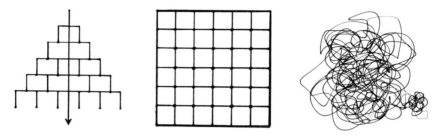

Fig.4 Branching Structure, Matrix Structure, Schizo Structure.

information which now contains movement, dynamic action, and sound in addition to written words, artists know that there must be more out there than this. Even though the technology is interactive, this is still the same old linear logic system in a new bottle.

As a start, we can propose new diagrams, such as the "matrix" structure (fig.4). This would be a non-linear array of information. The viewer could enter at any point, move in any direction, at any speed, pop in and out at any place. All directions are equal. Viewing becomes exploring a territory, traveling through a data space. Of course, it would not be the obviously literal one like the Aspen project.[4] We are moving into *idea* space here, into the world of thoughts and images as they exist in the brain, not on some city planner's drawing board. With the integration of images and video into the domain of computer logic, we are beginning the task of mapping the conceptual structures of our brain onto the technology. After the first TV camera with VTR gave us an eye connected to a gross form of non-selective memory, we are now at the next evolutionary step—the area of intelligent perception and thought structures, albeit artificial.

Finally, we can envision other diagrams/models emerging as artists go deeper into the psychological and neurological depths in search of expressions for various thought processes and manifestations of consciousness. Eventually, certain forms of neurosis, so long the creative

4. A landmark interactive laserdisc project by MIT Media Lab, in the late 1970s, that mapped the city of Aspen, street by street, with moving cameras so that the viewer could take a "ride" through the city, going anywhere at will—one of the first visual-mapping database moving-image projects related to data space ideas and today's virtual reality technology.

fuel of the tormented artist in the West, may be mapped into the computer disc. We may end up with the "schizo" or "spaghetti" model, in which not only are all directions equal, but all are not equal (fig.4). Everything is irrelevant and significant at the same time. Viewers may become lost in this structure and never find their way out.

Worlds are waiting to be explored. It is to be hoped that artists will be given their share of access to experiment with this exciting new technology. I recently had a glimpse of some of the possibilities for art when I met a designer who had first encountered computers while working at a large French fashion design firm in New York. There, the graphics artist worked at computer terminals. With a light-pen, he could draw various designs, working with functions of computer memory and data manipulation. Furthermore, his terminal was linked to a large databank of fabric designs and images from around the world and throughout history. After completing a sketch, for example, he could call up a seventeenth-century Japanese kimono design, look at it or superimpose it with his own idea. Then he could call up a turn-of-the-century European dress pattern, combine that with his design or integrate it with the kimono, all the while storing the various stages in memory. When all of this was completed and the final design chosen, he could then tie into other offices in Europe and the Orient right on the same screen. Designers could compare notes, get availability data on his fabric from the mills (i.e., where is the best silk, who has stock, what is the order time, etc.). All phases of his work could occur on the same screen as digital information. He could travel in space (Europe, the Far East), as well as in time (art history), all in an instant and available either as written text or visual images.

Despite the anti-technology attitudes which still persist (some, it should be added, for very good reasons), the present generation of artists, filmmakers, and video-makers currently in school, and their instructors, who continue to ignore computer and video technology, will in the near future find that they have bypassed *the* primary medium, not only of their own fields, but of the entire culture as well. It is imperative that creative artists have a hand in the developments currently underway. Computer video discs are being marketed as a great new tool in training and education. At this moment, there are creative people experimenting with the technology, ensuring that innovative and unique applications will emerge; but for now, many of the examples return to the boring domain of linear logic in the school classroom. The Aspen city map project is perhaps one of the more interesting examples of new program formats. We are at the beginning, but even so, for the artist, standard educational logic structures are just not that interesting. Artists have been to different parts of the brain, and know quite well that things don't always work like they told you in school.

It is of paramount importance now, as we watch the same education system that brought us through school (and the same communications system that gave us the wonderful world of commercial TV and AM radio) being mapped onto these new technologies, that we go back and take a deeper look at some of the older systems described in these pages. Artists not shackled to the fad and fashion treadmill of the art world, especially the art world of the past few years, will begin to see the new meaning that art history is taking on. As I have begun to outline in this article, the relation between the image and architecture (as in Renaissance art), the structuralism of sacred art (Oriental, Early Christian, and Tribal art, with their mandalas, diagrams, icons, and other symbolic representations, including song, dance, poetry), and artificial memory systems (the first recording technologies from the time of the Greeks through the Middle Ages), are all areas that require further investigation.

As we continue to do our dance with technology, some of us more willingly than others, the importance of turning back towards ourselves, the prime mover of this technology, grows greater than the importance of any LSI circuit. The sacred art of the past has unified form, function, and aesthetics around this single ultimate aim. Today, development of self must precede development of the technology or we will go nowhere—there *will* be condominiums in data space (it has already begun with cable TV). Applications of tools are only reflections of the users—chopsticks may be a simple eating utensil or a weapon, depending on who uses them.

The Porcupine and the Car

Late one night while driving down a narrow mountain highway,
I came across a large porcupine crossing the road up ahead.
Fortunately, I spotted him in time to bring the car to a stop a short
distance from where he was standing. I watched him in the bright
headlights, standing motionless, petrified at this "close encounter of
the third kind." Then, after a few silent moments, he started to do
a strange thing. Staying in his place, he began to move around in a
circle, emitting a raspy hissing sound, with the quills rising up off
his body. He didn't run away. I realized that this dance was actually
a move of self-defence. I cut the car headlights to normal beams,
but he still continued to move around, even more furiously, casting
weird shadows on the trees behind. Finally, to avoid giving him a
heart attack, and to get home, I cut the lights completely and
turned off the engine. I watched him in the dim moonlight as he
stopped his dance and moved off the road. Later, while driving off,
I realized that he was probably walking proudly away, gloating
over how he really gave it to that big blinding noisy thing that
rushed toward him out of the night. I'm sure he was filled with
confidence, so pleased with himself that he had won, his porcupine
world-view grossly inflated as he headed home in the darkness.

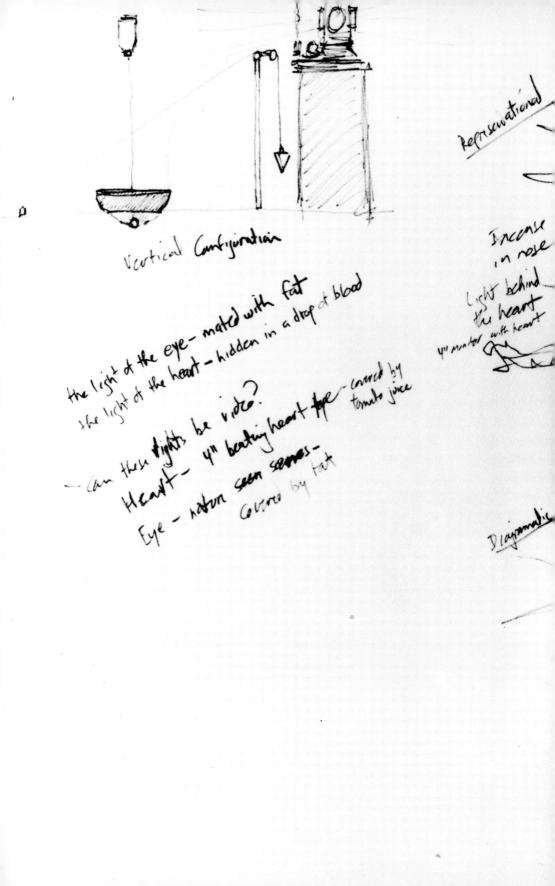

Vertical Configuration

the light of the eye - mated with fat
the light of the heart - hidden in a drop of blood

— can these lights be video?

Heart — 4" beating heart tape — covered by tomato juice

Eye — nature seen scenes — covered by fat

Incense in nose

Light behind the heart

4" monitor with heart

The Right Use of Forms

Soul is linked to the body
though it in no wise resembles the body

Lamp of reason

Fat in eyes

Skull.
— Sound from mouth

℞ Tomato juice
dripping from
heart

Stretched wire
running from mouth
transduced vibration
with pick-up

The power of the light of the
eye is ~~mated~~ mated ~~to~~ with fat

The light of the heart is hidden in
a drop of blood.

Joy harbors in the kidneys
Pain in the liver

The lamp of Reason in the
brains of the head

Smell in the nostrils
and speech in the
tongue

Reason

Sight
Smell

Heart

(sound)   Horizontal Layout

An Instrument of Simple Sensation 1983

The Right Use of Forms

Soul is linked to the body
    though it in no wise resembles the body
The power of the light of the
    eye is mated with fat
The light of the heart is hidden in
    a drop of blood.
Joy harbors in the kidneys
    Pain in the liver
The lamp of Reason in the
    brains of the head.
Smell in the nostrils
    and speech in the
        tongue

—Jallaludin Rumi (1207 –1273), *The Masnavi*

Previous page: notebook, 1983

Origins of speech
Origins of sight
Origins of thought

The regular rhythm of a live beating heart.
The light of an object and its internal image.
The sound of a tuned wire in vibration.
The weight of a stone.
The reflection in a bowl of clear water.

—Note, 1983

An Instrument of Simple Sensation, 1983, video/sound installation　115

Room for St. John of the Cross 1983

The Spanish poet and mystic St. John of the Cross
(1542–1591) was kept prisoner by the religious
establishment for nine months in 1577. His cell had
no windows and he was unable to stand upright.
He was frequently tortured. During this period St. John
wrote most of the poems for which he is known.
His poems often speak of love, ecstasy, passage
through the dark night, and flying over city walls and
mountains.

Above: installation text panel for *Room for St. John of the Cross*, 1983

To reach satisfaction in all,
desire its possession in nothing.
To come to the knowledge of all,
desire the knowledge of nothing.
To come to possess all,
desire the possession of nothing.
To arrive at being all,
desire to be nothing.

To come to the pleasure you have not,
you must go by a way in which you enjoy not.
To come to the knowledge you have not,
you must go by a way in which you know not.
To come to the possession you have not,
you must go by a way in which you possess not.
To come to be what you are not,
you must go by a way in which you are not.

When you turn toward something,
you cease to cast yourself upon the all.
For to go from the all to the all,
you must leave yourself in all.
And when you come to the possession of all,
you must possess it without wanting anything.

In this nakedness the spirit finds its rest,
for when it covets nothing,
nothing raises it up,
and nothing weighs it down,
because it is in the center of its humility.

—St. John of the Cross (1542–1591)

Anthem 1983

Anthem originates in a single piercing scream emitted by an eleven-year-old girl standing in the reverberant hall of Union Railroad Station in Los Angeles. The original scream of a few seconds is extended and shifted in time to produce a primitive "scale" of seven harmonic notes, which constitute the soundtrack of the piece. Related in form and function to the religious chant, particularly tantric Buddhist and Gregorian chants, *Anthem* describes a contemporary ritual evocation centered on the broad theme of materialism—the architecture of heavy industry, the mechanics of the body, the leisure culture of southern California, the technology of surgery, and their relation to our deep primal fears, darkness, and the separation of body and spirit.

—1983

AMERICA HAS NO DEMONS
The demon and the dark forces in Contemporary America—
Technological death
Cancer as the demons
Mechanical death—eating away of the body, physical processes
disturbed. Machines fail to do their job.
Hospital ward—wires, electrodes, chemicals, oscilloscopes, charts, tubes
life-support structures
    [—A life-support machine operating on nothing—]
Lying in the technological hospital as facing death
The hospital techno-ward as the living death.

—Note, January 1982

Anthem will be based entirely on contemplative vision—the original
source of true and balanced art—the original realism. . . .

The process of producing *Anthem* is the process of coming to terms
with the environment in which I live. It is an attempt at integration,
interpretation, and penetration of this place and this culture.

—Note, July 1982

Anthem, 1983, videotape   119

Anthem—Develops the image symbols idea—
each shot is a discrete ideogram—
the shots must be still and short—motion is minimal,
if so, it is concise and gestural. . . .
The shots must present everything that can be gathered in one glance—
they become like thought forms, or idea phrases.

In the string of image symbols there is repetition and patterning—this
becomes part of the piece and changes the meaning of the images as they
reappear in a different context.

—Note, February 14, 1982

Anthem—the paintings of the deities are not
representations, they *are* that energy.
The unseen world—the unknown, it is
threatening, archetypal images of danger,
fear, ominous, expectation, anticipation
Yantra, Mantra, Anthropomorphism
Understanding the spirit world—the key
to understand your own death and transience.

The images of the deities represent different
stages of growth—inner symbols, and all
illusions to be broken through/transcended.

—Note, April 14, 1982

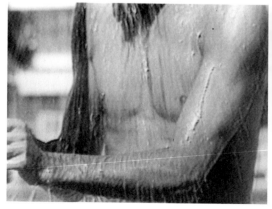

120   *Anthem*, 1983, videotape

History, 10 Years, and the Dreamtime

I remember a story:

> On a mountainside one afternoon about 2,500 years ago, the
> historical Buddha, Shakyamuni, delivered what has come to be
> known as the "silent sermon." He was offered a yellow flower and
> was asked to preach the Law to a large congregation of his
> followers assembled there. Shakyamuni held out the flower in his
> hand before the group. There was a hushed silence as the people
> waited for him to speak. They waited and waited, but he remained
> silent, firmly holding up the flower. Shakyamuni's gaze caught the
> eye of his foremost disciple, Maha Kashyapa, who smiled broadly
> in recognition. With the exception of Maha Kashyapa, no one could
> understand what the Buddha meant.

I remember thinking that here is one of the earliest accounts of
direct communication through the use of an image ... a real object
of nature, but framed as an image through the context of a formal
sermon. This famous story has been especially treasured by Zen
Buddhists because it illustrates the principle of understanding directly
through one's experience. It remains one of the special properties and
silent powers of the image. In our deepest past, of course, before
attempts such as this to reconcile nature as an image within the context
of high culture and language were even necessary, the natural environment itself was an image-symbol. There were no nouns, only verbs.
We were living within, instead of outside, the image.

> "If I seem to be on the verge of superstition, please recall that the
> images we make are part of our own minds, they are living
> organisms that carry on our mental lives for us, darkly, whether
> we pay them any mind or not."
> —Hollis Frampton, 1974

First published in *Video: A Retrospective, Long Beach Museum of Art 1974–1984*,
ed. Kathy Rae Huffman (Long Beach: Long Beach Museum of Art, 1984), 18–23.

This was around the same time that I attended the "Open Circuits" conference at The Museum of Modern Art in New York. I remember Hollis Frampton gave a talk there. It was January in 1974. I was studying human memory at the time—the senses, perception, the brain, memory—human "hardware," having realized that by concentrating so much on technology's hardware, I was missing the other half of the equation. The idea of images as living organisms fascinated me. Burroughs had been talking about images as a virus, but here Frampton was almost admitting them to the animal kingdom. I was also reading Aldous Huxley—his pioneer excursions to the interior via his work with mescalin, *The Doors of Perception* and *Heaven and Hell*:

"Like the earth of a hundred years ago, our mind still has its darkest Africas, its unmapped Borneos and Amazonian basins. In relation to the fauna of these regions, we are not yet zoologists, we are merely naturalists and collectors of specimens. The fact is unfortunate; but we have to accept it, we have to make the best of it.

"Like the giraffe and the duck-billed platypus, the creatures inhabiting the remoter regions of the mind are exceedingly improbable. Nevertheless, they exist, they are facts of observation; and as such they cannot be ignored by anyone who is honestly trying to understand the world in which he lives."

—Aldous Huxley, 1956

I remember reading about history. History as a filter ... it was constantly being rewritten. Human memory (like the five senses) was also a filter. Rather than being a past sense, memory becomes the future, informing all present actions and continually being updated, modified, and invented. They described psychological studies that showed that after witnessing an accident people would invent things that had never actually occurred, based on the nature of the questions asked of them later. History serves the present. It exists in the present. The concept of history is inextricably linked to the process of recording (i.e., historical "records"). What is recorded (whether it be a computer disc or a stone, intentional [photograph] or not [petrified forest]) is history. What is not recorded does not exist. It was an interesting book, but I have forgotten the title. I lent it to someone and never got it back.

"There is a myth that TV is an 'instant' medium, whereas metal sculpture is a 'permanent' medium. The irony is that metal sculptures have often been destroyed due to lack of storage space, and that instant and fragile electronic information often gets kept for years due to the convenience in storage and retrieval. E.g., the 1920s are gone, but the thirties are alive every day, as late-night TV shows. This strange phenomenon is bound to continue forever and someday, for some new generation, the demarcation line between the twenties and thirties will be as unreconcilable as B.C. and A.D."

—Nam June Paik, 1973

In 1974, the Everson Museum published the catalogue of a retrospective exhibition of work by Nam June Paik entitled *Videa 'n Videology*. It remains the best document of his work and vision. I still have it on my shelf. In 1974 people were already talking about a video history, and had been for a few years. I remember sitting in a Chinese restaurant in New York on a cold February evening with some friends. In my studies of memory, I had tried to trace the process of encoding an image backwards, from a stored mental image back to a real-time pattern of light. Up from Long Term Memory (where your address and name are) to Short Term Memory (which you must continuously refresh by repeating a 'phone number over and over on the way to writing it down) and then to the retina, I had just learned of Iconic Imagery. It seems that images are retained in all their complete detail for as long as a second after exposure. Most of the time we assume that these are live images of the world. So where does memory begin and direct stimulus end? It seemed as if all images were memories. I was confused.

Someone started talking about video history: "Video may be the only art form ever to have a history before it had a history." Video was being invented and simultaneously so were its myths and culture heroes, was what they were saying. Someone thought that young curators, writers, and artists were looking for a way into the already crowded art scene and were simply interested to stake claims and legitimize the medium as soon as possible. The waiter brought too many dishes—we never ordered chow mein. "The interesting thing about considering a history of video is that the medium itself is coming to be considered as history," someone said (TV as the conscience of the culture). "The value of documentation, publicity, and the self-conscious sense of history-as-media was right there from the start, in fact that's what most of it was about." (You are Information, remember?)

I recall first encountering descriptions of this newly formed feedback loop—history as media about history—in McCluhan. Everyone had read McCluhan in those days (also amplifying that feedback loop in the process). The original video field was greatly informed by the intellectual currents of the time—the McCluhan, Weiner, Fuller media culture self-consciousness constellation. Video had it in itself to be history right from the start—thus the tremendous emphasis on recording, expressed in those days as the "process v. product" rap. It's easy to forget that in the beginning it was enough simply to take part in this phenomenon of "recording-simultaneously seeing-instantly playing-back" something, anything, whatever. This certainly was, and underneath all the sediment today still is, a remarkable and profoundly fundamental characteristic of the medium, worthy of all the attention it received. In the seventies I wrote about the end result of an over-enthusiastic interpretation of these revelations:

> "Once, a friend of mine gave me a shopping bag full of used audio cassette tapes that he had retrieved from the garbage at his office. Thrilled at the prospect of unlimited free recording time, I got an idea to set up a tape recorder right in the center of activity in my house, the kitchen, and to try and record everything that went on. My idea was to have an ongoing, almost continuous record of all sonic activity in that space. When played back, it would create a sort of stream-of-consciousness parallel world to the present, but displaced in time. I kept the recorder loaded with tapes all the time I was at home, which then being my summer vacation was practically all the time. By the end of the week, when I had accumulated well over 24 hours of tape, I suddenly realized a distressing thought. I would need 24 hours, exactly the time it took to record, to play all this stuff back. Furthermore, if I kept this up

say, for a year, I would have to stop after six months to begin playing back, and if I really got ambitious and made it my life's work, I would have to stop my life when it was only half over to sit down and listen to all the material for the rest of my life, plus a little additional time for rewinding all the cassettes. It was a horrible thought, so I took down my tape recorder and immediately stopped the project.

"Information is in a way the opposite of garbage, although in our contemporary commercialized world they may at times appear identical. Both are products of man-made processes, and, despite what a few crazy artists now, and some archeologists far in the future, may say, it is a generally held view that garbage loses value over time, while information seems to be in the process of something gaining value over time. As a rule, information is something to preserve, garbage is something to be destroyed. However, both can be looked on as a kind of waste product, a physical burden, and for contemporary society both are among the most pressing problems of the day. An ancient Sufi saying states that a heavy load of broken pottery and a heavy load of books are the same for the donkey. . . . Consider for a moment the total amount of books, magazine and newspaper articles, radio and television programs, records, videotapes, and films produced in the world in one week alone, and it becomes clear that the major task of today is not information production, but information management. . . . In this light, the main problem for artists using video these days lies in deciding what *not* to record. Making a videotape, therefore, might not be so much the creation or building up of something, but more like the cutting or carving away of everything else until only a specific thing remains."[1]

Video archives as a sort of magnetic city dump—they are certainly almost as much of a bother to maintain. I like the idea of garbage pickers as intellectuals, of a culture's shit being the key archeological prize revealing its identity, and of the possibility that in our uncertain

1. Bill Viola, "The Porcupine and the Car," *Image Forum* (Tokyo) (September 14, 1980).

future it will most likely be only those die-hard survivors, the cockroaches, who will be left to go through our trash. Someone once told me that they thought it was interesting that the past and history were so connected to the earth, to dirt and rock, that we speak of layers of history or strata and how this is reflected in the expression, "down through history and up through evolution." It made me think of digging in the dirt when I was a kid.

Around this time I remember reading about Jacques Sandulescu. He was trapped in a collapsed Russian coal mine. Buried alive, he couldn't move an inch. Sweat ran down his face as he cried and screamed, only to fill his mouth with choking coal dust. Fear overwhelmed him. He wrote:

> "...at that moment I remembered finding some wild strawberries in the forest miles away from home. I had brought them to my mother inside a large green leaf; I knew she loved them. As I gave them to her, she looked at them, the first strawberries of the season, and then gazed at me a long time. That look in her eyes was the most beautiful and tender thing I have known in my life."

I used to leave a lot of books I was reading in Chinese restaurants and on subways and buses. I lost my copy of *Guerilla Television* that way. It seems like we were all reading more in those days. Those books were so important, now I don't seem to have as much time any more. Last week I borrowed a copy of *Guerilla Television* and have been reading through a lot of old stuff trying to remember what it was like in 1974, the year the video program began at the Long Beach Museum of Art. We forget things so easily.

> "to write about ... to write ... about ... tape is like explaining a trip to someone who's never dropped acid."
>
> —Marco Vassi in *Radical Software*, no.1 (1970)

I started to remember things that I had forgotten. From *Guerilla Television* I re-learned that Michael Shamberg, the author, was a writer with the "establishment's" *Time* magazine when he covered the "TV as a Creative Medium" exhibition at the Howard Wise Gallery in 1969, and soon after got into video and the Raindance group; that the group Videofreex came together, around a substantial chunk of money provided by CBS TV, to produce a pilot to broadcast entitled "Subject for Change" about alternate media and all the new stuff that was going on; that one of the innovative technical projects of the time, the automated Video Matrix information switcher, was actually designed first to be used to hype cans at an industrial trade show; that Global Village was set up as a sort of new light show, with people paying to come in and watch a bank of nine monitors playing back multiple channels of tapes during Thursday, Friday, and Saturday night shows with ads describing sex acts placed in the New York newspapers; that Raindance was started as a profit-making corporation, had financial advisors, and planned to sell stock.

It was all beginning to sound like the eighties and not the late sixties. And so it should—the art of survival hasn't changed in centuries. It's strange how our tinted rear-vision mirror changes and projects our own values and desires, distorting the past. We view distant events through a polarizing filter of black and white, a lowering of resolution. Some people may feel that these video facts don't fit into their idea of what the late sixties should be, but actually they are thoroughly late sixties. This is why all this stuff was right there in print as necessary survival information in one of the most important media survival manuals of the time. It is historical necessity that new things are always composed of opposites (synthesis as the true creative principle)—how, for example, the Hippies needed the establishment to define themselves, how the two halves of the A-frame need each other in order to stand, and how the ambiguous vase / two faces of the famous Gestalt psychology image are each composed of *both* figure and ground.

With all these "historical records" in front of me, I found myself always referring to the books for dates, for the numbers I have never been able to remember since school. History had always seemed to be numbers. I was relieved years later to read that the brain seems to function with images, a language of mental pictures, visuo-spatially derived, and even when recalling numbers it will tend to do so by visualizing the shape of the symbol for the number "5." William the Conqueror, 1066; Nam June Paik, Wuppertal Gallery, 1963. Thinking of events as numbers, as lists of dates, can trivialize them and revive the old "quantity over quality" attitude. (Older is better.) Although it is certainly important to know when things happened, all the old debates I came across about whether it was Paik or Vostell who first used a TV set in their work seemed just plain ridiculous. It totally ignored the reality of the situation—that Paik's contribution to video art is vastly more important, substantial, and far reaching than Vostell's. I was reading that the mind by nature will do precisely that—distill and synthesize concepts, trends, and content while glossing over actual figures and sequences.

Poking through the past, I also saw the continuation of a clear line of demarcation that previously had always seemed to fade the farther one went back in time into the infant video history. Apparently, that great common primordial soup of the sixties, where we tried to merge everything into a common single-celled media egg, never really existed. Right from the start there were at least two different clearly isolated streams: the video groups, just mentioned, and the individual artists. They existed in parallel, and the reason for these two divergent approaches, the group/communal and the personal/individual, was not as much economic, technical, or political, as simply psychological, or possibly even biological. The type of person drawn to do something with a group and the person who goes off somewhere to work alone are just two different animals. Artists have always been solitary individual characters. Bruce Nauman began using video alone in his studio in 1968 on the West Coast. Les Levine began that year in New York. Keith Sonnier followed in 1969, and soon after William Wegman, Richard Serra, Vito Acconci, John Baldessari, Paul Kos, Joan Jonas, Peter Campus, and many others all began making highly personal, individual tapes, most commonly characterized by the presence of the solitary artist on the screen, often in his or her studio, performing some activity.

The video groups emerged in the communal context of late-sixties politics and were communications oriented (including technological development), while the other "group" of individuals was emerging from the established art world. These "art world artists" were not included in the first two landmark exhibitions in the field, Howard Wise's "TV as a Creative Medium," in New York in 1969, and Russell Connor's "Vision and Television" at Brandeis University in 1970. (This was partly because it was a bit too early. Work by Les Levine was also shown at Brandeis.) They were also slow to be accepted by the newly forming public television artists' facilities, which preferred working with the documentary and technological videomakers and conventional forms like dance and drama, easier to assimilate into the context of mass-media broadcast.

These factors caused an early separation, which has persisted, and put the technologists, the so-called "video synthesizer artists," initially on the side of the communications media activist and video groups, altogether not an accurate or comfortable position. Furthermore, Howard Wise had already proposed a relation to video and kinetic/technological art by showing video in his gallery, although by the early seventies this work had faded from fashion in the art world.

The exhibition for the "art world artists" that proved to be their "TV as a Creative Medium" (and clearly acknowledged the link between video and performance) was the "Ten Video Performances" exhibition at the Finch College Museum of Contemporary Art in New York in 1971, although this third landmark exhibition is not discussed as much in the recent written video histories. Soon after that show, the effects of classifying all this activity by the media being used, rather than according to the nature of the work itself, would begin to show up in the gradual intermingling of these two directions in the many video exhibitions and events to follow. The museums and media programs became neutral ground where the various gallery artists, video groups, and independent individuals could be seen under the catch-all umbrella of "video art," and throughout the seventies up to the present they have remained the only real showcase for all the diverse work in the field.

Meanwhile, back in the seventies, I continued losing books and continued my studies of memory and images. I had become interested in images of time, which soon led me into diagrams, mapping, and geometry —the arts of the sky (astronomy-led architecture and navigation). Time was often described as a spiral. Galaxies, vortexes, tree rings ... Growth became concentric—a radiation, not a line. Things happened from the inside out, not from down to up. I began to think of human growth, my own life, in the same way—ideas can grow too ... their expression as images ... images are living things ... they must all share this pattern.

History became all out of sequence, progressing into the past as well as the future. If I was losing books I could always find them again.

This out-of-order history was confusing, but somehow made sense. I was always learning earlier things later. The tremendous and seemingly unprecedented exuberance that was in the air in those days, which is absolutely necessary to contact in order to understand the work that was being done then, and which I was having such a difficult time recalling ("rekindling," connoting a creative act, is a better term we use in connection with emotions), that total deluge of newness and images, I discovered to be mirrored in the past in a book I picked up in 1974, Lázló Moholy-Nagy's *Painting, Photography, Film*. It was 1927, but he might have been describing video and the expanded cinema of 1967. Here were the first telegraphed cinema images, microscopic images, astronomical plates, X-rays, photograms, lightning, extreme oblique angles, "arrested laughter,"—exhilarating extensions of the senses interspersed with prophetic quotes like:

> "Gigantic sums are often spent making a feature film. Compared with the technique and instrumentation of this film, present-day painterly technique is still at an infinitely primitive stage."

This could be the 1973 Nam June Paik catalogue from the Everson:

> "… the cathode ray tube will replace the canvas."

> —Nam June Paik, 1965

I discovered the films of Oskar Fischinger and the "pure cinema" of Hans Richter from the twenties—patterns of pure light and abstract movement flickering across the screen, like the Kubelkas later, and the video synthesizers after that, and the incredible sophistication and intelligence of the abstract Islamic art of pattern before them all. One of the tricks of the information age, compounded by experiencing it in contemporary America, is that everyone's attention is focused on the present. There is just too much stuff coming at you to think about anything else. In the age of self-consciousness (the media age), we are like a brain that has been deluded into believing that self-consciousness is the highest state and finds that it now has to think each and every heartbeat, each and every flexing of the lungs. So ten years begins to seem like a long time, the Rolling Stones start being described as "old music," Michael Jackson "new," classical pianists are "contemporary artists," and video-makers are allowed to cut on the frame, thanks to the equipment manufacturers, and "discover" montage editing ("never before in the history of video"), while Sergei Eisenstein (and all who know him) are out there somewhere smirking.

> "When the pianist becomes conscious, i.e., becomes aware of the present and thinks about striking each individual note as he or she once did in painstaking practice, it becomes impossible to play. The fingers trip over each other. It is impossible to be spontaneous, somewhat like trying to be creative in the eighties."

> —Edmundo Soto, 1984

In 1974 I remember David Ross going "way out there to California" (as in Saul Steinberg's New York "way out there") to head up the newly forming Long Beach Museum video program. I remember coming here ("there") to live in 1981, and thinking now I had to go "way out there" to New York (even though this was still not the accepted designation of "back East" and "out West," with its implicit indication of past and future, going and coming, left and right, history [the Old World] and the future [the New Frontier]).

I was having a hard time figuring out where I was in time and space, but here I am, writing an article for the Long Beach Museum of Art's ten-year video anniversary, gathering all this material, going through the old books and articles, planning to start out by decribing the environment in 1974. I make some notes, trying to remember what it was like:

> "In 1974, when the Museum's program came into existence, the first phase of video art had already played itself out. It was five years since Howard Wise's "TV as a Creative Medium." Raindance had already disbanded. Electronic Arts Intermix had launched its videotape distribution a year earlier in 1973. EAI handled primarily the "video" artists, while the Castelli Gallery had begun distributing the "art world" video artists. Video media access centers were in

full swing, and many art schools had begun regular programs in video. The first generation of video artists was well established and exhibiting regularly.

"But something was up and 1974 proved to be a pivotal year. The first two major conferences were held that year—"Open Circuits" at The Museum of Modern Art, an international meeting of artists, critics, curators and scholars who discussed ideas and issues, and the "Video and the Museum" conference at the Everson Museum in Syracuse, bringing together museum, gallery, media center people and artists from around the country.

"In technology, the video frame was just coming into existence, or rather, access, with the appearance of time code and computer editing, and the first low format automated editing controllers. Color was just becoming a reality with the introduction of the first portable color cameras. (Jon Alpert made the first color video program in the field, *Cuba—the People* in 1974.) The Time Base Corrector was introduced that year, providing the missing link between low format and broadcast standards. Advent introduced the first color video projector. There was no home video, no home computers, no video games, no videotape slow-motion, no one-inch VTRs, no digital video effects, no music videos/MTV. TV news was still shot on film. Soap operas still looked different from regular shows. Cable TV was barely a presence despite earlier optimistic prophecies. Three-quarter-inch videocassettes, first marketed only two years earlier, were only beginning to take hold, existing side by side with half-inch open reel in most facilities.

"The second stage of video, characterized by the shift from black-and-white to color, the emphasis on editing (and thus closer relation to cinema), the move to individual activity in the breakup of the video groups, the relocating of the field off centerstage and out to the fringes of the mainstream art world, the increased access to higher format equipment and emerging "professionalism," was just beginning. "Process" was giving way to "product." However, technically and experientially the video community was still ahead of the industry, reinforcing the sentiments of an alternative and somehow better media practice. Within a few years this would change—the industry would catch up, and soon, as today, greatly surpass the artists in technical innovation and expertise (something which ironically has a strengthening effect on the most important thing from the start—the actual "art" in the art form)."

This is as far as I got. I realized I was describing a totally different world, a landscape that no longer exists. All this discussion and thought about early video—I was starting to get dreams, past images, flash-backs. One was exceptionally vivid. We all get dreams like this every once in a while throughout life. What is interesting is that their vividness is not really about visual clarity or detail—it is a fidelity of *experience*, of being. The total sensation of what it is really like to *be* there fills your body—what it felt like to breathe air then. These are real "images." It is always a shock. We may be able artificially to record images, sounds, and words, but we are a long way from recording anything resembling experience. The shock is the realization of how much of the stuff of the past actually slips by.

Compounding this is the realization that our society has evolved such a warped sense of time. As technology accelerates everything into a higher and higher velocity, and as our dreams become centered on becoming more efficient, we are finding that we actually have less and less time. Lack of time is one of the greatest problems haunting the video field and all our modern institutions. It is why things sometimes get done in a haphazard and patchy manner, or not at all. People barely manage to keep their heads above the man-made institutional waters. The central problem of the day is how to maintain sensitivity and depth of thought (both functions of time) in the context of our accelerated lives.

"The spiritual life is something that people worry about when they are so busy with something else that they think they ought to be spiritual."

—Thomas Merton

I remembered an experience shooting video up on Mt. Rainer in 1979. I thought I would do a deep study of the mountain, and decided to fix the camera in one posittion for a week, observing the mountain passing through different stages of time and weather. I felt it important to devote so much time to what in the end would be a very short scene.

It was only after I finished and was proudly coming back down the mountain with my hours of tape in a big box that I realized what I had done. For the mountain, that time was like a puny little flashbulb that fired off so quickly it was almost invisible. One week—it was almost an insult.

I still think of watching that mountain move . . . and it *is* moving. I think about the words "the moving image." What is this movement? What is this process that transforms a living constellation of events into a history, a memory? I remembered again being at the "Open Circuits" conference in 1974. There, Hollis Frampton described the unity of the film and video media as "the mimesis, incarnation, bodying forth of the movement of human consciousness itself."

I was "back East" not too long ago and ran into an old friend on the street. I hadn't seen him for years. He had changed so much, I was frantically trying to update the old image I had been carrying around inside. He had just come from a Woody Allen movie. We began talking about video history of all things. He said he didn't know if he believed in history. I told him Woody Allen didn't either, and I paraphrased a quote of Allen's: "When I started working as a comedian," he said, "I just did those jokes which I thought were funny and I didn't give it a second thought. I'm sure Mort Sahl or Lenny Bruce and those guys didn't either. And then you find, when the press takes a look at your work after a year or two of performing, they see so many recurring themes that they say, 'Well, this guy Mort Sahl is really a political commentator.' I don't think he ever sat down in a room and said, 'Shall I talk about women, or shall I talk about politics?' It's never a conscious choice you make, never a conscious choice."

"In an age where there is much talk about 'being yourself'
I reserve the right to forget about being myself, since there is very
little chance of being someone else."
                                                    —Thomas Merton

I was getting cold standing on the street. We both agreed that something was shifting and that we seemed to be moving into a new phase. "You know," he said, "I suspect that this new shift will have a fair amount to do with all this talk of television art, but eventually in a totally different way than anyone today can even imagine." We parted.

I was thinking about our meeting and about the key issue of distribution on the way home. A young woman came on the bus with a small child. She was holding a bunch of brightly colored flowers. I looked at the flowers, and I looked at the child. I love to watch small children, to try and get some sense of what the world may be like for them—what it was like for each of us—that exhilarating sense of total open wonder at the nature of things. I picked up my book, making sure not to leave it on the bus. I was reading *The Cloud of Unknowing*, a classic in Christian mysticism by an unknown author in fourteenth-century England. Here was this voice from the past speaking out so clearly and directly to me. I read these words:

> "I charge and beg you, with all the strength and power that love can bring to bear, that whoever you may be who possess this book (perhaps you own it, or are keeping it, carrying it, or borrowing it) you should, quite freely, and of set purpose, neither read, write, or mention it to anyone ... unless that person is in your judgement wholly determined to follow Christ perfectly. ... And he should be, in your estimation, one who has for a long time been doing all he can to come to the contemplative life by virtue of his active life. Otherwise, this book will mean nothing to him. Moreover, I charge you and beg you by the authority that love gives, that if any shall read, write, or mention this book ..., you should charge them (as I do you) to take time over their reading, writing, speaking, or hearing.
>
> "I do not mind at all if the loud-mouthed, or flatterers, or mock-modest, or fault-finders, gossips, tittle-tattlers, talebearers, or any sort of grumbler, never see this book. I have never meant to write for them. So they can keep out of it. And so can those learned men (and unlearned too) who are merely curious. Even if they are good men, judged from an active standpoint, all this will mean nothing to them."

The bus was passing by a sign advertising the promise of cable TV. There was some old guy rummaging through the garbage. This was my stop.

To the memory of Hollis Frampton (1936–1984) and Barbara Latham (1947–1984)

Heaven and Hell 1985

Heaven and Hell, 1985, video/sound installation

SAN FRANCISCO 1985   Installation

. HEAVEN and HELL

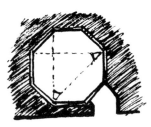

Projector alignment
with ~~blank walls~~
blank walls mirrored

1. LIVING ROOM SCENE.

TV: Close ups of birds eyes.
    Still standing birds (living trophys)
    Natural landscapes

Background: Large blow-up of 'pretty'
    B/w mountain panorama

Floor Lamp is on, soft orange glow

2. WILD FLIGHT IN DARKNESS:

White doves on black.
Wildly moving handheld camera.
Birds flying everywhere

Possibly also cut with
    Ferocious Barking Dogs at Night

Expanded Version: THE LIVING ROOM / THE DYING ROOM

In the dark room:

- White birds ~~at last~~ on black
= Attack Dogs at Night
- Night City Lights
- Sex Porno Clips
- Violent Crime
-

In the living room:

- Still Standing Birds
- Pastoral Landscapes
- The Moon crescent
- Suburbia
- Baby Birth
- Surgery

HEAVEN and HELL 2.

The same videotape is screened
in both rooms. The only difference
is the scale and the sound

One Monitor / One Projector
White Room | Black Room
   Silence | Sound
(or muzak)

Images on the monitor are just as
chaotic and violent (ie. a TV
metaphor)

CONTEXT as TOTAL POWER

Grazing as Pure Meditation

Remember—my plan for living with grazing
animals came from shooting the storms out
on the Saskatchewan prairies.

    Those cows and I sat there for eight hours.
They were much more at home than me.
They just "sat." Pure meditation, prairie
mind, at one with the landscape.

    I desired to record this state of mind
as the first idea to do the animal piece.

—Note, 1986

140   *I Do Not Know What It Is I Am Like*, 1986, videotape

I Do Not Know What It Is I Am Like

The tremendous energy released by a bolt of lightning is potential energy. Latent in the atmosphere, inverse charges build up within the mounting storm-clouds until a critical threshold is reached, and in an instant (about one tenth to half the speed of light) hundreds of thousands of volts of electrical energy are discharged, the stream of electrons forcibly burning a path through the non-conducting air, often jumping the gap between sky and earth.

And all this in a moment, in a time narrower than our tiniest thought, yet the image of lightning, in addition to leaving a momentary afterimage on the retina, is forever imprinted in the mind's eye of all who have ever experienced an electrical storm. We realize that we have seen this image before and are constantly seeing it as the diverse forms of nature continue to reveal their deeper common origins. We see the tree against the gray November sky; we see the river and its tributaries from an airplane window; we see the array of blood vessels in the body or the web of the brain's interconnecting nerve cells in a medical film; we sense a thought as it grows and branches out in our minds and lives.

The axis of the lightning bolt is the vertical; it travels along the line connecting heaven and earth. It is the same axis on which the individual stands when he or she walks out onto the great plain under the dome of the sky. It is the line that connects the ground they stand on to the deepest layer of time-lines in the geological strata of the earth far below, visible in the slice of the canyon wall. It is the path that the tree reveals as it stands and that is already contained in its seed. It is the same path along which the tree at the center of the world grows, the "axis mundi" described by Mircea Eliade, Joseph Campbell, Carl Jung, and others in their re-searches and reintroductions of that which we already have known into our newly conscious contemporary minds.

First published with the video disk *I Do Not Know What It Is I Am Like* (Los Angeles and Boston: Voyager Press/The Contemporary Art Television Fund, 1986). Extract published in the exhibition catalogue *Bill Viola: Installations and Videotapes*, ed. Barbara London (New York: The Museum of Modern Art, 1987), 59–62. See bibliography p.294.

In our horizontal models of time and movement, our image of the sediments of time, our expressions of "down" through history and "up" through evolution, the vertical pole becomes the continuous present, the connecting thread, the simultaneous, perpetual "now" that we are living at this instant and have always lived. It is the single point that, when displaced becomes the line, becomes the surface, becomes the solid forms of our world and minds, and that, without the imparted energy of movement (time) or the direction of movement (space), becomes the point once more, a process incremented by our breath as we each recapitulate its great form in the course of our individual journey.

There was a moment in prehistory when a large animal slumped down with its last breath and thoughts to leave its bones in the earth that the researcher is carefully sifting through in the fossil pit. There was a moment when the Cro-Magnon artist lifted the pigment-dipped natural-fiber brush to the walls of the cave that one now enters with electric light to view the image of the ancient bison on its walls. There was a moment when your father died, and his before that, and the same moment when the impulse and attraction between two human beings fused into the one that is yourself, as you will do/have done so many times in the past. There is a moment when the newborn first lets out a cry into the dry air, when the pressure of light first falls on the virgin surface of the new retina and is registered by some pattern of nerve impulses not yet fully "understood." There is a single moment when the flash of insight bursts into your unguarded mind, when all the pieces fall together, when the pattern is seen or the individual element uncovered ... when the breath of clarity opens the mind and you "see" for the first time in a long while, remembering what it was like again as if suddenly jolted from sleep. There is a moment when a single neuron fires in the darkness within the brain, when a threshold is reached and a tiny spark jumps the gap that physically separates one cell from another, doing the same shimmering dance when the heat of the flame touches the skin or when a deep memory replays on the surface of the mind. There is a moment, only truly known in anticipation before it happens, when the eyes close for the last time and the brain shuts down its circuits forever (the end of time). There is also the moment of recognition, the return of the familiar, the second-time perception that releases the latent energy and excitement of the first. It can be in a face, in a landscape, in a desire.

Then there is the moment of awareness of the other, embodied in the physical separation of mother and child, and restated from the first conceptualization of persons and objects in a space outside the skin, to the first encounter with an animal in the wild. The power of the gaze crystallizes these moments, and the eyes become the conduits of the exchange of energies between the organism and the environment, between the observer and the observed. A line of sight can just as easily slice through the separation between subject and object as it can define it.

As the gateway to the soul, the pupil of the eye has long been a powerful symbolic image and evocative physical object in the search for knowledge of the self. The color of the pupil is black. It is on this black that you see your self-image when you try to look closely into your own eye, or into the eye of another ... the largeness of your own image preventing you an unobstructed view within. It is the source of the laughter that culminates the staring game that young children play, and the source of the pressure that a stranger feels on their back in public as they turn to meet the eyes they know are there. It is through this black that we confront the gaze of an animal, partly with fear, with curiosity, with familiarity, with mystery. We see ourselves in its eyes while sensing the irreconcilable otherness of an intelligence ordered around a world we can share in body but not in mind.

Black is a bright light on a dark day, like staring into the sun, the intensity of the source producing the darkness of the protection of the closed eye. It is the black we "see" when all the lights have been turned off, the space between the glowing electron lines of the video image, the space after the last cut of a film, or the luminous black of the nights of the new moon. If there is a light there, it is only the light searching in the dark room that, limited by the optical channel within its beam, assumes there to be light everywhere it turns.

In memory of Ingrid Oppenheim (d. 1986)

144   *I Do Not Know What It Is I Am Like*, 1986, videotape

I Do Not Know What It Is I Am Like, 1986, videotape   145

Vision as reception
Vision as reflection
Vision as projection

—Note, 1986

The body as the unconscious.
The body as mind.
Landscape as the body.
The mind as landscape.
The dissolution of the self in the breakdown
    of inside/outside.
The skin as conceptual membrane.

Pain as knowledge.
Pain as beauty.
Satisfaction as stupification (as catatonia).

The mortification of the appetites.

—Note, January 1, 1987

Problems of vision

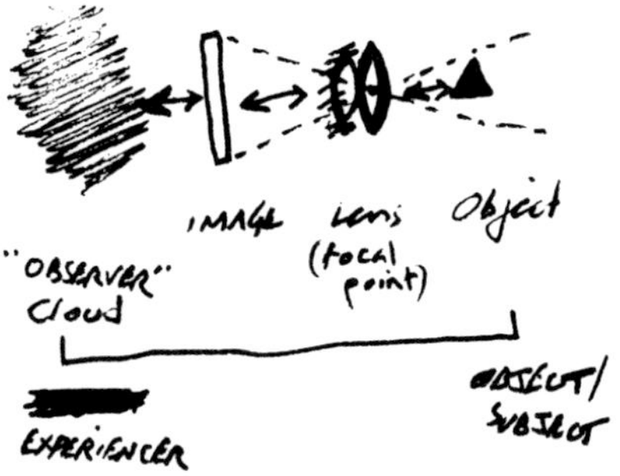

"OBSERVER"
Cloud

IMAGE   Lens   Object
         (focal
          point)

EXPERIENCER

OBJECT/
SUBJECT

Lens + Image are intermediaries
between object and ~~experience~~ perception/conception
Uncollomated light becomes the void of all possibilities.*

The observer deduces a position
in relation to the object. A "line
of sight" or direction to it, and
this distance becomes the degree of
separation of object (reality) and the
observer. All intermediaries, lens
and image, fall away in the final
perception. Sense of touch
becomes the unifying
sense.

The missing part of video is the viewer.
The dark room (the screening room) is the viewer's mind, the
space (cloud) behind the image — this completes the "backward
looking" sightline (the line of conception) in the vision process.

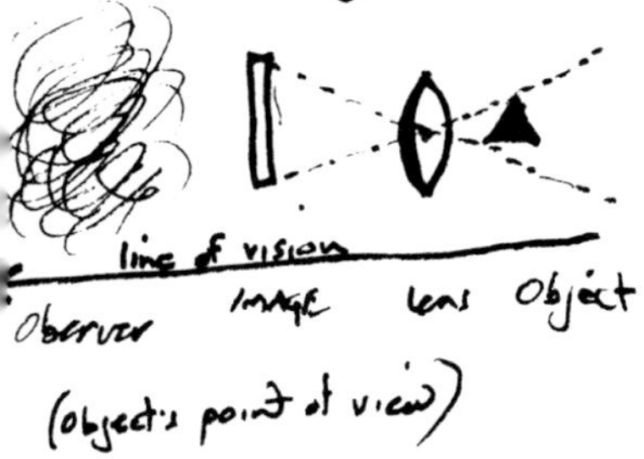

line of vision
Observer   Image   Lens   Object
(object's point of view)

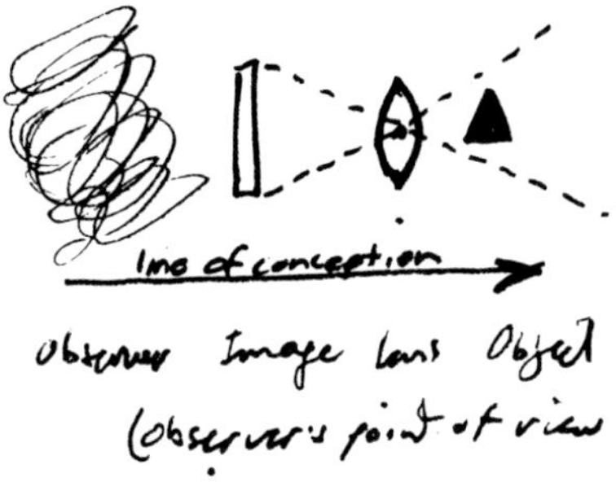

line of conception
Observer   Image   Lens   Object
(observer's point of view

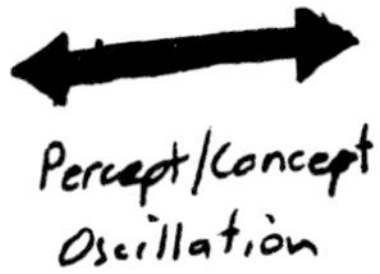

Percept/Concept
Oscillation

* Research, develope! lensless Video

The power of concentration—the energy of a thought to transform. The "ground"—the still object—the field on which thought energy manifests itself. When your world changes, it is your ideas which cause the radical shifts, the great realization overturns mountains, but the world itself does not change.

In order to realize the great shift, the mind must be tuned. The power of concentration is our most important faculty to be developed. Beyond physical maturity, strength, and sex, the metamorphosis is the ultimate desire and aspiration in adult life. Once we have procreated, the next transition is death, but somewhere in between these two posts we look for something else—we know there must be something that lies deeper. . . .

In my work I have most strongly been aware of the camera as representation of point of view—point of consciousness. Point of view, perceptual location in a space, can be point of consciousness. But I have been interested in how we can move this point of consciousness over and through our bodies and out over the things of the world. I especially identify with artist's, like Rilke's, location of this point out over the vastness and tremendous distances of open space—it is hard to locate his point of view in the poems if you are looking for it in the usual places. I want to make my camera become the air itself. To become the substance of time and the mind.

—Note, September 30, 1984

Statements 1985

Sense of place has been of primary importence in my work. I have
traveled all over the world to gather images for my videotapes.
I have found that the more intense my experience at a place
making a tape, the more power the piece absorbs for itself. My
travels have taught me that there is always just one "right place"
where an idea can come to life; that the single effort in making a
video piece is finding this "right place;" that video is sensitive to far
more than what the camera sees and what the microphone hears;
that what we call culture and the human spirit can be viewed as
the collective expression and interpretation of the overwhelming
power of the landscape.

—Note, 1982

For most viewers of my work, this "sense of place" is manifest as an
apparent concern with landscape—when the landscape becomes the
subject of a work, and other times when the landscape shares the
moment in balance with an action taking place in it, usually mediated
through a solitary individual. Yet these "landscape" works, in addition
to the other works I've done, are all landscape works in a larger,
extended sense. They find their unification in what for me is the
original place of the landscape in art and culture: the natural raw
material of the human psyche.

I do not distinguish between inner and outer landscapes, between the
environment as the physical world out there (the "hard" stuff) and the
mental image of that environment within each and every individual
(the "soft" stuff). It is the tension, the transition, the exchange, and the
resonance between these two modalities that energize and define our
reality. The key agent in this exchange of energies is the image, and
this "space between" is precisely the place in which my work operates.

From statements first published in the group exhibition catalogue, *Summer 1985*, ed.
Julia Brown (Los Angeles: The Museum of Contemporary Art, 1985), parts of which
were originally published in an interview with the artist by Deirdre Boyle in *Sight-
lines*, vol.16, no.3 (Spring 1983). Revised by the artist for publication in this collection.

In 1976, I made a piece called *Migration* in which I focused a camera on a single drop of water, revealing that the optical properties of the water drop created a miniature fish-eye lens; consequently, an image of the entire room and anyone in it was visible in each falling drop. In 1979, I went to the Sahara Desert in Tunisia and, using a special telescopic lens attached to the video camera, recorded mirages and other visual phenomena caused by the effects of the intense heat on light waves traveling across a vast, open distance. I have always considered that these two works are ultimately united — one pushes outwards, an investigation of infinite space, the other closes inwards, an investigation of the micro-world, and by doing so they both arrive at the same place.

When I was living in Japan I became fascinated with how notions of the landscape and space were integrated into traditional culture. (The rock gardens and tea houses are obvious examples of this.) Even Japan's written language, specifically the ideographic script imported from China, directly incorporates images from nature. The features of the natural environment as visual images *are* the origins of most written notation (such as hieroglyphs and picture writing, which led to the modern alphabet). Our brains contain the images of all landscapes, real and remembered. This is the original language. In a written Japanese poem, the characters on the paper serve as triggers that evoke responses contained primarily in the viewer. But in the romance languages, the words describe these responses as occurring to some implied generic observer.

I think it is important to emphasize the role of time in all this. Although we are talking about images, the existence and transformation or growth of the image in time (the "moving" image) is at the center of this whole process. Perception over time equals thought.

Just glance at an object as you pass it by. This is the physical realm— we avoid bumping into things when in this mode, without really thinking about them. But then grab an object with your eye and stare at it for a long time. It gradually takes over your psyche and becomes your thoughts. This is why duration is an important element in my work—cultivating the ability to see "through" objects.

In 1981 I made a videotape in Japan, *Hatsu Yume (First Dream)*, in which there is one sequence where a fixed camera views a rock on a mountainside over a long period of time. When it comes on the screen, the images are moving 20 times normal speed, and gradually, in a series of stages, it slows down to real-time, and eventually to extreme slow motion. People usually describe that scene by saying, "... the part where the people are all slowed down while moving around the rock." What I look at in that scene is the rock, not so much the people. I thought it would be interesting to show a rock in slow motion. All that is really happening is that the rock's time, its rate of change, exceeds the sampling rate (the recording time of the video), whereas the people are within that range. So the rock just sits there, high speed, slow speed ... it doesn't matter. I think about time in that way. There are windows or wavelengths of perception. They are simultaneous and interwoven at any one moment, but we are tuned only to a certain frequency range. This is directly related to scale changes in space or sound, proportion in architecture and music. A fly lives for a week or two, and a rock exists for thousands or millions of years.

In 1973 I met the musician David Tudor and became part of his *Rain-forest* project, which was performed in many concerts and installations throughout the seventies. One of the many things I learned from him was the understanding of sound as a material thing, an entity. My ideas about the visual have been affected by this, in terms of something I call "field perception," as opposed to our more common mode of object perception. In many of my videotapes, I have used the camera according to perceptual or cognitive models based on sound rather than light. I think of all the senses as being unified. I do not consider sound as separate from image. We usually think of the camera as an "eye" and the microphone as an "ear," but all the senses exist simultaneously in our bodies, interwoven into one system that includes sensory data, neural processing, memory, imagination, and all the mental events of the moment. This all adds up to create the larger phenomenon we call experience. This is the real raw material, the medium with which I work. Western science has decided it is desirable to isolate the senses in order to study them, but much of my work has been aimed at putting it all back together. So field perception is the awareness or sensing of an entire space at once. It is based on a passive, receptive position, as in the way we perceive sound, rather than an aggressive, fragmented one, as in the way our eye works through the narrowing function of focused attention. This perception is linked more to awareness than to momentary attention.

I have learned so much from my work with video and sound, and it goes far beyond simply what I need to apply within my profession. The real investigation is that of life and of being itself; the medium is just a tool in this investigation. I am disturbed by the over-emphasis on technology, particularly in America—the infatuation with high-tech gadgets. This is also why I don't like the label "video artist." I consider myself to be an artist. I happen to use video because I live in the last part of the twentieth century, and the medium of video (or television) is clearly the most relevant visual art form in contemporary life. The thread running through all art has always been the same. Technologies change, but it is always imagination and desire that end up being the real limitations. One of my sources of inspiration has been the thirteenth-century Persian poet and mystic, Rumi. He once wrote, "New organs of perception come into being as a result of necessity. Therefore increase your necessity so that you may increase your perception."

The Sound of One Line Scanning

"Our greatest blessings come to us by way of madness."

—Socrates

The ancient Greeks heard voices. The homeric epics are full of instances of people guided in their thoughts and actions by an internal voice to which they responded automatically. This suggests a people, as Julian Jaynes has pointed out, not fully exercising what we would consider free will or rational judgement.[1] As with most of us, there was a conversation going on in their heads, but it was not with themselves. Jaynes calls this distant mental landscape the "bicameral mind," and claims that, prior to the transition period of the Greeks, all ancient cultures were not fully conscious as we know it. In other words, they possessed many gods. Today we are suspicious of persons exhibiting such behaviors, forgetting that the term hearing refers to a kind of "obedience" (the Latin roots of the word are *ob* plus *audire*, or "to hear facing someone"). So rooted is our need for the concept of the independent mind, that we categorize those hearing voices as: a) mildly amusing, b) a poet, or c) confined to a mental institution. A possible fourth category might be "watching television." The prophets and gods have departed our world and the confused chatter in their wake must now be exorcized by someone called a "therapist."

> "A woman named Be was alone in the bush one day in Namibia, when she saw a herd of giraffes running before an approaching thunderstorm. The rolling beat of their hooves grew louder and mingled in her head with the sound of sudden rain. Suddenly a

First published, in a shorter form, in the catalogue for the National Video Festival (Los Angeles: The American Film Institute, 1986). Also published in *Sound by Artists*, eds. Dan Lander and Micah Lexier (Banff: Walter Phillips Gallery; Toronto: Art Metropole, 1990), 39–54; and as "Le son d'une ligne de balayage," *Chimères* (Paris), 11 (Spring 1991), 98–120.

1. Julian Jaynes, *The Origin of Consciousness in the Breakdown of the Bicameral Mind* (Boston: Houghton Miffin Co., 1976).

song she had never heard before came to her and she began to sing. Gauwa (the great god) told her it was a medicine song. Be went home and taught the song to her husband Tike. They sang and danced it together. And it was, indeed a song for trancing, a medicine song. Tike taught it to others who passed it on.

—!Kung Bushman story from Botswana,
as told to Marguerite Anne Biesele[2]

Consciously or unconsciously, most people assume the existence of some sort of space when discussing mental functioning. Concepts and terms for the manipulation of solid objects are constantly used to describe thoughts, as in "the *back* of my mind," "*grasp* an idea," "*over* my head," "*cling* to beliefs," "a mental *block*," and so on. This mental space is directly analogous to the "data space" in our first brain-child, the computer, being the field in which calculations occur and where the virtual objects of digital graphics are created, manipulated, and destroyed. Like a fundamental ontology, this given space is perpetually before or after what is done, an *a priori* existence from birth in the flip of a switch until the lights finally go out. If there is a space of thinking, either real or virtual, then within it there must also be sound, for all sound seeks its expression as vibration in the medium of space. The acoustic properties of this space, then, become the subject of this article.

To the European mind the reverberant characteristics of the interior of the Gothic cathedral are inextricably linked with a deep sense of the sacred and tend to evoke strong associations with both the internal private space of contemplation and the larger realm of the ineffable. Dream-image or flashback sequences in cinema have often utilized reverberation effects in the sound-track to signify both subjectivity and detachment. Cathedrals, such as Chartres in France, embody concepts derived from the rediscovery of the works of the ancient Greeks, particularly those of Plato and Pythagoras, and their theories of the

2. Recounted in Joseph Campbell, *The Way of the Animal Powers* (San Francisco: Harper and Row, Alfred Van Der Marck Editions, 1983), 163.

correspondence between the macrocosm and the microcosm, expressed in the language of sacred number, proportion, and harmony, and that manifest themselves in the science of sound and music. These design concepts were not considered to be the work of man, or merely functions of architectural practice, but represented the divine underlying principles of the universe itself. By incorporating them into the body of the church it was intended to establish a harmonic reflection of their form here on earth.

Chartres and other edifices like it have been described as "music frozen in stone." References to sound and acoustics here are twofold. Not only are there the actual sonic characteristics of the cavernous interior, but the form and structure of the building itself reflects the principles of sacred proportion and universal harmony—a sort of "acoustics within acoustics." When one enters a Gothic sanctuary, it is immediately noticeable that sound commands the space. This is not just a simple echo effect at work, but rather all sounds, no matter how near, far, or loud, appear to be originating at the same distant place. They seem to be detached from the immediate scene, floating somewhere where the point of view has become the entire space.

Ancient architecture abounds with examples of remarkable acoustic design—whispering galleries where a bare murmur of a voice materializes at a point hundreds of feet away across the hall, or the perfect clarity of the Greek amphitheaters where a speaker, standing at a focal point created by the surrounding walls, is heard distinctly by all members of the audience. Modern techniques of architectural acoustics, pioneered at the turn of the century by people such as Wallace Sabine, were derived in response to the severe unintelligibility of sound and lack of clarity due to room reverberation. This is doubly ironic, both in terms of the 2000-year-old Greek theater and the fact that the acute reverberation in the Gothic cathedral, although a result of construction and not specific intention, was considered an essential part of its overall form and function.

The science of acoustics is the study of sound in space. It assumes strong architectural associations because, although it can be described as simply the study of the behavior of sound waves, sound manifests itself at its most complex and interesting when bouncing off solid forms, most noticeably those of man-made interior spaces. In the rural world of the Middle Ages, it is doubtful that the awesome reverberations inside the cathedral had ever been heard before by the members of the clergy. A partial list of some of the most basic physical phenomena studied by acousticians reads like a set of mystical visions of nature.

Refraction: The bending of soundwaves due to a change in speed as they pass through different media, such as two layers of air of different temperatures. At Queen Victoria's funeral in London in 1901, rounds of artillery were fired and, although not heard in the surrounding countryside, the loud roar of cannons suddenly materialized 90 miles away.

Diffraction: Sound turning a corner, when the edge of a barrier generates a new series of waves. We hear invisible persons talking on the other side of a high wall.

Reflection: The rebounding of soundwaves off a surface, the angle at which they bounce off being equal to the angle at which they arrive. With multiple surfaces this becomes an echo, and it is then possible to hear one's own voice, possibly multiple times, as it existed at a previous point in time. One can sing with one's self. Multiple regular reflections produce the conditions of reverberation, where a sound can be repeated over and over on top of itself, the past becoming indistinguishable from the present.

Interference: Two sounds collide with each other, the wavefronts of each alternately reinforcing and inhibiting themselves. In a large hall the sound of a loud instrument suddenly drops to a barely audible whisper at a certain location in the room.

Resonance: Soundwaves reinforce themselves, either by the addition of an identical sound or when the material properties or spatial dimensions match the physical shape of the soundwaves themselves. A singer's voice becomes louder, gaining energy when released into a small enclosure, or an object produces a specific tone when struck. The shape and materials of an object represent a frozen sound potential.

Sympathetic Vibration, related to resonance and possibly the most evocative of all: When a bell is struck another one across the room begins vibrating, giving off the same sound.

Each of these phenomena evokes wonder, even after their scientific representations have been rationally understood. There is something of the immortal in an echo, for example: we can easily imagine an ultimate state of reverberation—a space where everything that has ever happened continues to exist—the end of time, where everything is live, perpetually present. If we sense that the description of sympathetic vibration bears some resemblance to radio broadcast, it is no coincidence, the same principle is at work. The processes of contemporary media systems are latent in the laws of nature—they have existed in various forms since the beginning of history.

We can also see, in resonance, that all objects have a sound component, a second shadow existence as a configuration of frequencies. In 1896, Nikola Tesla, one of the great geniuses of the electrical age, strapped a small oscillating motor to the central beam in his Manhattan laboratory and built up a powerful physical resonance that conducted through the building and into the earth, to cause an earthquake in which buildings shook, panes of glass broke and steam pipes ruptured over a 12-block area. He was forced to stop it with a blow from a sledge hammer. Tesla stated that he could calculate the resonant frequency of the earth and send it into strong vibration with a properly tuned driver of adequate size and specific placement.[3]

"Palongawhoya, traveling throughout the earth, sounded out his call as he was bidden. All the vibratory centers along the earth's axis from pole to pole resounded his call: the whole earth trembled: the universe quivered in tone. Thus, he made the whole world an instrument of sound, and sound an instrument for carrying messages, resounding praise to the creator of all."[4]

—Hopi Indian myth of the creation of the First World

3. Described in John J. O'Neill, *Prodigal Genius: the Life of Nikola Tesla* (New York: Ives Washburn Inc., 1944), 159–62.
4. Frank Waters, *Book of the Hopi* (New York: Ballantine Books, 1963), 5.

"In the beginning was the Word ... " provokes one to ask, where was the image? But like the Biblical creation myth, Indian religion (for example Yoga and Tantra) and later Asian religions (for example Buddhism) also describe the origin of the world in sound, with the original creative potency still accessible to the individual in the form of sacred speech and chanting (sympathetic vibrations). This idea of the origin of images in sound is mirrored in the invention and development of communication technology. In the age of the electronic image, it is easy to forget that the earliest electrical communication systems were designed to carry the word. For example, Edison initially tried to market the phonograph to the business community as an automated replacement for the stenographer in the office. If speech is the genesis of the media body electric—the telegraph and the subsequent systems of the telephone, radio, and television—then acoustics (or general wave theory) is the basic structural principle of its many manifestations.

The video image is a standing wave pattern of electrical energy, a vibrating system composed of specific frequencies, as one would expect to find in any resonating object. As has been described many times before, the image we see on the surface of the cathode ray tube is the trace of a single moving focused point of light from a stream of electrons hitting the screen from behind, causing its phosphor-coated surface to glow. In video, a still image does not exist. The fabric of all video images, moving or still, is the activated, constantly sweeping electron beam—the steady stream of electrical impulses coming from the camera or video recorder. The divisions into lines and frames are solely divisions in time, the opening and closing of temporal windows that demarcate periods of activity within the flowing stream of elec- trons. Thus, the video image is a living dynamic energy field, a vibration appearing solid only because it exceeds our ability to discern such fine slices of time.

All video has its roots in the live. The vibrational acoustic character of video as a virtual image is the essence of its "liveness." Technologi- cally, video has evolved out of sound (the electromagnetic) and its close association with cinema is misleading since film and its grandparent, the photographic process, are members of a completely different branch of the genealogical tree (the mechanical/chemical). The video camera, as an electronic transducer of physical energy into electrical impulses, bears a closer original relation to the microphone than to the film camera.

The original television studio was a hybrid of radio, theater, and cinema. Its images existed in the present tense. Its construction was based on the radio studio with the isolated control room behind glass, "on air" signs, and cameras placed out on the floor to pick up the action. The structure of the elements in the studio can also be viewed as the physical embodiment of the aesthetics of cinema, an ingenious solution to the "limitation" of having to exist live. Multiple cameras, usually three (representing film's classic long, medium, and close-up shots), view the action from their individual points of view. Unlike cinema, where activity within a given scene must give the illusion of simultaneity and sequential time flow, with the action often shot out of order, video represents a point of view that is literally shifted around the space in the present tense, parallel to the action. The illusion that video had to work very hard to create was one of recorded time, doing so only where necessary by using different parts of the studio in combination with different lighting effects. Direct translations of a sister art form of present-tense time, the theater, were used to format early television dramas and many of the burlesque-like variety shows. They were almost always performed in a theatrical setting with a live audience, who functioned as surrogate home viewers until later re-placed by the laugh-track and applause machine.

The fundamental aspect of cinema, the montage (an articulation in time), was interpreted by the fundamental aspect of early television, the live (an articulation in space), in a key piece of equipment in the studio, the video switcher. This was the central creative device for organizing what was finally to be seen by the viewer at home. The basic elements of cinematic language were hard-wired into its design. A simple switch button represented Eisenstein's paramount montage, the cut, and with a switch on each camera, cuts could be made to any point of view desired. Griffith's fade to black became a gradual reduction in signal voltage with a variable potentiometer. Wipes and split-screens were translated by engineers into circuit designs to electro-nically interfere with and offset the regular voltages in the signal flow, the most symmetrical stationary wipe patterns being harmonic overtones of the fundamental frequencies of the basic video signal. Thus, without the ability to record, a simulation of cinematic edited time was constructed by a live electronic instrument.

It was not until the late 1960s that this emulation of cinema was broken, when artists began poking beneath the surface to uncover the basic characteristics of the medium and release the unique visual potential of the electronic image, now taken for granted with a yawn, and oftentimes a grimace, as standard TV fare. The video switcher was redesigned into the first video synthesizer. Its principles were acoustic and musical, a further evolution of early electronic music systems such as the Moog. The videotape recorder was the last link in the chain to be developed, coming a good decade after the arrival of television and only fully integrated into video's image processing system with the introduction of the time-based corrector in the early 1970s. With the seamless incorporation of recorded material into the image stream, and the advancements of electronic editing, a need arose to identify remote feeds specifically as "live." Not only did video begin to look and act like cinema, but it began to look and act like everything else—fashion, conversation, politics, visual art, and music.

––––––––––––

"A single neuron operates on the power of about a thousandth-millionth of a watt. Hence, the entire brain operates on about ten watts." [5]

—Sir John Eccles

Musically speaking, the physics of a broadcast is a type of drone. The video image perpetually repeats itself without rest at the same set of frequencies. This new common condition of the drone represents a significant shift in our culturally derived thought patterns. It can be evidenced by contrasting another drone-based system, traditional Indian music, with our own European classical music.

Western music builds things up, piling notes on top of notes, forms on top of forms, in the way one would construct a building, until at last the piece is complete. It is additive: its base is silence, all musical sounds proceed from this point. Indian music, on the other hand, begins

5. Sir John Eccles, "The Physiology of the Imagination," *Scientific American* (1958).

from sound. It is subtractive. All the notes and possible notes to be played are present before the main musicians even start playing, stated by the presence and function of the tambura. A tambura is a drone instrument, usually of four or five strings, that, due to the particular construction of its bridge, amplifies the overtone or harmonic series of the individual notes in each tuned string. It is most distinctly heard at the start and end of the performance, but is continually present throughout. The series of overtones describes the scale of the music to be played. Therefore, when the primary musicians play, they are considered to be pulling notes out of an already ongoing sound field, the drone.

This music structure reflects the Hindu philosophical concept of the origin of all things in sound, represented by the essential vibration "Om," which is believed to be always present, without beginning or end, everywhere in the universe, generating all forms of the phenomenal world. In the music, there is great emphasis on tuning, while the philosophers speak of "tuning the individual" as a means to contact and replenish these fundamental energies. The idea of a sound field that is always present shifts the emphasis away from the objects of perception to the field on which the perception is occurring; a nonspecific viewpoint.

As a drone, video's significant aspect is that its electronic images exist everywhere at once, the receiver is free to pull the signal out of the line at any given point along its path or at any location out in the broadcast field. Children have been known to pick up radio signals in their dental braces, a contemporary manifestation of "speaking in tongues." The "space" of broadcast recalls the acoustic space of the Gothic cathedral, where all sounds, no matter how near, far, or loud, appear to be originating at the same distant place. They seem detached from the immediate scene, floating somewhere where the point of view has become the entire space. In technology, the current shift from analog's sequential waves to digital's recombinant codes further accelerates the diffusion of the point of view. Like the transformation of matter, there is a movement from the tangibility of the solid and liquid states into the gaseous. There is less coherence, previously solid barriers become porous, and the perspective is that of the whole space, the point of view of the air.

Within several weeks of launching its satellite, Brazil established communication links with all corners of the country and mapped every square mile of one of the largest uncharted territories left on the planet, the Amazon basin. One can now, theoretically, make a phone call relaying one's position from anywhere in the jungle, and even watch "Dynasty" if a TV set and generator are on hand. A system is already in place in the United States for new cars, where the vehicle's position and direction can be relayed to a navigational satellite that can pinpoint its location and display it on an electronic map on a dashboard screen. On the map every street in the country is selectable in varying scales down to a few blocks, with all the individual street names noted. It is now impossible to get lost—a disturbingly boring thought, not to mention a paranoid one.

In the late twentieth century, the Unknown, the "other side of the mountain," so central to the structure of our thoughts, has ceased to exist in geographic spatial terms. By the early 1980s the entire surface of the earth had been satellite-mapped down to a resolution of 30 feet or more. This "Known" of everything creates some bizarre new models of consciousness, such as the military's computer navigation system where there is no direct sensory link to the outside world. Here, a jet rocket can travel at high velocities, hugging the landscape, while relying solely on information of the precise terrain and features ahead stored in the on-board computer memory: data gathered again from satellite remote sensing. Memory replaces sensory experience; a Proustian nightmare.

Space without a container is the mental world of thoughts and images. Many of the techniques of the shaman rely on gaining a masterful, uncanny control over one's "point of view," a realization that a point of view is not necessarily synonymous with physical position. Mircea Eliade, tracing the origins of religious thought, suggests that the emergence of upright posture reorganized consciousness along the vertical axis, initiating the existence of the four cardinal directions of space (front, back, left, right, with the possible addition of two more, up and down) and, along with it, the privileged center, the self ego

6. Mircea Eliade, *A History of Religious Ideas*, Vol.1 (Chicago: University of Chicago Press, 1978), 3.

Ptolemaic focal point thus implied.[6] The four-walled, six-faceted room is the archetypal distillation of this mental foundation, and Brunelleschi's perspective, an urban fabrication, further articulates it. The mind is not only confined by three-dimensional space, it creates it.

Hard walls, with their recursive enclosing reflections, are dissolving into the transparent spaces of information architecture. The same mathematics that describe an acoustically flat non-reverberant space, a "neutral" room completely void of echos or reverberation, also describe a large expansive plain. The term "flat" is used in both situations. For the Native Americans who once inhabited the open plains, or the Aboriginal peoples of the Australian desert outback, there are no *acoustics* as such. Their acoustic spaces are internal.

> "When a man is far away down on the plain and I am on the hill, I look towards him while I am quietly talking to myself. He sees me and turns towards me. I say, 'Do you hear?' I move my head from side to side glaring at him, and at last I stare at him, and then turning I say, 'Come on, quickly,' As I stare at him fixedly, I see him turn as he feels my stare. He then turns and looks about while I continue staring at him. So I say, 'Walk this way, right along, where I am sitting.' Then he walks right up to me where I am sitting behind a bush. I draw him with my power (miwi). You do not see any hand signs or hear any shouting. At last he comes up and nearly falls over me. He says, 'You talked to me and I felt it. How did you talk so?' I explain, and he adds: 'I felt your words while you were talking to me, and then I felt that you are there.' I answer, 'True, it was in that way that I talked to you, and you felt those words and also that power.'"[7]

> —Australian Aboriginal medicine man, as told to
> Ronald M. Berndt, Lower Murray River, Australia

As the telegraph and subsequent "wireless" communication technologies were provoked by a response to the separation of individuals over

7. Quoted in A. P. Elkin, *Aboriginal Men of High Degree* (St. Lucia, Australia: University of Queensland Press, 1977), 45.

the vast spaces of the New World, so thought transference and "seeing at a distance" for the Aborigines are a manifestation of the vastness and stillness of the Australian desert. Desert solitude is an early form of visionary technology. It figures strongly in the history of religion. Individuals have used it to hear the voices of the past and future, to become "prophets," to receive images or, for Native Americans, to host "vision quests." It seems that when all the clutter and noise of everyday life is reduced to such brutal minimalism, the usual "control valves" are released and images well up from within. The boundary between the software of the private interior and the hardware of the exterior landscape is blurred; their forms intermingle and converse.

Evidence of synaesthesia, the crossover between and interchangeability of the senses, has been reported in individuals since the earliest civilizations. It has been particularly evocative for the artists who have dreamed of the unification of the senses, and there are many examples in recent art history, ranging from the Russian composer Scriabin's chromatic piano, which played colors from a keyboard, to the nausea of the *son et lumière* shows of public tourism. Visual artists have often described hearing music or sounds when they work, as composers have mentioned perceiving their music in imagistic form.

> "My whole imagination thrilled with images; long lost forms for which I had sought so eagerly shaped themselves ever more and more clearly into realities that lived again. There rose up soon before my mind, a whole world of figures, which revealed themselves so strangely and plastic and primitive, that, when I saw them clearly before me and heard their voices in my heart, I could not account for the almost tangible familiarity and assurance in their demeanor."[8]
>
> —Richard Wagner

Synaesthesia is the natural inclination of the structure of contemporary media. The material that produces music from a stereo sound

8. Richard Wagner, *My Life* (New York: Dodd and Mead, 1911), quoted in C.E. Seashore, *Psychology of Music* (New York: Dover Publications Inc., 1967 reprint of 1938 original), 166–7.

system, transmits the voice over the telephone and materializes the image on a television set is, at the base level, the same. With the further implementation of digital codes to bring personal banking, buying gas, cooking with the microwave, and other functions into this same domain, there will be an even more extensive common linguistic root.

Efforts with artificial technology have made it necessary to distinguish between synaesthesia as an artistic theory and practice, and synaesthesia as a genuine subjective ability or involuntary condition for certain individuals. There is a natural propensity in all of us to relate sound and image. The beauty of these experiences is in their fluid language of personal imagination, and in their ties to mood and moment. As long as their individual subjective nature is understood, that is, that they can never become conventional, we will be spared the tedium of the dogma and proprietary theorizing of the practitioners, from the visual musicians to the music videoists.

The free-translation between all sensory modalities, however, is only the first stage toward the transcendence of the ultimate barrier between the domains of the physical body and the luminous mind. In extreme cases, this physical threshold has been crossed. E. Lucas Bridges, son of a late nineteenth-century Christian missionary living with the Ona, an indigenous people of Tierra del Fuego, gives a vivid example:

"Houshken ... broke into a chant and seemed to go into a trance, possessed by some spirit not his own. Drawing himself up to his full height, he took a step toward me and let his robe, his only garment, fall to the ground. He put his hands to his mouth with a most impressive gesture and brought them away again with his fists clenched and thumbs close together. He held them up to the height of my eyes, and when they were less than two feet from my face drew them apart. I saw that there was now a small, almost opaque object between them. It was about an inch in diameter in the middle and tapered away into his hands. It might have been a piece of semi-transparent dough or elastic, but whatever it was it seemed to be alive, revolving at great speed, while Houshken, apparently from muscular tension, was trembling violently.

"The moonlight was bright enough to read by as I gazed at his strange object. Houshken brought his hands further apart and the object grew more and more transparent, until, when some three inches separated his hands, I realized it was not there anymore. It did not break or burst like a bubble; it simply disappeared, having been visible to me for less than five seconds. Houshken made no sudden movement, but slowly opened his hands and turned them over for my inspection. They looked clean and dry. He was stark naked and there was no confederate beside him. I glanced down at the snow, and, in spite of his stoicism, Houshken could not resist a chuckle, for nothing was to be seen there."[9]

When the first technologies of image and sound codified the functioning of the human senses into a surrogate artificial form, a tremendous and unpredictable understanding was gained of the operations of human perception. Similarly, as the implementation of the computer becomes an embodiment of mind, the new links to the "mind stuff" of digital data processing will certainly provide even more potent translation possibilities beyond basic sensory inputs. Although it is tempting to ponder a possible synaesthetic "putting back together" of science's discrete perceptual and cognitive compartments, inspired by these electronic free and fluid interchanges of our ways of seeing, what seems to be emerging at the moment is the amnesia and anaesthesia of a vast, cluttered, and confused landscape of image fragments, a semiotician's field-day of delights.

This condition of our contemporary media culture is hauntingly embodied in a single individual of the early twentieth century, a remarkable mnemonist to whom all sensory modalities were fluidly and uncontrollably connected; who was assaulted by a barrage of images and associations that remained for hours, days, or even years; who constantly found that the distinctions between the past (memory), the present (sensate experience), and the future (fantasy) were blurred or non-existent. The great Russian brain researcher A. R. Luria

9. E. Lucas Bridges, *The Uttermost Ends of the Earth* (New York: E.P. Dutton, 1948), quoted in Joseph Campbell, *The Way of the Animal Powers* (San Francisco: Harper and Row, Alfred Van Der Marde Editions, 1983), 163

conducted a 30-year study of this disturbingly prophetic character, whom he called simply S.

Luria described S flawlessly reciting dozens of pages of text filled with everything from a narrative story to a foreign language he did not speak, complex scientific terms, or even nonsense syllables. His memory was also spatial—he could remember the positions of the individual elements on the page or blackboard in any order presented, and did so even when asked to repeat them years after the original tests. When he was a child, his imagery of school was so real that he sometimes failed to get out of bed to get ready to go. A characteristic of S's inner world that greatly impressed Luria was his effortless ability at synaesthesia, a fact that Luria realized was precisely the reason that he was able to perform such amazing feats of recall. S described his procession of thoughts:

> "I heard a bell ringing. A small round object rolled right before my eyes ... my fingers sensed something like rope.... Then I experienced a taste of salt water ... and something white."

> "I'm sitting in a restaurant—there's music. You know why they have music in restaurants? Because it changes the taste of everything. If you select the right kind of music, everything tastes good. Surely people who work in restaurants know this."[10]

Gradually it became impossible for S to function:

> "I always experience sensations like these. When I ride in a trolley I can feel the clanging it makes in my teeth. So one time I went to buy some ice cream, thinking I'd sit there and eat it and not have this clanging. I walked over to the vendor and asked her what kind of ice cream she had. 'Fruit ice cream,' she said. But she answered in such a tone that a whole pile of coals, of black cinders, came bursting out of her mouth, and I couldn't bring myself to buy an ice cream after she'd answered that way.... Another thing ... if I read when I eat, I have a hard time understanding what I'm reading—the taste of food drowns out the sense."[11]

10. A.R. Luria, *The Mind of the Mnemonist* (New York: Basic Books, 1968), 81–2.
11. *Ibid.*, 159.

As he grew older, S's inability to forget began seriously to affect his life, and he eventually quit his job and began a life of exhibiting himself as a public attraction. Luria commented on the difficulty of compiling a final report on his subject, since during the sessions images would come into S's mind that constantly slipped him out of control and he would begin to "operate automatically," becoming verbose, his mind cluttered with details and irrelevances as he digressed endlessly. S lived with an image stream that he could not turn off. Out of his possession of a super-human indelible memory he developed an overwhelming, disturbing sense of everything being temporary.

If S had been an ancient Greek, he might have been one of the most extraordinary individuals that the culture had produced. Instead, he ended up as a contemporary tragic hero, immortalized in the pages of scientific journals, his experiences sometimes reading as the vengeful curse of a bad music video director. Today, our self-created media systems offer us creative potential previously available only to individuals with special powers. The synaesthetic possibilities in the sensory and conceptual domains are inspiring, but instead, as victims of "sane" communicators with equally "sane" imaginations, we are becoming like Luria's mnemonist—overwhelmed and incapacitated by rootless images and amplified voices. It is the village "seer" that we sense the absence of, not the formal structures of efficient information management systems and professional communicators.

Artists, poets, composers, and scientists who have heard the voices know that they are not mad—their work testifies to this fact. However, severe mental breakdown can be a type of occupational hazard for persons working at the boundary of commonly accepted consensus reality; a space culturally fabricated by the perceptual conventions imposed by the structuring devices of language, customary behavior, and forgotten histories. Creative "madness" might simply be a disorder of history, "cured" by the passage of time, as visionary insights become the commonplace facts of culture. In all their sessions, S never once said that he thought himself possessed by madness. He once told Luria that until he became an adult and got his first job, he just assumed that everyone's mind functioned in exactly the same way his did.

"All men are capable of having dreams and seeing visions."
—William Blake (1757–1827)

Interpreting a Broken Wineglass 1988

The question of explaining or interpreting art is a complex and profound one that will not be answered (if it is indeed answerable at all) by critical theorizing, or dialogues such as this one, or one more major thematic art exhibition. Rather, any hope for its articulation is to be found in the practical and functional results of a cultural crisis, a genuine cultural shift that becomes reflected in the actual work, physical efforts and intuitive responses of artists and other creative individuals. One point of interest here is that the further afield from Western industrial culture's ideas of art we go, for example into the highlands of New Guinea, the villages of Bali, the Buddhist monasteries of Tibet, or even the European Renaissance cathedrals of 400 years ago, the need for "explaining" art, and the complementary condition of an alienated and bewildered public, disappears. So "explaining" contemporary art and educating the public can be seen as a particularly modern problem. The confusion and bewildering plurality of images, ideas, and styles in this period, which cause many to feel overwhelmed, is a necessary condition of change and reconfiguration, as some artists and organizers alike are recognizing that the reestablishment of the broken link between art and the public, the restoration of art to a functional place in people's lives, is a necessity for the practical survival of a living art practice.

When I think of how to explain much of contemporary art to the public, the first thing I would recommend would be to inform them as clearly as possible, in published reports, articles, and TV programs, the precise figures of the costs of artworks in today's market and exactly how much individual works are selling for. This would certainly help my parents, for one, to understand what all the fuss is about certain works they see from time to time. It will also serve to explain to the general audience the behavior and rationale of a great many artists and art professionals, and to give a value to artworks to a public which

First presented as part of a panel discussion entitled "Contemporary Art: Intent and Interpretation" at the National Art Education Association conference in Los Angeles on April 9, 1988. The topic for discussion was "Can contemporary art be explained and interpreted, and what is the role of the artist's intentions in such efforts?"

already equates monetary quantity with cultural quality. Look at all the publicity that the sale of the Van Gogh for 40 million dollars generated, never mind if the piece was worth that much (of course, as we all know, it was worth a lot more). However, with contemporary art it is a bit different, and this approach only really serves to explain most of the mediocre artworks and exhibitions and collections that are around. It doesn't really help with the good art.

So what to do. I feel that the answers lie within ourselves. One thing would be to look at how we are living for clues. We live suspended, like fish in water, within a media system that processes all culture as entertainment and an educational system that processes knowledge as product, both reflecting their positions within an entrenched capitalist system that has pervaded even the private inner lives of its citizens. These are deep-seated beliefs and attitudes that cannot be overturned by a single informative afternoon at the local museum. Art educators and museum and gallery personnel are confronted with a public that has been programmed into expecting that appreciating art, like everything else, must rely on the uncovering of a single answer or meaning, in this case which the artist has cleverly concealed within the work. In other words, that art is something which one "gets." They wait to be told. This thing found, then, frees the person to get on with the other works until they are all finished in this manner and one may then leave the museum or gallery to continue with the afternoon's entertainment. Art becomes a "return" on their "investment" of time.

The majority of people today feel isolated and detached from art, and all the well-meaning orientations and explanations that fill them with facts about the meanings in the work and intentions of the artists, in my opinion, only serve to separate them further from the inner life of the art before them. As countless artists have stated before, the appreciation, as well as the making, of art demands a primacy of perception, an open child-like state of vulnerability and emotive sensi-tivity. Education and extended knowledge can certainly be important, but the essence of the moment of confronting an art work is a purely individual encounter, an individual experience on individual terms, something that cannot be taught, and which increasing amounts of rational explanation and verbal discourse will proportionally diminish.

I quote René Magritte: "People who look for symbolic meanings fail to grasp the inherent poetry and mystery of the image. No doubt they sense this mystery, but they wish to get rid of it. They are afraid. By asking 'What does this mean?' they express a wish that everything be understandable. But if one does not reject the mystery, one has quite a different response. One asks other things."

This is the seed-core of the place of art in our lives. Now, of course there will be relatively few artworks that will have this special impact on one's inner life. Someone having this experience with every single artwork by every artist encountered would be highly suspect (extremely heightened sensitivity is one clinical definition of schizophrenia). So beyond this there is the branching out into the majority of other works that, although not crucial to a particular individual, nonetheless have something interesting to say and to offer. This is where a wider appreciation of art and the importance of education comes into play.

The following is a true story: I was on a New York subway car with a friend, when the train pulled into a station and the doors opened. There was a mass of people before us. It was rush hour. I had this remarkable momentary rush of feeling. I could feel every one of those people. I had a powerful visceral flash of the entire mass of humanity in the city at that instant, as if everyone's feeling of being alive had pressed into me at once, right into my bones—a moment of Walt Whitman-like luminous intensity. I was deeply moved, almost over-whelmed. After a few long seconds of speechless immobility, I finally turned to my friend and said, "Wow, there are a lot of people in New York." He looked at me and said, "Good, Bill ... very good. When it rains it's wet, right?" I was shocked and embarrassed. I shut up. Of course, when it rains it is wet, but the experience of wetness, the feeling of being caught in a downpour, with clothes cool and clinging to a wet body, that's something else.

Van Gogh, writing in his journals, quoted Sainte Beuve: "One may have a blazing hearth in one's soul, yet no one ever comes to sit by it. Passers-by see only a wisp of smoke rising from the chimney and continue on their way."

When we discuss explaining contemporary art to the public we must, I feel, first ask ourselves what is our purpose for doing so.

As people drawn to the field of art, it is, most fundamentally, the basic human characteristic of wanting to share and give others an experience that has been profound and important in our own lives. If it is our desire to perpetuate our own experience of personal meaning and transformation, then the question becomes, how do you start the fire in the individual? You can't just reach in there and strike a match—they must do it themselves. The fire, once ignited, will grow to consume all the necessary fuel in its path, a process we call "an individual educating themselves."

Explanation, or raw facts and rational discourse, or understanding the artist's intention, or anything else under discussion here is not really the problem. A good teacher or an inspired presenter will do just what I am saying—start the fires burning, no matter what the nature of the raw materials. The problem is that people with this gift are few, as is art of the most profound nature, while the job positions for educators and gallery time-slots/wall-spaces are many.

I don't really have any answers to these problems. Jallaludin Rumi, the great Persian poet and mystic of the thirteenth century, has made two statements which are relevant here. Rumi used to throw up his hands in despair at the scholars and theorizers of his day huddled in the mosques in intense intellectual debate. He preferred to go out into the fields and get stung by the flies and kiss the stones and the flowers to write his poems. He used to say, "All of this talk is like stamping out gold coins, while the real work is being done outside by someone digging in the ground." Rumi, encouraging his students to penetrate beneath the many forms of surface appearance in this world, often used to scream at them and say, "Break the wineglass and fall towards the glassblower's breath!" I think that if we are going to get anywhere at all, then all of us—artists, exhibitors, and educators alike—have to start breaking more wineglasses, the more expensive the better.

Statement 1989

I have come to realize that the most important place where my work
exists is not in the museum gallery, or in the screening room, or on
television, and not even on the video screen itself, but in the mind of
the viewer who has seen it. In fact, it is only there that it can exist.
Freeze a video in time and you are left with a single static frame,
isolated from context, an abandoned image, like a butterfly under glass
with a pin through it. Yet, during its normal presentation, viewers can
only physically experience video one frame at a time. One can never
witness the whole all at once; by necessity it exists only as a function
of individual memory. This paradox gives video its living dynamic
nature as part of the stream of human consciousness.

It is not the monitor, or the camera, or the tape, that is the basic
material of video, but time itself. Once you begin to work with time as
an elemental material, then you have entered the domain of conceptual
space. A thought is a function of time, not a discrete object. It is a
process of unfoldment, an evolving thread of the living moment.
Awareness of time brings you into a world of process, into moving
images that embody the movement of human consciousness itself. If
light is the basic material of the painter or photographer, then duration
is the *materia prima* of the time-based arts of cinema and video.
Duration is to consciousness as light is to the eye.

Once involved with time, it becomes clear that one must also
embrace the first stages of an insight as being just as important as the
insight itself. This is the state of confusion, unclarity, non-
understanding that precedes all creative breakthroughs. It is the time of
an unfinished thought, the time that the painter must go through (not
the painting itself), the time behind the facade of all great discoveries.
The still turbulence of being up alone working at three-thirty in the
morning. It is the time of risk, the point of unification between art,

First published as "Statement for this Festival," in *Delicate Technology* (supplement),
eds. Video Gallery SCAN (Fujiko Nakaya) and I&S (Japanese and English) (Tokyo:
2nd Video Television Festival at Spiral, 1989).

science, and all the creative activities. Its center is personal transformation. The medieval Christians called it "the cloud of unknowing," or, in the words of St. John of the Cross, the "dark night of the soul."

In this domain of the unknown, the uncertain, the "great ball of doubt" talked about in Zen practice (which is so necessary for spiritual development), the only light to follow is faith—faith in that other thing, that something else dimly felt behind the veil of daily life.

The late Mircea Eliade, extraordinary scholar of world religions, described the socio-historic roots of this feeling in a discussion on the emergence of paleolithic culture 25,000 years ago:

"It is difficult to imagine how the human mind could function without the conviction that there is something irreducibly REAL in the world, and it is impossible to imagine how consciousness could appear without a meaning on man's impulses and experiences. Consciousness of a real and meaningful world is intimately connected with the discovery of the sacred. ... In short, the sacred is an element in the structure of consciousness and not a stage in the history of consciousness."

This was such a significant discovery for me—"the sacred as an element in the structure of consciousness." It is within us all. The intuitive awareness and unwavering belief in this other world interwoven with our own, this other place, the "separate reality," or whatever it has been called, has been the fuel for the fire of almost every artist who has left his or her mark on the earth.

Interview with Michael Nash

A while ago, in a discussion that we had, you used the expression "living within the frame" to describe an ambition of your work at a particular point in its development. It's a statement that I feel could also serve as a kind of ethical philosophy of your artistic practice. What led you to this approach rather than to some of the alternatives your contemporaries have chosen, such as appropriation, semiotic orientation, performative dramatization, or manipulation of visual technology?

I think primarily it was curiosity about life. Curiosity about what would happen when relatives died. Where did they go? Could they still be reached? Curiosity about seeing a new member of the family born. Where did it come from? What were they before they were here with us? Curiosity about personal experiences that seem to indicate an existence of another order or another domain of experience. I remember falling into a lake when I was 10. I almost died. The thing I remember is the imagery of this incredibly beautiful, serene blue-green world that I had no idea existed below the surface.

When I started making videos I was caught up with the current issues of the day, structuralism being probably the most dominant. This was in the early 1970s. A lot of my work ostensibly started out by trying to prove something, much like a scientist does. You start with a premise or hypothesis or an observation and you want to create an arena that acts as a symbolic representation of that aspect of the world in you. The idea of the controlled experiment is what I think a lot of early performance and conceptual art was very much taking on—that kind of pragmatic positivistic approach of the experiment that exists in a kind of rarefied state outside normal existence. But video would not let me do that because the camera, as it was evolving, became better and more portable, and all of a sudden you could take this thing outdoors instead of working within the confines of the electronic studio. I found that you could just take a camera outside, walk down the street,

First published in *Journal of Contemporary Art*, vol. 3, no. 2 (Fall/Winter 1990), 63–73.

bring it back, and then integrate it into this electronic domain. You would just take life as it comes, which is what happens when you take the lens cap off.

I'm moving away from that kind of empirical scientific paradigm. The stuff I did when I was still in art school and right after was literally modeled on that approach, and the influences were obvious. I was interested in the "body artists"—Vito Acconci, Terry Fox, Dennis Oppenheim, and others—who used that device to frame experience. It was one of those rare historical moments that artists find themselves in from time to time, incorporating experience itself directly into what was being called a work of art. It was a major shift, not making something about an experience but making something of an experience, like when Acconci blindfolded himself in 1969 or 1970 and had someone he didn't know that well lead him around the pier on the Hudson River in New York, not knowing if he was going to be led to the edge or not. That's a very real experience.

I found myself being influenced by that. Living within the frame is living within the experience. Art has to be part of one's daily life, or else it's not honest.

The juxtaposition of some of the concerns in your work with dominant concerns in current critical inquiry draws out this failing.
I think it's a great failure that critical discourse today in art—which exists supposedly on the edge of some of the higher aspirations we have as human beings—does not encompass the very, very human qualities of our emotional lives. You never hear love coming up in critical discourse today. I had my first child about two years ago, and the most incredible thing about it is just living with and coming to really understand what love means, and where it comes from. It's been so profound for me to see the joy upon my son's face when we play, when we're together. You have all of the difficulties and the problems associated with bringing up a child, having it infringe on your work, and all these other things we're all so worried about, and you have days where you just want to throw him out the window with the bath water. But there is this larger thing called love that binds the whole situation, and it's very deeply rooted. It's being created for him right in front of my eyes as he matures as a human being. I could never make any

work of art that would come even close to the immensity of that as an experience. A lot of other things involved with our inner lives are just not being addressed, because they're not the property of any specialized group of people. They exist in each and every one of us. Love and hate and fear, the great themes of birth and death and consciousness are age-old themes, the fascination of understanding them in a historical context, to see how different cultures dealt with them, solved their equations. They're unsolvable and mysterious in the positive sense of the word, and therefore life-giving. Something that is not solvable and doesn't have an answer gives life because it propels one to continue with the quest. I get somewhat frustrated that more people aren't thinking of the great themes in life as being in the domain of art.

Could you talk about the matrix in which the work operates, its relationship to the context of art, television, and home videos, and how you see the future of the video medium in general in relationship to these venues?
After I went through an early infatuation period with the technology, I obliterated it—literally and metaphorically—in 1973 in a piece I called *Information.* I've chosen to work with images of the real world, camera images, recorded outside on the streets or in the mountains, images that obviously are representations, and those issues now are very current. I think we were aware of them back in the early 1970s. They've now been articulated quite eloquently by people such as Baudrillard. They are representations, and that leads to a whole other set of issues. Nonetheless, they have been taken for the truth, as Baudrillard mentions, they've become what they represent. One becomes what they behold. For that reason there is a kind of cultural currency with these images, as they are part and parcel of the mass media. There was always the physical possibility for people to understand my work outside the confines of the specialized issues of the art world. That for me solved a lot of problems I was having at the time with Clement Greenberg's theories, and with a lot of those approaches that seemed to be about narrowing down and limiting discourse and dialogue to a group of the initiated. That finally turned me around, from the time I was in art school and detested anything I made that my mother would praise, to coming completely full circle and understanding that I had to make work that my mother could get something out of—not

understand, because that is a very tricky word, but get something out of. The context changes the work, obviously; we know that not only from contemporary art theorists, but from people like Heisenberg, that the observer and the observed are this interactive system. I feel fortunate that a lot of different people from very different backgrounds have been able to, on their own terms, appreciate what I do. That's very important for me.

But it's not a situation where the fact of the context affects the work.
It's a given. It's something that's there. It's not something that I deny or want to ignore, but something that is absolutely, fundamentally, in the work. I mean, what is a birth? A birth of a human baby can mean so many different things to so many people, because of the power of the mind to speculate, to fantasize, to project onto another, and therefore to create metaphors. That's a very fundamental pattern in the human mind; it's been there for millenia. You can see it in operation in the paleolithic age on the walls of Lascaux. It's something that we just do as human beings, and it's a beautiful, beautiful thing. That meaning is relative, an active agent that gives life to objects, is the essence of their existence as living things. When we say everything is alive, we don't mean a stone is going to jump up and run away—biologists and scientists worry about using those all-expansive so-called mystical terminologies. What that means is that everything has some kind of essence that can be reached through human thought. Thought is the animator. That's a principle of nature, that's not the property of the art world.

Recently you brought up an interesting relationship between the current political situation with the National Endowment for the Arts and how television's disempowerment of an individual action works to negate individual political response and allows a hysterical minority to be reached and politicized. In some way television's perceptual imperialism has produced this art crisis. Is this also a reflection on how artists are failing to challenge this imperialism, or do you think it's unfair to criticize artists for the dilemma that we find ourselves in?
That's a very complicated question. There are many issues and elements in that. I think artists have to bear some of the blame for the current situation. I don't mean that literally in the sense of not

mobilizing fast enough politically to avoid the current dismal situation in the US Congress with the NEA. But I mean in general that artists are basically out of touch with what people are feeling and thinking as participants in a specialized dialogue. There are a lot of different aspects to art, and I think it's arrogant of the art world to believe, or unconsciously promote the assumption, that it has some kind of monopoly on creativity. I consider Sunday painters in the park to be just as valid artists as people showing in galleries in SoHo. The common human trait of creativity is something that's going to link people from all different walks of life to art. I think it's important for people who are involved as professional artists to come out of their little cubbyholes and begin to acknowledge the rest of society.

At the same time we need in art an area of specialization, in the same way scientists need to have conferences of physicists where they talk in equations that you and I could not possibly comprehend. That's absolutely necessary. I tend to look at this not so much as avant-garde, because that term carries a lot of political and sociological connotations, but as the research arm of the field of art, where people are going to be at the edge of pushing things, doing something that no one else is doing, putting two ideas together that haven't been put together before.

I would say that more than any other artist working in video, perhaps as much as any contemporary artist I can think of, your work asserts and elaborates upon the life of the soul. The idea of soul-life is not very much in theoretical vogue these days—many post-structuralists would reject any kind of notion of the essence, or would say that the perception of something like the soul is just the engine of language throwing off heat, a simultaneous by-product that's not active or operational in any way. What is your theory of the soul, and how is it reflected in your work? Or is it possible to assign to your thinking about the soul a notion like a theory?
No, I don't think you can assign a notion like a theory to it, because the reason that I make my work is to understand. I don't make my work to explain, to describe, or to state a position. I think this is a very big difference from science, because when scientists go out to prove something they're functioning exactly like lawyers who have a premise, and they're going to prove that premise, using the rules of the legal system. For the scientist, a set of relationships and interactions we call

the laws of nature exist to be manipulated in one's favor in order to prove whatever is one's point. So it's sort of dead thought in which we've come to exist, and it's one of the detriments of the evolution of logical empiricism. The Cartesian method was a major revolution in consciousness, no question about it, but as we're coming to its back-water period, you find that this way of thought has taken over to such an extent that people tend to approach life in those terms.

Then you have another type of scientist, who isn't going out to prove anything, but is just going out to learn something. All great scientific discoveries are accompanied by this kind of humility that is experienced when whatever thoughts, ideas, and preconceptions one has had in one's mind are completely blown away by seemingly incongruous and inexplicable behaviors of the natural world. That's the magic. I have questions and I'm interested in why things are certain ways.

Your work often exposes the edges of perception. I think of specific works such as Chott el-Djerid *where you pursue an absolute limit of visual perception until that perception becomes something else. There's a horizon line in that piece, and a life line in others, where finitude begets existence. Your recent works seem to particularly emphasize threshold moments of life, focusing on the coming into being, perhaps a bit more than on mortality, as a sort of an instigating factor in perception of experience.*

You refer to *Angel's Gate*. The notion of the boundary is a fundamental part of the structure of human consciousness. Finitude is really the essence of what being alive is all about. A baby is born, and immediately mortality has been created before your eyes. The desires of two individuals become coalesced into this physical being, who's created as a kind of condensation of possibilities into a singularity, into a thing. Often I've used water as a metaphor, the surface both reflecting the outer world and acting as a barrier to the other world. Without limits there is no energy created; physicists have taught us that limits create energy. If you have someone who believes in everything, then he doesn't believe in anything at all.

Could you talk about what you're reading right now that in some ways is being drawn into the work, or is just part of a larger intellectual inquiry that becomes manifested in the work you're doing now?

The area of intellectual inquiry, which for the most part had been coming from personal study of various books and texts, is currently coming directly out of my own personal experience. In one word, I would sum it up as "responsibility." Responsibility to myself, responsibility to family, and responsibility to the community (friends and strangers). You know, we all need each other in one way or another. Even though artists, like shamen, require time away from everyone else "out in the great loneliness" as the Inuit say, ultimately this time in solitude yields results that benefit the group. It must, or else you have a disconnected, ineffectual art practice, impotent in terms of inner power and/or solely economic; in other words, the definition of decadence and to a large part a description of our current situation regarding the commercial art world. So this responsibility I have been sensing lately, triggered by bringing up our two-and-a-half-year-old son, has to do with the recognition of art and artistic ability as a gift, rather than a possession or asset, that fits into the larger whole of self-family-community, with self-knowledge being the key thread that ties all of these things, our lives as solitary individuals and our lives as a group, together. In the past few years I have learned that what I previously considered to be an all-consuming physical practice, doing all-nighters (neglecting sleep, food, and socializing) has been gradually modulated into a deeper inner practice that is just as total and ongoing, but shares time and space with my wife Kira and my little boy Blake, with my parents, and with friends and people in my neighborhood here in Long Beach. I work in my studio on a schedule now, pretty much Monday through Friday, and spend the weekends doing things such as going to the park with the family, with other time squeezed in doing political work in the community with the Coalition for Freedom of Expression that we've formed. It's all creative energy, energy that's used to transform and transmute, and it's been very satisfying to see that the same creative energy that was driving my personal artwork for all these years can have such a commonly shared basis in a broader practice.

I have been trying for so long to show the side of life I believe in—to live in that space—to understand and use the language of that space as the formulas of my work. This is the real space—the danger place, under our feet, our nose, below our belly, after our death, before our birth, which we only get to glimpse occasionally, if lucky. I have looked for it everywhere—squeezed it out of rocks, out of the stones of buildings and the floorboards of rooms. *Anthem* was one of the first pieces that used the images of the other side—the daily-life side, the illusion, the place of the known that everyone believes in so strongly.... The key is getting beyond value judgments, and touching the pure mind.

—Note, November 2, 1984

I consider art to be a branch of knowledge, not a function of pleasure. Pleasure or taste leads from the senses. The sensory experience is the means of comprehending and encountering the invisible. I do not completely diregard or discount sensory phenomena, as in the ancient axiom that the sensory experience is an illusion not to be trusted.

I aim to connect the body and the mind. To understand the meaning and higher order correspondences of the image, sensory experience is required, particularly initially. Our culture is at a road-block because of the linkage between art and entertainment. The domain of the senses becomes key in this connection. Aesthetics is essentially sensationalist. The Greek word aesthetic means perception by the senses.

—Note, January 11, 1991

Death by beauty.
Death by sensitivity.
Death by awareness.
Death by experience.
Death by landscape.

The dark side of vision. Images of such striking beauty and clarity that they pierce the heart and inflict pain. Like heroin, the flirtation with mortality can be addictive. The drug of sense.

The trip to the desert is one of discovering the deep common roots of beauty and pain, of sensitivity and death.

To be sensitive to all frequencies at once, to be overwhelmed and delirious with sensory experience.
(Use of camera tubes sensitive to all frequencies—lenses sensitive to all distances.) The articulation of the self through the extreme sensitivity and heightened awareness (right mind) is the great work—the true medium. There is no other. It is the source of video. Where to put the mind is the primary question of composition, and of the creative act.

—Note, December 12, 1986

The Passing 1991

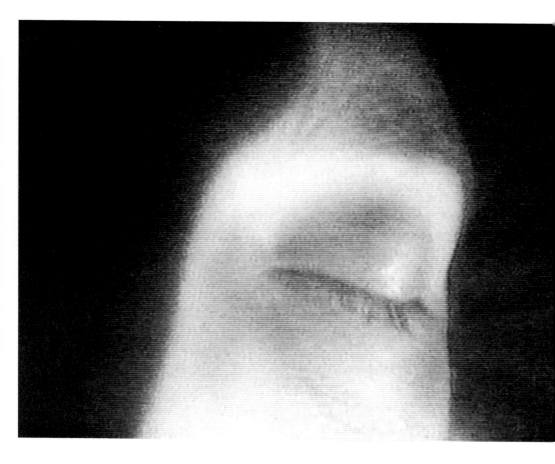

This and following pages: *The Passing*, 1991, videotape

Feb 17 1991   6 am
MOTHER leaves her body behind.

Video Black—The Mortality of the Image

Somewhere there is a video camera that has not been shut off for the last 20 years. Its rigid, unblinking eye has been tirelessly scanning a parking lot somewhere, silent witness to all the comings and goings of the past two decades. It has seen the same man get out of his car each morning, his body gradually sagging, less resistant to gravity, as his gait imperceptibly slows over the intervening time. It has seen the unbroken procession of days and nights, the cyclic changes in the sun and moon, the growth of trees, and the perpetual variations of weather with the accumulation of its harsh marks. It has seen the parade of fashion in car design and clothing, and witnessed the evidence of human intentions and impulses in the sudden material alterations of the physical landscape.

However, this perpetual observer has no stories to tell, no store of wisdom, no knowledge of the grand patterns. Locked within a great immutable Now, it has no sense of past or future. Without a memory to give it a life, events flicker across its image surface with only a split second to linger as afterimages, disappearing forever without a trace. Today it will be shut off, the world abruptly ending in an arbitrary cut-off point, as all endings are, and a new model camera installed. In another society, this camera, with its accumulated existence, would be graduated to an object of power to be venerated and reciprocated. At the least, the tubes of old cameras such as this should be installed in a shrine with the hope that someday some future technology could coax from their surface the subtle residue of a lifetime's experience. Today's event will pass with barely a notice.

The Eternal Image

"It is difficult to imagine how the human mind could function without the conviction that there is something irreducibly *real* in

First published in *Illuminating Video: An Essential Guide to Video Art*, eds. Doug Hall and Sally Jo Fifer (San Francisco: Bay Area Video Coalition: New York: Aperture, 1990), 476–86.

the world; and it is impossible to imagine how consciousness could appear without a *meaning* on man's impulses and experiences. Consciousness of a real and meaningful world is intimately connected with the discovery of the sacred. . . .

In short, the "sacred" is an element in the structure of consciousness and not a stage in the history of consciousness."[1]

—Mircea Eliade

The concept that objects can acquire power, that a human being's inner thoughts and impulses can have a residual effect on the outer physical world is of archaic origin. Reflecting a time when the material elements of nature were effused with mind or spirit, this timeless world view is confined today to the vague subjective sensations, often described as emotional, of empathy and an awareness of a "larger-than-me" order, that often mark encounters with the remnant of the natural landscape. The evolution in cultural memory (history) of the assumed location of the artificial image describes a progressive emergence from within the heart and mind of the individual outwards to its current residence as a depiction of the external world.

Sacred art in the Western tradition evokes images of the gold-leafed painted panels of the Middle Ages, a time when Asian and European art shared a common ground. One of the most striking things about medieval religious art is that the landscape (for us the *materia prima*; the physical, hard, "real" stuff of the world) appears as an insignificant element, a backdrop subordinate to the religious vision or epiphany. Space is a radiant gold and is substantially less real than the spiritual reality (scene or events) depicted. From our point of view, the inner and outer worlds have reversed their roles.

"The Indian or Far Eastern icon, carved or painted, is neither a memory image nor an idealization, but a visual symbolism, ideal in the mathematical sense. . . . Where European art naturally depicts a moment of time, an arrested action, or an effect of light, Oriental

1. Mircea Eliade, *A History of Religious Ideas*, vol.1 (Chicago: Universtity of Chicago Press, 1978), xiii.

art represents a continuous condition. In traditional European terms we should express this by saying that modern European art endeavors to represent things as they are in themselves, Asiatic and Christian art to represent things more nearly as they are in God, or nearer their source."[2]

—A. K. Coomaraswamy

Paramount to the notion of the image as sacred object is the icon, a form found in both oriental and occidental tradition. The term *icon* (ancient Greek for "image") as it is usually understood refers more to a process or a condition than to the physical characteristics of an object. An icon can be any image that has acquired power through its use as an object of worship. In fact, the status of icon was the goal and even the measure of success of the majority of visual artworks created in the great religious traditions of ancient Christianity, Buddhism, and Hinduism. The presence of art critics was not required as devotees instantly knew, at first glance, whether or not the work in question qualified. The artists created their works for God, not for the art world. Therefore the work had to be exceptional and as near perfect as possible, the personal devotion and insight of the artist being the main criterion and primary evidence of quality in the finished work.

Icons are timeless images, and even though in the West they often depict temporal events (the Annunciation, the Flight out of Egypt, etc.), the mythic or religious existence of those events (i.e., their present tense) is far more important. Icons maintain their currency by being continually updated to the present, by sustaining a constant relevance to Now. They are necessarily functional objects, their function fulfilling a most basic primary and private need within the individual.

Images become icons either through content alone, i.e., they were commissioned to perform such roles, or, more importantly, through the cumulative power of use, itself a reaffirmation of an image's intrinsic power. It is as if the continuous act of worship and veneration leaves a residue that builds up over the years. This aspect of the Christian icon is

2. A. K. Coomaraswamy, *The Transformation of Nature in Art* (New York: Dover Publications, 1956), 28, 30–31. (Reprint of original Harvard University Press edition, Boston, 1934.)

an echo of the animistic world view of older tribal, "pagan" societies. No wonder such a strong backlash was unleashed in the home of the classical Christian icon, the Eastern church of the Byzantine empire. There, in the eighth century, the so-called iconoclasts declared the worship of icons pagan, thus initiating a conflict that was to last more than a hundred years. Icon worship was finally restored by imperial decree.

Unlike the consumption-oriented mass-media images of contemporary culture, icons maintain their relevance by remaining the same for centuries. Giving form to eternal realities, their affinity is toward the eternal itself.

The Temporal Image

"As the eye, so the object."

—William Blake

One day in 1425, Filippo Brunelleschi walked out onto the Piazza del Duomo in Florence. Standing at the main doors to the cathedral, facing the baptistry across the piazza, he set up a small wooden box on a stand. He had invited various influential friends and *cognoscenti* to witness his experiment. One by one they stepped up to this curious device and closed one eye to stare through a small hole in one side.

To a twentieth-century observer, the only interpretation of this scene could be that of a photographer demonstrating a new camera. By expanding the definition of photography perhaps more than is acceptable, Brunelleschi's box could be considered a crude camera. For a citizen of fifteenth-century Florence, the effects of looking into this device were as mind-boggling and astounding as if seeing an actual camera for the first time. Peering into the small hole, they first saw a direct monocular view of the baptistry across the way. Then, by the flip of a lever, a mirror was moved into position and a small painting of the baptistry appeared, exactly in line and proportional to the direct view. In fact, with regard to geometry and form, the two were barely distinguishable. Brunelleschi had made a sharp right-hand turn out of the Middle Ages.

That Brunelleschi's demonstration seems so obvious to us today is a measure of its intellectual achievement—the more a revolutionary discovery shifts or even shatters the world view, the more commonplace it seems to the observers of subsequent ages. What he accomplished that day must have seemed to his contemporaries to be at the very limits of knowledge, as incredible, for example, as some of the quantum physicists' descriptions of our world seem to people of today. Prior to 1424, no one had ever painted an image that way. Historians describe this event as Brunelleschi's public pronouncement of the laws of linear perspective, which he is credited with discovering. There is certainly no doubt that his new system, along with its formalization and publication by his friend Leon Alberti 12 years later, irrevocably altered the history of painting and accelerated the development of techniques of artificial image making.

Describing Brunelleschi's breakthrough simply as the discovery of the vanishing point, however, places an inordinate emphasis on the picture itself as the locale of this revolutionary change. What Brunelleschi achieved was the personification of the image, the creation of a "point of view" and its identification with a place in real space. In doing so, he elevated the position of the individual viewer to an integral part of the picture by encoding this presence as the inverse, *in absentia*, source of the converging perspectival lines. The picture became an opaque mirror for the viewer, and the viewer, in turn, became the embodiment of the painter, "completing the picture" as art historians like to say, with the two points of view merging in a single physical spot. The painter now says when he or she paints, "See things as I see them. ... Stand in my shoes." Consequently, the picture plane and the retina became the same surface. Of course, "Whose retina?" was the key question, as the manipulation of the viewer, an early form of behaviorism, was added to the list of artistic techniques.

In the dialogue between viewer and image, there were now three entities where formerly there had been two, or possibly even one. (One in the sense that most images, as thoroughly two-dimensional diagramatic and/or schematic representations, were previously used as a sacred vehicle to achieve a state of union between the viewer and the divinity.) The image was to be taken to heart within the individual, with the concurrent loss of self-identity so common to religious experience, thus forming the single image of "self/deity." It was an evocation rather than a description (the picture evoked the god or goddess within, it did not describe him or her without).

With the new identification of the viewer with the painter, rather than with the sacred object, came the placement of both of them relative to a third entity, the nearby physical object(s) or subject of the painting, and along with this possibly the inauguration of the process of encroachment of the individual ego (i.e., the artist's) onto the image in the visual arts.

In the Brunelleschian world, the mechanism is perception, the image retinal. When the emphasis is on the act of seeing at a physical place, then time enters the picture as well ("if it's here, it's not there— if it's now, it's not then"). Images become "frozen moments." They become artifacts of the past. In securing a place on earth, they have accepted their own mortality.

The Temporary Image

"For the memories themselves are not important. Only when they have changed into our very blood, into glance and gesture, and are nameless, no longer to be distinguished from ourselves—only then can it happen that in some very rare hour the first word of a poem arises in their midst and goes forth from them."[3]

—Rainer Marie Rilke

More than 400 years after "the Fall" of the image, when the original powerful realization of the optical image was transforming itself into the physical form of the photographic picture machine, it was no coincidence that at the same time the painters were advancing their discoveries of light and image as palpable substances independent of the object. The physical act of rendering the visual world as-the-eye-sees-it was being taken out of their hands, while the image had once again diverged to begin a slow return to dematerialization and internalization.

3. Rainer Maria Rilke, *The Selected Poetry of Rainer Maria Rilke*, ed. and trans. by Stephen Mitchell (New York: Random House, 1982), 91.

The inevitable mechanization of the image made possible two things that led to its liberation from the prison of frozen time: machine nature introduced automated sequential repeatability, and advances in the material sciences made possible the fixing of light impressions on a durable surface, both necessary for the advent of the first moving pictures. It is important to note that the invention of photography was not the invention of the camera, but that of the process of fixing an image onto a plate. Real-time viewing boxes, similar to today's view cameras without the film, were available from the late eighteenth century, the projections of magic lanterns were known in the seventeenth century, and the camera obscura has been around for millennia, probably arising in ancient China. (It is most likely that Brunelleschi was aware of the camera obscura, and he was certainly influenced by the new concepts in all fields, including optics, that were then being imported from the Arabic and Persian cultures of the East, through the translation of the ancient manuscripts of the Greeks, and by more recent texts by great Arabic thinkers such as Alhazen (Ibn al-Haytham).)

In this sense, moving images had been around for a long time. Technically, however, the first imparting of movement to artificial images (in this case drawings) occurred in 1832 with the simultaneous inventions of Joseph A. F. Plateau's Phenakistiscope and Simon R. von Stampfer's Stroboscope, soon followed by others, leading up to the eventual integration of the photographic image into the process at the Edison laboratory during 1888–9, and thus to the birth of true cinema. The emphasis of the term *moving image* is somewhat misleading, since the images themselves are not really moving and the art of cinema lies more in the combination of image sequences in time (montage) than it does in making the images move.

A thought is a function of time, a pattern of growth, and not the "thing" that the lens of the printed word seems to objectify. It is more like a cloud than a rock, although its effects can be just as long lasting as a block of stone, and its aging subject to the similar processes of destructive erosion and constructive edification. Duration is the medium that makes thought possible, therefore duration is to consciousness as light is to the eye.

Still, the question remains, exactly what is this movement in the moving image? Clearly it is more than the frenetic animation of bodies. Hollis Frampton, the great American avant-garde filmmaker, described it as "the mimesis, incarnation, and bodying forth of the movement of human consciousness itself." The root of the cinematic process remained the still picture, but images now had behavior, and the entire phenomenon began to resemble less the material objects depicted and more the process of the mind that was moving them.

Time itself has become the *materia prima* of the art of the moving image. The "unsticking" of the image in time has been a gradual process, and its effects are permeating art and culture in the late twentieth century, moving beyond the domain of conventional cinematic form and serving to dislodge the dominant compositional model of the dramatic narrative (based on Aristotle's theories of 400 B.C.). This chapter in art history is potentially as significant as the introduction of three-dimensional space originally was to painting. No doubt the first examples of time-based visual art in the twentieth century will be regarded by future observers as being clumsy and childlike, much in the way the modern eye tends to see the medieval painter's first attempts at three-dimensional representation as somewhat naive.

If from the medieval vantage point, the post-Brunelleschi optical painting seemed to be not all here (the illusion of someplace else compared to the concrete, immediate, nondescriptive existence of the icon image), then cinema was "really" not here. The physical apparatus of the moving image necessitates its existence as primarily a mental phenomenon. The viewer sees only one image at a time in the case of film and, more extreme, only the decay trace of a single moving point of light in video. In either case, the whole does not exist (except in a dormant state coiled up in the can or tape box), and therefore can only reside in the mind of the person who has seen it, to be revived periodically through his or her memory. Conceptual and physical movement become equal, experience becomes a language, and an odd sort of concreteness emerges from the highly abstract, metaphysical nature of the medium. It is the concreteness of individual experience, the original impetus for the story—"I went here and this happened ...." Sitting in the dark room, we sense a strange familiarity—an image is born, flashes before our eyes, and dies in blackness.

Once there was a train of images sequentially unfolding in time; there was "a moving image" and with it, by necessity, a beginning and an end; mortal images, with the camera as death. As long as perpetual motion remains an unrealized dream, there will always be a last image, usually with darkness as a final punctuation. Fade to black . . .

The Last Image

"I raise the mirror of my life
Up to my face: sixty years.
With a swing I smash the reflection—
The world as usual.
All in its place."[4]

After writing these lines in 1555, the Zen priest Taigen Sofu put down his brush and died. (From the Japanese tradition of *jisei*, poems written by Zen monks and Haiku poets on the verge of death.)

In many countries throughout the world, black is the color of mourning. Echoing this ineffable finality, in European culture black is considered to be outside color, the condition of the "absence of light." The focal point for black in our lives is the pupil of the eye, portal to the tiny chamber in the center of the eyeball, where darkness is necessary to resolve the original parent of the artificial image.

Since the means of the artistic creation of images are now the laws of optics and the properties of light, and the focus is the human eye, it was only a matter of time before someone thought to hold up a mirror. The ideal mirror, around since the beginning of humankind, is the black background of the pupil of the eye. There is a natural human propensity to want to stare into the eye of another or, by extension of oneself, a desire to see seeing itself, as if the straining to see inside the

4. Yoel Hoffman, *Japanese Death Poems* (Tokyo: Charles E. Tuttle Company, 1986), 118.

little black center of the eye will reveal not only the secrets of the other, but of the totality of human vision. After all, the pupil is the boundary, and veil, to both internal and external vision.

Looking closely into the eye, the first thing to be seen, indeed the only thing to be seen, is one's own self-image. This leads to the awareness of two curious properties of pupil gazing. The first is the condition of infinite reflection, the first visual feedback. The tiny person I see on the black field of the pupil also has an eye within which is reflected the tiny image of a person ... and so on. The second is the physical fact that the closer I get to have a better view into the eye, the larger my own image becomes, thus blocking my view within. These two phenomena have each inspired ancient avenues of philosophical investigation and, in addition to the palpable ontological power of looking directly into the organs of sight, were considered proof of the uniqueness and special power of the eyes and the sense of sight.

Staring into the eye is an ancient form of autohypnosis and meditation. In the *Alcibiades* of Plato, Socrates describes the process of acquiring self-knowledge from the contemplation of the self in the pupil of another's eye, or in the reflection of one's own.

Socrates (describing the Delphic inscription "gnothi seauton"): I will tell you what I think is the real advice this inscription offers. The only example I find to explain it has to do with seeing. ... Suppose we spoke to our eye as if it were a man and told it: "See thyself" ... would it not mean that the eye should look at something in which it could recognize itself?

Alcibiades: Mirrors and things of that sort?

Socrates: Quite right. And is there not something of that sort in the eye we see with? ... Haven't you noticed that when one looks someone in the eye, he sees his own face in the center of the other eye, as if in a mirror? This is why we call the center of the eye the "pupil" (puppet): because it reflects a sort of miniature image of the person looking into it. ... So when one eye looks at another and gazes into that inmost part by virtue of which that eye sees, then it sees itself.

Alcibiades: That's true.

Socrates: And if the soul too wants to know itself, must it not look at a soul, especially at that inmost part of it where reason and wisdom dwell? ... This part of the soul resembles God. So whoever looks at this and comes to know all that is divine—God and insight through reason—will thereby gain a deep knowledge of himself.[5]

The medieval Neoplatonists practiced meditating on the pupil of the eye, or *speculation*, a word that literally means "mirror gazing." The word *contemplation* is derived from the ancient practice of divination, where a *templum* is marked off in the sky by the crook of an auger to observe the passage of crows through the square. *Medi*tation and *concen*tration both refer to the centering process of focusing on the self.

The black pupil also represents the ground of nothingness, the place before and after the image, the basis of the "void" described in all systems of spiritual training. It is what Meister Eckhart described as "the stripping away of everything, not only that which is other, but even one's own being."

In ancient Persian cosmology, black exists as a color and is considered to be "higher" than white in the universal color scheme. This idea is derived in part as well from the color of the pupil. The black disc of the pupil is the inverse of the white circle of the sun. The tiny image in "the apple of the eye" was traditionally believed to be a person's self, his or her soul, existing in complementary relationship to the sun, the world-eye.

"There is nothing brighter than the sun, for through it all things become manifest. Yet if the sun did not go down at night, or if it were not veiled by the shade, no one would realize that there is such a thing as light on the face of the earth. ... They have apprehended light through its opposite. ... The difficulty in knowing God is

5. Quoted in Wilhelm Fraenger, *Hieronymus Bosch* (New York: G. P. Putnam and Sons, 1983), 42.

therefore due to brightness; He is so bright that men's hearts have not the strength to perceive it. ... He is hidden by His very brightness."[6]

— Al-Ghazzali (1058–1111)

So, black becomes a bright light on a dark day, the intense light bringing on the protective darkness of the closed eye; the black of the annihilation of the self.

Fade to black ...

[Silence]

A voice is heard in the darkness: ... but wait, fade to black is just one of the blacks in video—there are actually three states of video that can be black like what you're talking about.

Narrator: And what are they?

Voice: Well, there's video black, as in "fade to black." Then there's snow, when the set is on but there is no signal present—you can also see this as a blank, dark screen on video monitors. And then there's nothing, when the plug is pulled out and the set is cold. In terms of our bodies, these are like closing your eyes, sleep, and death.

Narrator: I see. So, if I understand what you're saying, as long as there is the kernal of self-consciousness, as in the first two stages and sometimes even in the darkest depths of the inter-mediate zone between stages two and three, "near-death" or "beyond-death" experiences, then there is always the possibility for renewal.

Voice: That's it. Self-consciousness is the awareness of context—you know ... the view from above, the motivation to keep flipping the power switch back on.

Narrator: That reminds me of a recurring dream I have.

6. Quoted in N. Ardalan, L. Bakhtiar, *The Sense of Unity* (Chicago: University of Chicago Press, 1973), 47.

Voice: Tell me.

Narrator: Well, there is nothing but black. I am awake. Lying on my back, I sense my breathing, quiet and regular. I roll over and stare upwards. I see nothing, or rather I am trying to understand what I am seeing. There is the sensation of space, palpable in the blackness, but it is depth without the reassuring content of an image. There is the sensation of my body, its extension and weight pressing downwards. And there are these questions in silent dialogue with the darkness. I bring my hand up to my face. There is nothing. I turn it over, wave it, and the slight brush of the movement of air is felt against my cheek. I lie motionless. There is a slight ringing sensation in my ears, and my mouth feels dry because I haven't wanted to move, not even to swallow. Without motion, I slowly become aware of the loss of sensation in my limbs. I don't know how long I have been lying like this. I imagine the darkness as an immense soft black cloud of cotton wool, silent and weightless, gradually pressing in around my body. Everything seems to be closing down to a small opening just around my face; outside of this small area, the oblivion of nothing. Finally, like a body under water focused on breathing through a tiny straw, I let that go and feel myself submerged in the great comfort of the senseless and weightless void.

Voice: [Dumbfounded silence]

Fade to black.

In two minutes, the tape runs out and the screen is plunged into snow. The hissing sound jars the viewer from sleep. A hand slowly comes in and fumbles for the power button. There is a click, silence, and the snow on the screen abruptly collapses into a momentary point of light, which gradually fades while the glass screen quietly crackles, dissipating its static charge, and the internal circuits begin to lose their heat to the cold night.

Statement 1992

I do not accept the category of "television art." Television is a means of transmitting ideas in the form of moving images and sounds. To say that it has a special case called "television art" is to accept the political consequences of commercial television's present hegemony (particularly in America) over the full spectrum of imagery representing the infinitely varied, rich, often chaotic, conflicting, and contrasting forms of consciousness that make up the full range of human experience on this planet. The American media writer Gene Youngblood has called television "perceptual imperialism," underscoring the fact that the medium is not only a political tool but a physiological one as well, and that its effects in conforming each individual's psycho-physical make-up cannot be underestimated.

Art that conforms to established rules, specifically those rules that have been instituted outside of the practice of art, becomes a form of propaganda. Even if its "message" is subversive, its form will always be conformist, underlying form being the true residing place of power in any system of communication. Whoever controls the rules of the conversation controls the conversation. This is why people talk about the phenomenon of interesting innovative ideas or new image forms getting "swallowed up" or "co-opted" by the media powers-that-be. In political terms, propaganda is a form of obscenity in relation to the original idea of democracy, where contrasting ideas were meant to be discussed openly and rationally and not coerced or deviously misrepresented, and where individual voices were meant to be heard and not modified or supressed.

Television has always been fearful of unrestricted individual expression. Until the television system gives artists total open creative freedom and control over the form and content of their works, either by open acceptance of existing works or the commissioning of new works,

Comment on art for television, and/or idea for a future TV art channel, for 3rd Video Television Festival at Spiral Hall, Tokyo, February , 1992. First published in *Japan 92*, eds. Haruo Fukuzumi and Keiko Tamaki (Tokyo: Video Gallery SCAN, 1992), 152–3.

there will be no "television art." Until artists who work with video become, through self-discipline, devoted practice, and selfless knowledge, deeply aware and compassionate human beings, there will be no "television art." The rules for the artist ultimately do not come from art history, or from current trends, ideas, and fashions, or even from the materials themselves. These are merely resources to draw on. The real rules come from the Self. The only method is Self-knowledge, and its only parameters are that of the Gift, of receiving and in turn passing it on. These rules are the same and only rules for the creation of a true "television art."

The Stopping Mind 1991

"The mind of attachment arises from the stopping mind. So does
the cycle of transmigration. This stopping becomes the bonds of life
and death.... Stopping means that the mind is being detained by
something, which may be any matter at all....

"When facing a single tree, if you look at a single one of its red
leaves, you will not see all of the others.... Similarly, the wheels of
a cart go around because they are not rigidly in place. If they were
to stick tight, they would not go around and the cart would not
move. The mind is also something that does not function if it
becomes attached to a single situation.... The mind that stops or is
moved by something is sent into confusion—this is the affliction of
the abiding place, and this is the common man. To be called, to
respond without interval, is the wisdom of the Buddhas.... Not
stopping the mind is object and essence. Put it nowhere, it will be
everywhere."

—Takuan Soho (1573–1645), "The Mysterious
Record of Immovable Wisdom," *The Unfettered Mind*

The Stopping Mind is a video installation for projected images and
sound based on the age-old human desire to stop time. It deals with the
paradox of thought (memory) and experience—the underlying propensity of the mind to retain or arrest experience and the dynamic nature
of both the experience and the perpetual movement of consciousness
itself.

Four large screens are suspended from the ceiling and float in space
in the center of a large dark room. They are positioned to describe the
sides of an open cube. Four separate but related images are displayed on
the screens. The images are static, the room is silent. Suddenly, without
warning, the images simultaneously lunge into movement, momentarily coming to life in a burst of frantic motion and cascading sound.
After only a few seconds, and equally without warning, they are seized
again and become frozen as still frames.

The image sequences center on the theme of memory, and include archival footage (cultural memory) as well as home-movie-style created footage (individual childhood memory). The material is characterized by constant activity and motion.

The imprisoned time of the still images can unleash itself at any moment, and once witnessed, the immanent potential for violent reactivity is constantly present in the space. If allowed to play continuously, the material would be overwhelming and unbearable. The dominant state of the images as still frames becomes a kind of relief after each burst of activity as the "disarmed" images subside into the pictorial. The intervals between each onslaught of motion are random and unpredictable, occurring anywhere from several seconds to over a minute apart. The duration of each movement burst is likewise of random length, varying between one and fifteen seconds.

Unpublished project proposal for the Museum für Moderne Kunst, Frankfurt am Main, April, 1990.

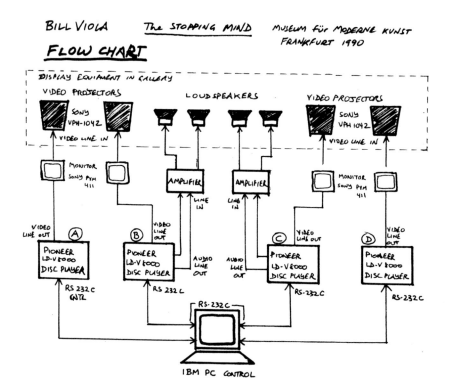

The Stopping Mind, 1991, video/sound installation

PROPOSAL for INSTALLATION - FRANKFURT 1990

ARCHITECTURAL PLANS: TOP VIEW

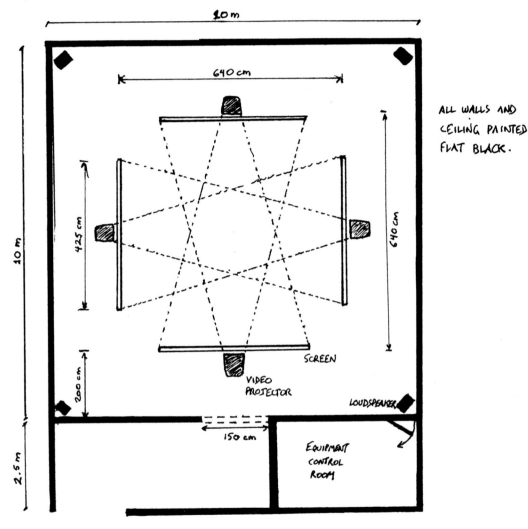

ALL WALLS AND
CEILING PAINTED
FLAT BLACK.

10 m

640 cm

425 cm

640 cm

200 cm

150 cm

2.5 m

SCREEN

VIDEO
PROJECTOR

LOUDSPEAKER

EQUIPMENT
CONTROL
ROOM

PROJECTORS: CEILING MOUNT. (Possibly sound proofed)
SCREEN DIMENSIONS: 425 × 320 cm (14 × 10.5 ft.)
             ALUMINUM FRAME, 2 SIDED MATERIAL
             SUSPENDED from CEILING, (Bottom edge appx. 1 m from floor)

Overleaf: voiceover narration for *The Stopping Mind*, 1991   215

oblivion of nothing. Outside of this there is only darkness. There is only blackness. There is nothing. I am
like a body under water breathing through the small
opening of a straw. A body under water breathing.
Breathing through a small opening. Finally, I let that go.
I let it go. I feel myself submerge. Submerging into the
blackness. Letting go. Sinking down into the black
mass. Submerging into the void. The senseless and
weightless void. The great comfort of the senseless
and weightless void, where there is nothing but black.
There is nothing but silence. I can feel my body. I am
lying in a dark space. I can feel my body lying here. I am
awake. I feel my breathing, in and out, quiet and regular.
I can feel my breathing. I move my body. I slowly roll
over and look up. I see nothing. There is nothing. There
is no light. There is no darkness. There is no volume.
There is no distance. There is no sound. There is no
silence. There is the sensation of space, but there is no
image. There is the sensation of my body with its extension and the weight pressing down. I can feel my body
pressing down. And there is this silent voice ringing in
the darkness. A voice ringing in the blackness. I bring
my hand up to my face. I move my hand but there is
nothing. I move my hand back and forth and I feel the
slight movement of air across my cheek. The air moving
across my cheek but I see nothing. Nothing in the
blackness. My body does not move. I lie completely
still. I don't move. I don't move my body, not even to
swallow. Slowly I become aware of the loss of sensation in my limbs. The loss of sensation of my body. I
don't know how long I have been lying like this. I don't
know how long I've been lying here. Lying in the
silence. I imagine the black space. I imagine the
silence. The darkness of no image. The silence of no
sound. I imagine my body. I imagine my body in this
dark space. The space is like a large black cloud of soft
cotton, silent and weightless. A soft black mass slowly
pressing in around my body. I can feel it slowly pressing
in around my body. Pressing in around me. Everything
is closing down. Closing down around my body. It's
closing down around me until only a small opening
remains. A small opening around my face. Only a small
opening around my face remains. Outside of this – the
oblivion of nothing. The oblivion of nothing. Outside of
this there is only darkness. There is only blackness.
There is nothing. I am like a body under water breathing
through the small opening of a straw. A body under
water breathing. Breathing through a small opening.
Finally, I let that go. I let it go. I feel myself submerge.
Submerging into the blackness. Letting go. Sinking
down into the black mass. Submerging into the void.

It only takes an instant for an impression to become a vision.

—Note, January 21, 1985

The Visionary Landscape of Perception

The Landscape is the Imagination

Our landscape and our imagination seem to represent opposites. I think of the difference between soft and hard, the mental and the physical, a thought and a rock. But I also think of the equality of these two things, the transformation of one into the other. For example, a thought can move a rock. A mountain can inspire a thought.

I think of infinities and limits. The imagination is infinite; the landscape is limited. As William Blake said, "Everything to be believed is an image of truth." Yet today satellites have mapped the entire surface of the earth, the entire landscape, down to a resolution of 30 feet or less.

The landscape is infinite and the imagination limited. I see an endless plain under a blue sky while I think of all the places on earth that cannot be touched in a single life time. Yet try as I might, I cannot image the moment of my death.

The unknown territory is an important traditional aspect of our environment and a vital part of the structure of our minds. The unknown place on the other side of the mountain, across the sea, around the corner ... unknown because the senses do not penetrate.

I think of lying in bed as a child, staring at the dim ceiling, gripped in terror trying to imagine what they could possibly mean when they said, "the universe is infinite and goes on forever." I realized then that there is a limit to my mind's reach.

Then I try to capture all of the thoughts I have had since then. All of the directions my work has taken me, and the endless stream of idea possibilities that lie before me. I sit down to write this, and I am aware

Transcript of the original version presented in August, 1989, as part of a panel discussion at the 2nd Video Television Festival at Spiral Hall, Tokyo, and first published in *Delicate Technology*, eds. Video Gallery SCAN (Fujiko Nakaya) and I&S (Tokyo: Video Television Festival Organizing Committee, SCAN, 1989), 129–48. Also published as "Perception, Technology, Imagination, and the Landscape," in *Enclitic 11*, no. 3 (July 1992), 57–60, and as "Perception, technologie, imagination et paysage," in *Trafic 3* (Summer 1992), 77–82.

of myself, thinking about myself writing this, while thinking about myself while writing this, while thinking about myself....

Perception over Time Transforms the Landscape into Story

The Bushmen of the Kalahari desert in Africa have a tradition of story-telling, where the events of mythic time, as well as human memory time, are superimposed on the landscape. Certain places and natural features become charged from previous events and are later reactivated by walking through them and telling their story. Many ancient tribal cultures share this tradition, especially the grand master of ancient societies, the Aborigines of Australia, who brought it to an extremely high level of sophistication. They are probably the oldest continuously evolving culture on earth, with 40,000 years of continuously evolving traditions.

The concept of Dreamtime and its song lines is an extraordinarily complex and beautiful system. In it, the landscape is engaged as a living thing, and the earth's features are revealed as places where the totemic beings of the mythic time, called "the Dreaming," emerge, re-enter, and/or transform the surface of the earth. The landscape itself is an imprint, the living embodiment of the mythic time still accessible to those living today. Walking through the landscape then becomes a re-telling of the stories of these beings, usually through singing. The entire continent of Australia is criss-crossed by trails that represent lines of song, linking the individuals who sing them to the ancient times of creation. After 40,000 years, the land has become a story.

Anthropologists have documented examples of ESP, communication at a distance, among the Aborigines, and this also seems to be a natural result of a continuous social presence over the millennia in such a vast open land. Just as the wind and rain impress forms on land over geological time, the long-term effects of perception imprint the mind on the land. The physical and mental landscapes superimpose.

In Japan too, although its culture is not as old, we can see the merger of inside and outside space beginning to occur. We think of the special significance conjured by the names of places such as Mount Fuji, Ise, or Lake Biwa. With the continued presence of people over long periods of time, geographical features become story points in a mental landscape.

The object of the fascination that foreigners have with American culture is also a source of its problems. The human presence of the newly arrived Europeans on this continent is not enough established to develop a story. People are floating on top of the land, like boats on an opaque sea. The deepest past of America is first of "the other," a separate race of dispossessed or disposed people; second, and finally, it is solely geological, the bare earth of The Grand Canyon, Monument Valley, etc. The distorted idea that the natural landscape is dead ("inanimate matter") comes from living on land without a story.

Images tell Lies

Perception is the way we contact the world, it is the language of being, yet the senses have traditionally been considered the source of illusion.

An old expression from sound recording technology is "fidelity," fidelity of a recording. We talk about high fidelity, low fidelity. The real question is, of course, fidelity to what: to the object, the hard reality, or to the image, the soft reality?

Traditionally in television, fidelity has been to vision, to the visual image and not to reality, and rarely to the retinal image in the eyeball, even though the camera can be considered a crude and very rough model of the eye. The human visual image is binocular, it includes overlapping areas, double images, indistinct edges, and only a very small part of the center, called the fovea, shows focus in rich detail. Of course, human software, the mind, integrates this with information from the other senses and smoothes out these problems.

Artificial images do not portray reality accurately. They aspire to the image and not to the object, to visual perception and not to the experiential mind field. They do not, for example, show all sides of an object that we know from our experience to exist. The camera only sees three faces of a cube, for example, yet our hands can tell us that the other three simultaneously exist. The "realistic" way of showing all of the sides of the cube as an object in the visual image, specifically in the medium of painting, died out in Europe at the end of the Middle Ages, and was finally eliminated with the advent of vanishing-point perspective. After that, the "photo-realist" tradition, if we can call it that, developed from the Renaissance onwards. The back side of the object disappeared. Of course, the reason why artificial images succeed is that they rely heavily on the viewer's prior knowledge that, for example, objects do have all their sides. They involve the viewer's knowledge base in their functioning.

Human beings, therefore, have always been an integral part of any technology of images. Perception is the input channel to the mind, and with new technologies, the call is first to the body, then the mind will follow. Therefore we talk about "user-friendly," the ease of human interface, comfort of use, the accuracy of human perception. To increase concentration and involvement, movies use the black room, soft seats, and a large screen to fully occupy the sensory field. Wilhelm Reich, the Austrian psychologist who was imprisoned in America because his work was too accurate and unsettling for the establishment, realized that in fragmented industrialized societies, the body was the neglected key. To reach the mind, his therapy focused on healing the body through touch. "When I put my hands on the body," he said, "I put my hands on the unconscious."

The Earth is the Ultimate High Definition System

High definition denotes higher resolution. It is the next step in a long series of steps. So, let's take it to the ultimate: what is maximum resolution? First we must realize that reality itself has no resolution. Resolution is only a property of images. It is a property of who or what is doing the looking, not of what is being seen.

Reality itself is infinitely resolvable. Therefore ultimate resolution is a function of scale. Magnify reality and you move through planes of meaning: first, the familiar world; then the macro, or the ant's eye view; then the microscopic; the molecular; the atomic; etc. This is the physical approach. It has a long history in Western culture. In some ways, the history of science can be viewed as the journeying through increasingly refined scales of reality; as knowledge increases, so does space.

The limits of the physical approach are apparent as we move through the last remnants of the machine age. Hollis Frampton, the great American avant-garde filmmaker, called film "the last machine." He said it was "as close to software as the machine age can get." In the software age, we transform scale into information, into language. We move into a huge close-up of a human hair, and as we approach the images of molecules in action, we encounter a strand of DNA—the shape of a code, the form of information and a new depth becomes possible.

In the software age we are beginning to model ourselves on information processing and not on machine construction. Limitations become merely local boundaries defined by lack of adequate translations and transformations. And just as the presence of human beings in a specific place over long periods of time creates a story, the electronic image landscape is beginning to create a layering of mental archeology. This is the world we are learning to inhabit as images become our tools.

Hardware equals Software

One of the original sources of all philosophy is the paradox of the hard and the soft: the body and the soul; the outer physical world and the world of thoughts and images within. This is one of the great mysteries of life, and the good thing about mysteries in the classic sense is that they don't have to be solved, only experienced. The great mystics of history bathed in the mystery. Their goal was to translate experiences, not images or descriptions. The original function of the statue of Buddha was simply as an image to aid in meditation. It was only later that, in some cultures, it became an object of divinity to be venerated and worshipped.

Technology, particularly imaging technology, exists on the border between the worlds. An unplugged TV set is not television. The time is past when we can discuss software apart from hardware. This is irresponsible and impractical. We are looking at a total living system. Software and hardware have always been related, ever since the days our monkey ancestors picked up the first tool and began to model nature. All hardware springs from a thought, a desire, or a need. The chair: to sit elevated in comfort. The telegraph: to speak over distances. All comes from the mind interacting with nature. Another example: the American urban landscape of today is a landscape formed in the shape of money. The desire to make money creates its form.

Suzuki Shunryu Roshi, the Zen master who founded the San Francisco Zen Center, said this about painting: "When you pick up the brush, you already know the results of your painting, or else you could not paint."

The Future of Technology is the Future of What is Real

With each new step in the evolution of technology, we take a step closer to our ideal of higher and higher quality, which actually means creating things that look more and more like nature itself. Signal-to-noise ratio in sound is a technical term referring to the measure of the strength, and therefore the purity, of the signal as it exists over the chaotic noise of a disorganized background. We can also speak of the "signal-to-noise ratio of life." How close can we come to the true nature of things? The implied goal of many of our efforts, including techno-logical development, is the eradication of signal-to-noise ratio, which in the end is the ultimate transparent state where there is no perceived difference between the simulation and the reality, between ourselves and the other. We think of two lovers locked in a single ecstatic embrace. We think of futuristic descriptions of direct stimulation to the brain to evoke experiences and memories. We think of experiments with drugs—LSD as a kind of movie to be taken internally. With advanced research on the brain it is possible that inner images can be accessed, but pure, transparent experience will probably remain an unattainable, implied goal, the measure for the connoisseur and the impetus for further refinement.

As human beings we require limits and boundaries to function. Our nervous system is one of difference registration. Boundaries create friction, and therefore create energy. Limits exist as challenges to provoke the means to transcend them and to propel us forward, with more limits coming into view as we arrive there—much like the mirage that continuously recedes on the road before us in the summer. Technology does constantly provoke us to ask what is real. Is television real? Some people say no, yet it has more effect on people today than the natural landscape does.

When asked what is real, most people turn inwards, to their individual experience. They think about hitting their head on a rock, an image of the face of their mother, or losing their job, or whatever. They do not necessarily think of themselves standing there at the moment the question was asked. At that moment, of course, all these things are memories, mental images. Memory is the residing place of life experience, the collection that reveals and/or fabricates order and meaning. What is real, therefore, is what is psychologically meaningful. At one time in the past, the mythic and symbolic were real. Today, physical science has influenced us to believe that the objects of the physical world are real. Yet, we surround ourselves with electronic images and transmitted information. Hollis Frampton called the movement in moving images "the movement of human consciousness itself. The images carry on our mental lives for us," he said, "darkly, whether we want them to or not." We already are, and always have been, in an imaginary landscape of perception.

Slowly Turning Narrative 1992

The work concerns the enclosing nature of self-image and the external circulation of potentially infinite (and therefore unattainable) states of being all revolving around the still point of the central self. The entire room and all persons within it become a continually shifting projection screen, enclosing the image and its reflections, including a self-reflection of the space

and viewer, and all locked into the
regular cadences of the chanting voice
and the rotating screen. The entire
space becomes an interior for the revelations of a constantly turning mind
absorbed with itself. The confluences
and conflicts of image, intent, content,
and emotion perpetually circulate as
the screen slowly turns in the space.

—1992

Following pages: The One Who..., voiceover, *Slowly Turning Narrative*, 1992   227

the one who goes
the one who does
the one who feels
the one who knows
the one who breathes
the one who moves
the one who stands
the one who sleeps
the one who turns away
the one who looks
the one who comes
the one who calls
the one who returns
the one who remembers
the one who fails
the one who runs
the one who lives
the one who expects
the one who sees
the one who allows
the one who forgives
the one who hates
the one who makes
the one who pleads
the one who cries
the one who falls
the one who creates
the one who forgets
the one who betrays
the one who screams
the one who loves
the one who smells
the one who feels
the one who lies
the one who agrees
the one who follows
the one who leads
the one who deceives
the one who doubts
the one who carries
the one who resolves
the one who discovers
the one who dies
the one who fights
the one who responds
the one who fears
the one who leads

the one who completes
the one who abandons
the one who receives
the one who surrenders
the one who avows
the one who prays
the one who gives
the one who denies
the one who takes
the one who stops
the one who sits
the one who kills
the one who rests
the one who dreams
the one who cuts
the one who pulls
the one who pushes
the one who destroys
the one who fires
the one who blames
the one who writes
the one who retreats
the one who lies
the one who drives
the one who gathers
the one who helps
the one who hurts
the one who eats
the one who robs
the one who keeps
the one who shares
the one who accuses
the one who cheats
the one who supplies
the one who demands
the one who buys
the one who swallows
the one who shits
the one who fucks
the one who increases
the one who threatens
the one who spits
the one who pisses
the one who blinks
the one who hears
the one who touches
the one who changes

the one who grows
the one who shrinks
the one who rots
the one who stabs
the one who brags
the one who whispers
the one who announces
the one who refines
the one who conceals
the one who chokes
the one who relies
the one who finds
the one who meets
the one who waits
the one who dives
the one who scrapes
the one who starves
the one who fills
the one who learns
the one who cleans
the one who uncovers
the one who disappears
the one who consumes
the one who solves
the one who flies
the one who crushes
the one who punctures
the one who upsets
the one who disturbs
the one who centers
the one who tells
the one who turns
the one who escapes
the one who lunges
the one who avoids
the one who sucks
the one who cares
the one who endures
the one who drops
the one who cracks
the one who interrupts
the one who annoys
the one who defines
the one who knocks
the one who reveals
the one who disturbs
the one who arrives

the one who embraces
the one who silences
the one who strikes
the one who nurtures
the one who catches
the one who drops
the one who adds
the one who removes
the one who distills
the one who reflects
the one who explains
the one who ignores
the one who hits
the one who delays
the one who keeps
the one who shoots
the one who hides
the one who accommodates
the one who heals
the one who describes
the one who defies
the one who closes
the one who informs
the one who travels
the one who speaks
the one who transforms
the one who overrides
the one who commands
the one who rules
the one who stifles
the one who judges
the one who fakes
the one who misleads
the one who releases
the one who contains
the one who gags
the one who farts
the one who squeezes
the one who shifts
the one who shuts
the one who stabilizes
the one who disables
the one who empties
the one who cripples
the one who bleeds
the one who thirsts
the one who desires

the one who obeys
the one who bathes
the one who hungers
the one who enlightens
the one who brushes
the one who tells
the one who prevents
the one who intervenes
the one who constrains
the one who mediates
the one who suppresses
the one who convinces
the one who disciplines
the one who complies
the one who retains
the one who comforts
the one who calculates
the one who climbs
the one who constrains
the one who crawls
the one who believes
the one who rejects
the one who covers
the one who copies
the one who wills
the one who donates
the one who recedes
the one who charges
the one who convinces
the one who qualifies
the one who achieves
the one who wins
the one who loses
the one who darkens
the one who opens
the one who finishes
the one who conceives
the one who purifies
the one who perpetuates
the one who reforms
the one who restores
the one who remains
the one who drowns
the one who refuses
the one who maintains
the one who prevails
the one who undresses

the one who washes
the one who kisses
the one who divides
the one who resists
the one who aligns
the one who measures
the one who delivers
the one who sends
the one who troubles
the one who signals
the one who confirms
the one who holds
the one who decreases
the one who removes
the one who cleanses
the one who negates
the one who signs
the one who extends
the one who profits
the one who fulfils
the one who speculates
the one who matches
the one who empowers
the one who simplifies
the one who multiplies
the one who disfigures
the one who clutters
the one who amuses
the one who connects
the one who sustains
the one who deserves
the one who practices
the one who asks
the one who bestows
the one who hides
the one who curses
the one who frees
the one who sets
the one who faces
the one who fixes
the one who deludes
the one who isolates
the one who recalls
the one who submerges
the one who engages
the one who bears
the one who pronounces

the one who pays
the one who responds
the one who sings
the one who lowers
the one who lessens
the one who earns
the one who crushes
the one who splits
the one who sows
the one who suppresses
the one who binds
the one who tightens
the one who operates
the one who stings
the one who plays
the one who nullifies
the one who grieves
the one who ends
the one who laughs
the one who encloses
the one who refers
the one who evolves
the one who declines
the one who searches
the one who discerns
the one who softens
the one who erodes
the one who mourns
the one who passes
the one who establishes
the one who detracts
the one who reproduces
the one who organises
the one who respects
the one who finances
the one who abstains
the one who summarizes
the one who shortens
the one who deals
the one who lifts
the one who leaps
the one who contracts
the one who damages
the one who cancels
the one who pressures
the one who restores
the one who aches

the one who itches
the one who worries
the one who infects
the one who invests
the one who wets
the one who stains
the one who fills
the one who stays
the one who advises
the one who plans
the one who battles
the one who relates
the one who dismantles
the one who understands
the one who contacts
the one who controls
the one who presses
the one who undermines
the one who spends
the one who speeds
the one who occurs
the one who rocks
the one who lights
the one who blinds
the one who gains
the one who covets
the one who indulges
the one who abuses
the one who instigates
the one who initiates
the one who renders
the one who effects
the one who sounds
the one who lengthens
the one who proceeds
the one who patches
the one who panders
the one who handles
the one who depends
the one who concedes
the one who envisions
the one who enters
the one who applauds
the one who regulates
the one who enforces
the one who suspends
the one who enrages

the one who rescues
the one who survives
the one who conforms
the one who rents
the one who employs
the one who behaves
the one who overstates
the one who concludes
the one who projects
the one who demeans
the one who subverts
the one who nourishes
the one who howls
the one who blows
the one who copulates
the one who supports
the one who eradicates
the one who confides
the one who serves
the one who permits
the one who reduces
the one who forgoes
the one who honours
the one who slows
the one who bans
the one who sanctifies
the one who secures
the one who locks
the one who attracts
the one who scratches
the one who erases
the one who appreciates
the one who confuses
the one who regresses
the one who degrades
the one who joins
the one who embodies
the one who creases
the one who stimulates
the one who obliterates
the one who anticipates
the one who supervises
the one who slumps
the one who slouches
the one who straightens
the one who migrates
the one who educates

the one who packages
the one who ties
the one who counts
the one who dignifies
the one who wastes
the one who designs
the one who investigates
the one who punishes
the one who categorizes
the one who strains
the one who masters
the one who converges
the one who converses
the one who repeats
the one who relinquishes
the one who authorizes
the one who defaults
the one who promotes
the one who produces
the one who ages
the one who clings
the one who decays
the one who subsidizes
the one who replenishes
the one who collapses
the one who descends
the one who distinguishes
the one who repairs
the one who exhausts
the one who ascends
the one who says
the one who seizes
the one who peeks
the one who works
the one who borrows
the one who belittles
the one who resumes
the one who misunderstands
the one who folds
the one who trembles
the one who hesitates
the one who leans
the one who burns
the one who renounces
the one who concentrates
the one who schemes
the one who sells

the one who stands by
the one who observes
the one who revokes
the one who strengthens
the one who shudders
the one who defends
the one who rages
the one who rapes
the one who masturbates
the one who hunts
the one who weakens
the one who wishes
the one who rises
the one who integrates
the one who trusts
the one who whistles
the one who performs
the one who intimidates
the one who inspires
the one who accumulates
the one who depletes
the one who chooses
the one who exceeds
the one who excels
the one who repels
the one who selects
the one who frightens
the one who denigrates
the one who feeds
the one who scatters
the one who shelters
the one who marks
the one who inflicts
the one who despises
the one who corrects
the one who deforms
the one who moderates
the one who wounds
the one who prides
the one who expires
the one who confounds
the one who penetrates
the one who eludes
the one who satisfies
the one who outlives
the one who uses
the one who breaks down

the one who weeps
the one who murmurs
the one who manipulates
the one who rectifies
the one who complains
the one who applies
the one who appoints
the one who reserves
the one who notifies
the one who clothes
the one who rebuilds
the one who realizes
the one who constructs
the one who wonders
the one who contemplates
the one who disposes
the one who preserves
the one who mobilizes
the one who disintegrates
the one who stores
the one who begins
the one who mistrusts
the one who worships
the one who carries
the one who repents
the one who defeats
the one who recommends
the one who drags
the one who bites
the one who beholds
the one who possesses

the one who is.

Sculpting with time. Time is the basic material of film and video.
The mechanics of it may be cameras, film stock, and tape, but what
you are working with is time. You are creating events that are going to
unfold, on some kind of rigid channel that is embodied in a strip of
tape or celluloid, and that thing is coiled up as a potential experience
to be unrolled. In a certain way it is like a scroll, which is one of
the most ancient forms of visual communication. It is a very potent
mechanical representation of our experience of time.

—Note, June 27, 1989

The Body Asleep

"...philosophical ideas by themselves change nothing in the life
of an individual. Without the practical knowledge of how to bring
great ideas into the heart and even the tissues of the body, philosophy cannot take us very far. Systems, explanations, clarifications,
proofs—through these modern man squanders his attention in the
intellectual function while remaining cut-off from the emotional
and instinctual sides of his nature, wherein reside the most powerful
energies of our being, and without the corresponding development
of which no authentic moral power is possible."[1]

—Jacob Needleman

Far more disturbing than falling asleep at the wheel while driving is
waking up. The fearful speculation of how long one has been asleep
punctuates the moving monotony with a shrill reminder of the uncertainty and fragility of existence. Walking home alone in the middle
of the night through a densely populated neighborhood is another
moment when being awake can be more disturbing than being asleep—
the thundering silence of masses of people sleeping behind walls and
closed doors rings throughout the emptiness of the immediate surround-
ings, as if a great tide has retreated for the moments far out to sea. The
monuments to the waking life stand hollow and still as if
a contemporary holocaust had rendered them useless, a silent vision
of the underworld that occurs every night on the unknown streets of
our cities.

However, there is another and perhaps most disturbing sense of
wakefulness that these events merely suggest, and that is being "awake"
while being alive—the only genuine "hyper-realism," the hardcore
immutable physical basis and conclusion of true "conceptual art," the

First published in *Pour la Suite du Monde: Cahier: Propos et Projets*, eds. Gilles
Godmer and Real Lussier (Montreal: Musée d'art contemporain, 1992), 56–7
(French), 80–1 (English).

1. Jacob Needleman, *Lost Christianity* (New York: Doubleday, 1980).

uncertain embodiment of the moment, the insecurity of the infiniteness of the present tense, all really made known only through pain. Lie motionless in a dark space, and it is the areas of discomfort that illuminate the body's being. Numb areas disappear. Numbness becomes the body's assimilation of the darkness. It is invisibility, obscurity, and anonymity. Anonymity is a form of social numbness. Common sense and convention become forms of mental numbness. Loss of sensation becomes pleasure.

When asked what is real, most people turn inward to their individual experience. They think about things like hitting their head on a rock, the face of their mother, or losing their job. They do not necessarily think of themselves standing there at the moment the question was asked. Being awake is much more difficult, unsettling, and uncomfortable than remaining asleep, even though it is often perceived as being transparent or invisible from the other side, as the many examples of the "dream within a dream" scenario that recur through-out various histories and cultures demonstrate. (A famous example from fifth-century B.C. China is "I do not know if I am Chuang Tzu dreaming he is a butterfly, or a butterfly dreaming he is Chuang Tzu.")[2] How do you know you are awake? Why, you pinch your body until it hurts, according to age-old advice.

The evolution of mental history in Western culture describes the displacement by reason and logic of the body as an instrument of knowledge. (In the same way that the pagan European "Day of the Dead" was replaced by the Christian "All Saints' Day" and yet remains on the same day; that the hostile designation "witch" replaced the vital role of the female "shaman;" and that unusual geological features in the landscape of the New World, acknowledged and/or worshipped by the Native Americans, were quickly labeled "The Devil's" by foreign settlers.)

The rich subterranean world of individual mental archeology vivifies the present by connecting us back to the mythic times of action and creation, a world which we today label the "unconscious." It bears

2. *Chuang Tzu: Basic Writings*, trans. Burton Watson (New York: Columbia University Press, 1964).

the same relation to our contemporary, modernized, conscious minds that the dirt under Main Street, visible occasionally between the cracks and in corners, bears to the shops and artificial structures above that rely on it for support, while at the same time rendering it invisible and insignificant. It is this same dirt that links our common day-to-day urban world to its ancient past, and that appears increasingly in abundance when we venture outside the city limits to confront the natural undeveloped landscape, even if increasingly isolated within defined preserves called "national parks." There, ancient unconscious feelings are aroused, more evidenced if time and place coincide with a solitary receptive state, an awareness that is both strange and familiar. Long dismissed as mere emotion or sentiment, these underlying feelings and capacities of the human heart and mind are central in traditional senior cultures to the acquisition and employment of knowledge, and knowledge would be meaningless without them.

In our daily urban world, increasingly and many times exclusively composed of people-made devices and structures, the body and its functions remain one of the last vestiges of nature, if not the ultimate, that we can live in close contact with. Its ineradicable nature may in the end save us from complete Cartesian collapse. Wilhelm Reich, the Austrian psychologist who was imprisoned for his work (so accurate and unsettling was it for the Establishment), realized that in contemporary industrialized societies, the body was the neglected key. To reach the mind, his therapy focused on healing the body through touch. "When I put my hands on the body," he said, "I put my hands on the unconscious." [3]

From Reich then to Robert Mapplethorpe now, direct images and acknowledgements of the body and its functions have been unsettling, disturbing, and threatening formulations that define the power that the separation from nature has generated. Unfortunately they often lead to damaged lives for their creators and a further polarization for the rest of the community. The Mapplethorpe/Serrano censorship controversy in the visual arts over the last few years, far from resolved in the United States, has to be seen as a fight over the body and therefore

3. Wilhelm Reich, *Selected Writings* (New York: Noonday Press, 1973).

part of the larger environmental battle, the body being one of the last battlegrounds between nature and old-world hostile human forces. The larger struggle we are witnessing today is not between conflicting religious moral beliefs, between the legal system and individual freedom, or between nature and human technology; it is between our inner and outer lives, and our bodies are the area where this is being played out. It is the old philosophical "mind-body" problem coming to a crescendo as an ecological drama where the outcome rests not only on our realization that the natural physical environment is one and the same as our bodies, but that nature itself is a form of Mind.

The term "ecology" is one of the most powerful descriptions of our present and future condition; not the ecology of the specifics of botany, biology, or climatics, but the broader, deeper Ecology—ecology as a philosophical and moral system (in a thoroughly contemporary and Zen-like way) where individual elements are not considered independently but as descriptions of the whole; where relationships, and not objects, take precedence; where value is based on interactive processes and not on some absolute hierarchy (the coyote is "bad" for the prairie dog, but "good" for the animal population balance). Our greatest responsibility today, and deepest moral crisis, is that we are increasingly asked to take over and perform, in a fully self-conscious manner, the actions that for Nature over the milennia have been a single great interconnected unconscious process. This burden of self-consciousness, for the moment extremely difficult and uncomfortable, may in itself be a continuing part of the process of Nature on the grandest scale.

In this light, the machinations of the majority of the present-day art world, mired in the commodity-bound confused wake of the breakup of nineteenth- and twentieth-century formalist "aesthetic" codes and undisciplined personal expression, seem increasingly trite, frivolous, and out of touch, except of course for the few individual lights that have always been around to show us the way. Twentieth-century artistic practice has been right, however, in its emphasis on individual vision and action. As with any true political change, any shift in environmental or social awareness and practice (the two should be considered as one) can only be authentic if it originates and resides concurrently within each individual on their own terms. This is the real political nature of spiritual practice, usually overlooked by political theorists, and also why Eastern religions, with their emphasis on individual enlightenment and self-awareness (devotees are called "practitioners" and not, as in Christianity, "followers"), represent such a vital resource for the equation of contemporary life. And finally, as Nature herself has shown us, any change to be successfully put into practice, whether it be playing the piano or recycling, must ultimately be unconscious and automatic—it's locus in the body must reside in the bones and not on the tip of the tongue (a favored place for art critics).

In 1977, during a time of severe drought, a caravan of whites and Aborigines in Land Rovers left the frontier settlement of Wiluna and headed out into the great Australian outback to bring back, or to confirm as dead, what were believed to be the last two human beings on the continent living the 40,000-year-old tradition of nomadic hunter-gatherers. As the grueling and painstaking expedition wore on and became more urgent (the two Aborigines were eventually found), friction arose between the head Aborigine tracker, an elder who had known the two when they were all still wandering through the landscape, and the white leader of the group.

It seemed that part of the tradition of the nomadic culture was to burn large tracks of spinifex grass which Aborigines would encounter on "walkabout." This served several purposes. First, it created "smoke," a plume visible for sometimes 100 miles that served as location signposts for the isolated bands of individuals simultaneously moving through the vast open landscape. Second, it fertilized the land, allowing certain plants to thrive by causing seeds to sprout and small green shoots to emerge which became the primary and sustaining food for populations of small birds in the area. (Some of the plants and birds are disappearing now that the Aborigines have moved off the land into settlements.) All of this was accomplished quite "unconsciously" (from our viewpoint) by the Aborigines.

The tension in the caravan arose from the fact that as travel became more rapid, the elder Aborigine became more grumpy and unbearable as they passed areas of unburnt spinifex without stopping. When asked, he was unable to explain his mood and hostility, saying simply that he was "grumpy and unsettled." Finally, in order to proceed, the whites agreed to stop every so often, on the way out as well as on the return with the two nomads, and as soon as they did, the Aborigines would get out and set fire to the spinifex, sending a huge cloud of smoke high into the air and feeling in high spirits for the trip after that.[4]

At this critical point in our collective history, our relationship to the landscape and its elements, both natural and human-made, to be successful must eventually become as unconscious as this. As the missing pieces in the puzzle become dimly visible from our viewpoint at the end of the twentieth century, our aspirations and actions, whether building a house, disposing of waste, making a business deal, or creating a work of art, if out of accordance with the natural world, both inner and outer, must elicit within us that grumpy, uncomfortable feeling, as if no other course of action is possible until that feeling is resolved. And, naturally, no other course of action is.

4. W. J. Peasly, *The Last of the Nomads* (Freemantle: Freemantle Arts Centre Press, 1983).

In Response to Questions from Jörg Zutter

When was your first direct encounter with European culture?
At the moment I was conceived. My mother was born in northern
England. My father's mother was German, and his father Italian, and
he first went to school as a child in New York speaking no English
whatsoever. This is the peculiar and particular nature of America—the
shadow of Europe always behind you, conscious or unconscious. It is
precisely this diffracted view, the fact that it is an angular shadow,
diffuse, shifting, amalgamated, and not a faithful image, that has
fascinated so many of the European intellectuals, from de Tocqueville
to Eco and Baudrillard.

*You have had over 20 years of involvement with Europe on various
projects. How does this first-hand knowledge of both the original object
and its "shadow" affect you and your work?*
It is of course interesting and at times amusing if you know the origin
of things. However, it doesn't particularly disturb or excite me that
here in southern California I can drive past a Spanish-style house with
authentic ceramic roof tiles, or houses of traditional New England wood
frame, English Tudor, and Japanese styles all standing next to each
other on the same street, or that I can go into the sterile and bizarre
setting of a shopping mall to purchase a genuine Tuscan leather bag
while a group of Mexicans with motors strapped to their backs are
blowing away fallen leaves from indoor Australian native trees while
Mozart plays from concealed loudspeakers at a nearby Japanese Sushi
bar. This is normal. This is how I grew up. It gives me energy. It is the
Europeans, I think, who are more likely to be concerned about the "crisis
of representation" these conditions appear to evoke. When I first went to
Japan I was concerned that a traditional Buddhist pagoda was standing
right next to a McDonald's. After living there later, I realized that the
Japanese aren't too worried about it—when they are hungry they go
to the McDonald's, when they want to pray they go to the temple.

First published in the exhibition catalogue *Bill Viola: Unseen Images*, ed. Marie Luise
Syring (Düsseldorf: Verlag R. Meyer, 1992), 93–111 (German, English, French).

The unique place of material culture in today's world is that, as a set of images, it is not proprietary any more. It is not national. It is the property of all—any time, any place, any material or style, any period in history. The key underlying common element now is not appearance, it is use. This is what is defining value. And the key currency of the interchange of this value is the image. This is why art is at such a critical point in its evolution and why many modes of artistic practice are being called into question. And this is also why there is so much uncertainty. As Rumi said in the thirteenth century, "Any image is a lie," yet as William Blake said 500 years after that, "Anything to be believed is an image of Truth."

But is there a course of action for the artist, or even the individual, on the basic survival level, that this situation provokes?
It is not the point to try and "resolve" these apparent collisions as much as it is to realize that they are the direct and predictable expression of a new and unfamiliar set of conditions now in place. These conditions are not geographic, climatic, conventional, or traditional. The real ordering forces at work today under the surface, that create these seemingly jarring juxtapositions, are alpha-numeric; they are informational and economic, and ultimately political. Their ground is transcultural and multinational. It is only because we are still viewing the landscape at the surface level, and don't see that what pops up and meets the eye in seemingly random or unrelated patterns from below is really integrally bound together, connected and coherent, just beneath the surface. To see the unseen is an essential skill to be developed at the close of the twentieth century.

Your first extended stay in Europe was when you were 23 years old, working for one and a half years at the Art/Tapes/22 video studio in Florence, Italy, in the early 1970s. Did this classical environment and birthplace of the Renaissance have any influence on your work?
It is always interesting to encounter with the mature intellect ideas that are practically instinctual and well instituted in our bodies as "common sense." The effects of the avant-garde thought of the Renaissance can be felt in every industrialized country on earth, Japan and the Far East included. So to some extent, these influences were already there. Personally, it was most important for me being there, to feel art

history come alive off the pages of books, to soak into my skin.

I probably had my first unconscious experiences then of art as related to the body, for many of the works of the period, from large public sculpture to the architecturally integrated painting in the churches, are a form of installation—a physical, spatial, totally consuming experience. Furthermore, in function, classic Renaissance art was a lot more like contemporary television than contemporary painting, with many of the images designed to communicate well-known stories directly to the illiterate masses in highly visible public spaces.

What kind of personal work did you do during your stay in Florence?

Actually, in Florence I spent most of my time in pre-Renaissance spaces—the great cathedrals and churches. At the time I was very involved with sound and acoustics, and this remains an important basis of my work. Places such as the Duomo were revelations for me. I spent many long hours staying there inside, not with a sketchbook but with an audiotape recorder. I eventually made a series of acoustic records of much of the religious architecture of the city. It impressed me that regardless of one's religious beliefs, the enormous resonant stone halls of the medieval cathedrals have an undeniable effect on the inner state of the viewer. And sound seemed to carry so much of the feeling of the ineffable.

Acoustics and sound, a rich part of human intellectual and speculative history, are thoroughly physical phenomena. Sound has many unique qualities compared to an image—it goes around corners, through walls, is sensed simultaneously 360 degrees around the observer, and even penetrates the body. Regardless of your attitudes towards the music, you cannot deny the thumping and physical vibration in your chest cavity at a rock concert. It is a response beyond taste. When I discovered standing wave patterns, and the fact that there is a total spatial structure of reflection and refraction, a kind of acoustic architecture in any given space where sound is present, and that there is a sound content, an essential single note or resonance frequency latent in all spaces, I felt I had recognized a vital link between the unseen and the seen, between an abstract, inner phenomenon and the outer material world.

Here was the bridge I needed, both personally and professionally, and it opened up a lot of things that were closed off, myself included. Here was an elemental force that was between being a thing and an energy, a material and a process, something that ranged from the subtle nuance of experiencing a great piece of music to the brute force of destroying a physical object by pressure waves, as any sound is well capable of doing. This gave me a guide with which to approach space, a guide for creating works that included the viewer, included the body in their manifestation, that existed in all points in space at once yet were only locally, individually perceivable. I began to use my camera as a kind of visual microphone. I began to think of recording "fields" not "points of view," I realized that it was all an interior. I started to see everything as a field, as an installation, from a room full of paintings on the walls of a museum to sitting at home alone in the middle of the night reading a book.

Many people are mistrustful of the physical effects of electronic images and sounds. What is the place of the body and physical sensation in your work and in the nature of the medium you have chosen?
At a time when the body has been neglected and/or rejected as a serious instrument of knowledge for so long, the physicality of these new media has been grossly overlooked. (In cinema, for example, this has been due to the dominance of the literary/theatrical.) There is still such a strong mistrust in intellectual circles about things which speak to the mind via the body. It's as if they can see that this direction will ultimately lead to opening the locked gate to the forbidden zone of the deeper emotional energies. In my opinion, the emotions are precisely the missing key that has thrown things out of balance, and their restoration to their rightful place as one of the higher orders of the mind of a human being cannot happen fast enough. The pitfalls of mere feel-good sensuality and sentimentality are clear enough. As the American philosopher Jacob Needleman has said, by ignoring the emotional side of our nature, we have turned our backs on the most powerful energies of our being, the source of the most human of qualities, compassion, and without which no authentic moral power is possible.

Just recently in an interview in Kassel, the questioner was describing my work as using "effects, the same as Hollywood," and suggested that somehow these were lesser elements, sensual and momentary, even seductive and therefore dangerous. We must revise our old ways of thinking that perpetuate the separation of mind and body. These attitudes negate much of the world culture's response to the questions of mind and being and self; for example, they deny the validity of such things as the 2,500-year-old history of Buddhism and the significance of the various disciplines of meditation throughout the world. Without this approach of understanding and controlling the mind through the body, we find that ironically one of the major problems in the West today arises from a lack of focused developed mind, neglected by an over emphasis on the body as a cosmetic self-defining image detached from any deeper function.

It is true that from an intellectual viewpoint the scary part of the body's mechanism is that it is purely responsive and mostly involuntary—instantaneous and therefore isolated from the normal mechanisms of rational analysis and logical thought. There is great potential for misuse and manipulation in work of this nature. And it is true that without an established wider cultural context of image language there can be a proliferation of misuse, either through ineptitude, misunderstanding, or deliberate abuses of the form that go unnoticed or uncriticized. These aspects are hopefully the result of a temporary transitional situation, as we move away from print and literary modes and into the world of the image, away from deductive reasoning and toward associative patterning. One of the greatest challenges in today's culture, urgently necessary from a political point of view, is how to bring analytical skills to bear on the perceptual physiological language of the image, an event and not an object— constantly changing, living, and growing.

As Neil Postman has observed, most media messages today exist in a zone beyond true or false and are impervious or irrelevant to traditional discursive logical methods of establishing their authenticity. Even a college education isn't enough. In America, Reagan-Bush media advisors like John Deaver and Roger Ailes have successfully utilized the circumstance of a largely media-illiterate population ill-equipped to read accurately the full information content of its dominant medium, television, with dangerous political consequences for the democratic system. Significantly, the skills required to successfully decode commercial and political messages have become associative and arise from the domain of art, not reason. This places a new importance on the skills and knowledge of the artist and the role of art education in daily life.

There are formal elements in your work that relate to the European tradition, such as the references to painting (Goya, Bosch, Vermeer, etc.), and particularly traditional structures such as the altarpiece triptych (The City of Man, Nantes Triptych). What is your interest in repeating such classical forms?

I consider myself to be part of a long tradition of art-making, a tradition that includes my own cultural background of Europe, as well as the late twentieth century's expanded range of Oriental and ancient Eurasion culture, and even embraces our current nineteenth-century French model of the post-academy avant-garde and its rejection of tradition. I do feel that there are serious problems with the conclusions of a 150-year-long evolution of the rejection of tradition, as necessary as it was in the first place. Especially, our connection to Eastern culture should not be undervalued.

Don't forget that one of the great milestones of our century has been the transporting of ancient Eastern knowledge to the West by extra-ordinary individuals such as the Japanese lay Zen scholar D. T. Suzuki and the Sri Lankan art historian A. K. Coomaraswamy, an event on a par with the re-introduction of ancient Greek thought to Europe through translations of Islamic texts from the Moors in Spain. The connection between Europe and the Orient runs deep and was over-shadowed by the developments of the Renaissance and later mass industrialization. In the age of air travel it is easy to forget that you can walk from Kamchatka to Iberia. There were Buddhist missionaries in Jerusalem at the time of Christ, and the apostle Thomas spent time in India.

Concerning my use of the classical triptych, the triple image is an ancient form. I am interested in its use as referent to the European Christian tradition, as an image that arises out of the culture and therefore resides within, not without, many of the people who have come to see it in Europe. I am less interested in its use as a quotation, or an "appropriated image," because I think that if one proceeds too readily down that path you can easily become enamoured with the process of quoting in and of itself and lose respect for the latent power of the objects and materials themselves, and the inner transformative reasons for appropriating them in the first place.

Beyond more technical reasons such as the delicate balance of the number three and its use for comparative contrast and interaction, both visually and especially temporally, ultimately my interest in the triptych form is that it is a reflection of a cosmological and social world view, "Heaven-Earth-Hell," and its tripartite structure is an image of the structure of the European mind and consciousness. These aspects can become activated energies when applied to images of a contemporary nature.

Your videotapes and installations are infused with emblematic transformations and archetypal images. Some works suggest subconscious dreams and remind us of the theories of Swiss psychologist C. G. Jung, to whom you have referred. What is this connection?

First of all, I think it important to recognize that it is no longer acceptable to scrutinize things solely from the perspective of our local, regional, or even "Western" or "Eastern" cultural viewpoints. We share a privileged position at the end of the twentieth century in possessing unprecedented, vast, readily available intellectual resources gathered from around the world and from diverse histories by the intensive labor of scholars and translators in many disciplines. Any contemporary comprehensive assessment and analysis of a set of ideas has to be based on its place in world culture.

The contribution of Freud and Jung and the European psychological movement was very great. It opened up to Western culture, for the first time in many centuries, the inner energies of the human mind. C. G. Jung particularly was more open to aspects of world culture and its precedents, and his theory of archetypal images, as a kind of visual archeology of the mind, is a very powerful model with important implications for the practice of art. Especially relevant is the notion, a basic component of ancient culture, that images have transformative powers within the individual self, that art can articulate a kind of healing or growth or completion process, in short that it is a branch of knowledge, epistemology in the deepest sense, and not just an aesthetic practice. The potent combination of this narrow aesthetic approach with the extreme progression of a commodity-based commercial system is largely responsible for the dismal state of the art world and the preponderance of trite, frivolous, empty art objects over the past decade and longer.

However, the work of Jung, Freud, and the others has also to be seen in the light of world history. In this sense, the nonmaterial-based cultures of Asia far outshine the Europeans in the depth and breadth of their speculations on the nature of mind and self. The-turn-of-the-century psychologists represented the first primitive, yet far-reaching, steps by the West towards illuminating the nature of the inner world. Recent work by psychologists now well-versed in Eastern thought, such as James Hillman, as well as the radical conclusions on the nature of matter (a term so long synonymous with the universe itself in the Western mind) by twentieth-century physicists such as Werner Heisen-berg, represent converging thought streams that redefine the world to include inner realities, that shift Western science on a track closer to the traditions of the East, and that indicate that this development of ideas is much larger than what Freud and Jung initially described. Several millenia of Buddhist sutras, texts, and philosophical science on the nature of mind greatly exceeds the Psychoanalytical Society archive in Vienna. Ancient Hindu texts and speculation on theories of representation far outnumber the writings of contemporary French intellectuals on the same subject. There is no excuse to ignore the larger picture any more, in science, philosophy, or art history.

Why have your interests in individuals been focused so strongly on the mystics of history, usually of religious traditions, rather than the principal artists of the past?

Actually I can see a strong connection between the outstanding mystics and artists. I think my interest in the mystics arose out of certain problems, initially unconscious, that I was having with the notion of art history itself. I later came to realize that the existence of what I studied in school, what we call "art history," is more circumstantial than actual. It exists because it has occurred but not because there is any more than only the most vague and general connection between the works as a whole. The use and creation of images is so fundamental to human beings since the beginning of time that it has to be considered an essential part of humanity's existence, like sex. So, if there is this natural propensity to create images, then there will always be this thing called "art history" and there will be as many artworks of as many varied forms and purposes and natures as there are babies. Furthermore, the majority of creative expressions in images by human beings will necessarily be excluded. The primary book I had in university, and still the dominant one in use, Janson's *History of Art*, never included Japanese, Chinese, or Indian art, although it wasn't called the *History of European Art*. In fact, much of the work I was seeing on my travels to Asia and the South Pacific, classical and contemporary, wasn't being discussed. Other things were being labeled "folk art" and excluded.

If the intentions, essences, purposes, and very nature of these creative expressions are so diverse and contradictory, then one of the only ways to link them all to include them in the same category is either circumstantial, i.e., that they all have condensed out of the linear accumulation of history, or formal, i.e., that this one exhibits these physical characteristics and not these, a form of zoology and an approach applied from nineteenth-century scientific materialism. What was missing for me was the essence of the artist's vision, the connection to the deeper levels of human life that I felt the great artists I was coming to admire all spoke to, since their techniques and styles were secondary elements that existed solely in service to this, "the great work," the real power of their accomplishments.

When I began to focus on this aspect of the work, I saw that what at first appeared to be independent shining lights, bursts of transcendent inspiration on a dull field, became linked by something unconsciously sensed below the familiar surface. I started to follow these lights, and the rest didn't matter, making my own alternative "history," an anti-history really since one of the primary qualities of what I was pursuing seemed to exist beyond historical time. I thought it was something that couldn't be described, that existed without precedent or models. Then I became aware of the existence of an established, parallel, alternative history running through the history of religion, with very elaborate descriptions and prescriptions for these creative states I was trying to understand. I became drawn to the work of the mystics, East and West, and people such as Jallaludin Rumi, Chuang

Tzu, St. John of the Cross, and Meister Eckhart began to embody for me the qualities and true nature of the work of the artist that I felt had been so confused and distracted throughout the course of material expression through the history of human affairs.

Is there a distinctive difference between European and American mysticism that is relevant to your work?

First it is important to look at the term "mystic." In Western culture, the term is imprecise, often applied by people with little if any experience or knowledge of the subject and living within a society with no criteria and poor terminology to judge or describe inner states. Historically, it becomes loaded down with the political history of the Christian church, which discouraged or brutally suppressed any deviations from the accepted canon. Not least, it includes a wide variety of individuals doing very different things and has become a catch-all phrase to include anyone doing something different.

Historically, the use of the term becomes more widespread and necessary the further European culture diverged from its original pagan shamanistic sources, the last great purge being the Inquisition and the persecution of female "witches" (the shamen), the place and energy of the woman being the last place these energies resided. Looking at rock and roll and the counterculture of the late 1960s, it is interesting to see a revival of what European culture has traditionally defined as "Dionysian" tendencies. That entire episode was really about a rediscovery of the body and the attempt to break out of (in America) the Protestant ethic's denial of the same and to bring the technologies of the body, from basic instinctual sex to high-level meditation, back into the discussion, on a par with the cornerstone of the European intellectual tradition, the faculties of reason in the mind alone. To return to your question, obviously most of the influential mystics in the Western tradition are European. In America, individuals such as Walt Whitman and Mother Ann Lee of the Shakers come to mind, but for the most part they are integrally bound up with the social reformist utopian directions that the promise of the New World offered. The European mystics, on the other hand, were primarily involved with individual vision, although many of them were reformers and definers of new social and political orders.

This is because many European mystics were concerned with reintegrating into the Christian tradition an ancient teaching that had been expelled since the early centuries just after Christ. This is traditionally called the *via negativa*, or negative way, and is a teaching traced directly back to Eastern religious concepts (Hindu and Buddhist), present in the teachings of the Gnostics of formative Christianity, and embodied most notably in an obscure shadowy figure from the fifth century called Pseudo-Dionysius the Areopagite. Most probably a Syrian monk, Pseudo-Dionysius' teachings of the Celestial Hierarchy (he introduced the word), and the inability to know or describe God directly, became central to the later Neo-Platonic movement of the twelfth century and beyond, and the source of inspiration for many notable mystics such as the anonymous English author of a classic fourteenth-century text who described it in the title as "The Cloud of Unknowing," and St. John of the Cross who called it "the dark night of the soul."

The basic tenets of the *via negativa* are the unknowability of God; that God is wholly other, independent, complete; that God cannot be grasped by the human intellect, cannot be described in any way; that when the mind faces the divine reality, it becomes blank. It seizes up. It enters a cloud of unknowing. When the eyes cannot see, then the only thing to go on is faith, and the only true way to approach God is from within. From that point, the only way God can be reached is through love. By love the soul enters into union with God, a union not infrequently described through the metaphor of ecstatic sex. Eastern religion calls it enlightenment.

The essence here is the individual faith, and as God is said to reside within the individual, many aspects of it bear a close resemblance to Eastern concepts and practices. The *via negativa* represented a place where Eastern and Western religion found themselves on common ground, but through the forces of the Inquisition and beyond, the *via negativa* was eventually dominated by the more familiar *via positiva* of today, a method of affirmation that describes positive, human attributes such as the Good and All-Knowing to the image of a transcendent God. Although still beyond all human understanding, the divine has an important connection to the human world through these attributes, expressed in orders of magnitude, a quantitative rather than qualitative difference.

After spending so long investigating Eastern religion and Islamic mysticism, and after rejecting my own Christian roots, I was so excited to find the same thread running through my own cultural history, something I never expected to find. I viewed it as a basic human tendency rather than a specific historical movement, and it clarified a lot of things about the universal nature of mystical experience, the essence of creativity and inspiration, issues of solitude versus community and the role of individual vision in society, as well as my own artistic practice. I relate to the role of the mystic in the sense of following a *via negativa*—of feeling the basis of my work to be in unknowing, in doubt, in being lost, in questions and not answers—and that recognizing that personally the most important work I have done has come from not knowing what I was doing at the time I was doing it. This is the power of the time when you just jump off the cliff into the water and don't worry if there are rocks just below the surface.

Notable in your work is the direct inclusion of fundamental aspects of human life, birth, and death, for example. What is the role of these direct, often documentary-like, elements?

Video currently bears the weight of the truth factor in our society. Most people feel that what they are seeing through a video camera is a truthful record of an actual event. This perception has its roots in certain characteristics of the medium such as its ability to display a "live" image and is often described pictorially as a quality of "immediacy." Think of the difference, for example, of displaying a painting of a woman in childbirth as opposed to a videotape of the actual event.

I have felt for a long time that contemporary art, as well as philosophy, has neglected the fundamental energies of our beings. It is easy to see how notions of a "progress" of ideas can pass over issues as basic as birth and death. Yet these are the great themes of so much of human creative expression. Since so much of my work has to do with "seeing" in an extended sense, I have found that raw and direct recordings in our current context can have great power. These essential experiences are universal, profound, and mysterious, and lie like unsolved equations in contemporary society that have been put off to the side of the mathematician's desk because they are unsolvable with the math currently in use. But that's the point, they are mysteries in the truest sense of the word, not meant to be solved, but rather experienced and inhabited. This is the source of their knowledge. It is my hope that for future generations, these images will lose their shock value because I feel that in some ways this clouds the real essence of their nature, even though at present the shock response is a necessary measure of how far from life's sources industrialized society has come. These "power images" are like wake-up calls, and I feel today there is a need to wake up the body before you can wake up the mind.

Despite the onslaught of media images that incessantly confront us and skew our perceptions. I maintain great faith in the inherent power of images (and by images I mean the information that comes through sight, hearing, and all the sensory modalities). The images we have created throughout history and prehistory are our companions and guides, separate selves with their own lives and beings. For the ancient Greeks, one of the main questions that fueled all philosophical specu-lation was what is alive and what is not, what is imbued with "psyche." For modern science, the question has become what has mind, what does not. This narrowing down of parameters to the realm of thought, specifically human thought, makes possible an attitude that divides and separates ourselves from nature and ourselves from our total beings, leading to disastrous consequences. It can allow nature to be exploited and abused. Animals can be eliminated, slaughtered, and even tortured with no moral consequences, or at least within no ritual framework.

For me, one of the most momentous events of the last 150 years is the animation of the image, the advent of moving images. This · introduction of time into visual art could prove to be as important as Brunelleschi's pronouncement of perspective and demonstration of three-dimensional pictorial space. Pictures now have a fourth dimensional form. Images have now been given life. They have behavior. They have an existence in step with the time of our own thoughts and imaginings. They are born, they grow, they change and die. One of the characteristics of living things is that they can be many selves, multiple identities made up of many movements, contradictory, and all capable of constant transformation, instantaneously in the present as well as retrospectively in the future. This for me is the most exciting thing about working as an artist at this time in history. It is also the biggest responsibility. It has taught me that the real raw material is not the camera and monitor, but time and experience itself, and that the real place the work exists is not on the screen or within the walls of the room, but in the mind and heart of the person who has seen it. This is where all images live.

Landscape as Metaphor 1993

In response to questions from Martin Friedman for the exhibition
"Landscape as Metaphor," Denver Art Museum, March 5, 1993

What is the relationship between the landscape sites you deal with and
the history of the land?
Apparently exterior, the true extension of any landscape traverses both
the exterior and interior of the individual. In short, landscape is the
link between our outer and inner selves. Its substance is as much of
mind as it is of body, and we cannot be considered distinct and apart
from it any more than a living cell can be considered autonomous
within the body of its host. The surprise and outrage that people register
on discovering that the chemicals that have been dumped in the river
now traverse their bloodstreams is a direct measure of the distance we
have artificially inserted between ourselves and the world around.

Can you define and comment on the relationship between the
landscape and the unconscious?
The natural landscape is the raw material of the human psyche. The
cumulative time that impressions of the urban, human-made environment have fallen on the surface of the collective retina is miniscule,
compared with the time we have spent hunting and gathering in the
great expanses of the untamed natural world. The accumulations that
constitute our inner archeologies speak more to the kinds of images
witnessed today in our national parks than to those we see on our
downtown streets; they lie beneath each action and thought, like a dark
untouched personal substratum. Through the clichés and stereotypical
sentimental banality of the idea of a "scenic viewpoint," a distant
familiarity and connection is nevertheless acknowledged. The last
remaining tracts of undeveloped land bear the same relationship to
our common daily world of the busy city street and office, that our
unconscious minds, broader, deeper, and darker, bear to the more
narrow spotlit view of our conscious rational self. In this sense, what
little truly wild lands are left in the world must be preserved, not only
for scientific or ecological reasons, but for our essential psychological
balance and well-being.

What is the perception of the American landscape at the close of the twentieth century, from a psychological point of view?
You park your car in a paved expanse of a parking lot and move towards the entrance of a shopping mall. Just before going in, you glance down but do not really notice a small patch of brown earth, some exposed dirt, on the edge of an enclosed strip of landscaping. This small opening, framed like the remnant of an unhealed wound, is the only visible presence of the underlying reality of the entire fabricated structure that you will momentarily become immersed in. It is the original essence of the site, glimpsed like a momentary flash of deeper awareness that occasionally punctuates our day-to-day mind. Although now paved over, excluded, put out of sight, and only allowed to exist in the rigid landscaping that makes it conform to our own terms, it is the ground of being that supports the whole artifice. The dirt under the shops on Main Street *is* our collective unconscious. In the heightened, material velocity of contemporary life, shops and constructions come and go, but the ground never moves. Perhaps this is why the effects of an earthquake are most felt as an extreme psychological dislocation and disorientation in the individual, unfortunately registered like some large-scale betrayal, rather than as the wake-up call to our deep psychological connection to the earth that these disturbing symptoms describe.

Can you discuss aspects of the animistic quality of land?
It is not hard to see why a great leap of the imagination is required to recognize that the material essence of the tools we engage in contemporary life, our telephones, color TVs, VCRs, and computers, are of the earth. All of these devices come from the ground, created from "nothing," the conforming of an immaterial idea onto raw materials, animal, vegetable, and mineral, gathered and distilled from the raw earth. Hidden presences all, from the metals in the chassis frame to the petroleum distillates that compose the tape and cassette boxes.

The culmination of the manifest destiny history of the America that regards the virgin nature of the New World as an inseparable part of a successful future, that approaches the landscape and indigenous people within it as a hostile Other to be tamed or eliminated outright, that sees the material substance of the land solely as a raw material to be forged and processed, and that therefore views all undeveloped land as unrealized profit, is the scarcity and elimination of the very fuel that has fired the engine of the nation. This is the rim of the crisis that we find ourselves poised on today, whether intuitively sensed or dramatically experienced. At the close of the twentieth century, the re-evaluation of our relationship to the land is essential to our survival, both physically and spiritually. This classic "mind-body" problem, the inability of Western science to reconcile the physical external world with the immaterial inner essence of the human mind, is reaching a climax on an unprecedented scale, with unprecedented consequences.

Between How and Why

The technologies of the optical image (photography, cinema, video) are machines for the close of the machine age. They are machines that produce content, that have as their product the direct imprints of the outside world. They give us the world back, and for this they are much more profound and mysterious than people realize. By nature they are instruments not primarily of vision, but of philosophy in an original ancient sense.

Looking at the videotape recorder, it is difficult to realize that this machine, this object, comes from the earth. The metals and plastics that comprise its physical mass are all earth materials. They come from the ground. Even the electricity that activates it is a fundamental element of the natural environment. The history of much of human culture, particularly in the Western world, has centered on the development of the material. The contemporary electronic technologies of video and computer are simply the most recent stage of this evolution. Historically in the West, the work of Isaac Newton, and the scientific revolution that followed him, greatly accelerated the emphasis on the material. His discoveries and new approach shifted the inquiry into the nature of the world from religious/philosophical to scientific speculation, from emotive affinities to material causes, from empathy to reason: the apple now falls not because it desires to be at its proper resting place, the earth, but because a physical force called gravity pulls it there; the celestial becomes mechanical, and the primary mode of questioning the world becomes not *why*, but *how*.

Today, at the close of the twentieth century, we are finding that questions of "how" are not enough to carry us forward through the millennium. The crisis today in the industrialized world is a crisis of the inner life, not of the outer world. It is focused on the individual, and on the confusing mix of signals and messages swirling around us that do not address a human being's fundamental need to know and

First published as a statement for the catalogue *Medienkunstpreis* (Karlsruhe, Germany: Zentrum für Kunst und Medientechnologie, 1993).

live the "why" of life. Talk of machines, technologies, capabilities, costs, markets, infrastructures, offers no guidance and is inadequate and irrelevant to the development of our inner lives. This is why art today, traditionally the articulation and expression of the "why" side of life, is now so important and vital, even though it remains confused and inconsistent in its response to the new demands and responsibilities placed on it in this time of transition.

The new technologies of image-making are by necessity bringing us back to fundamental questions, whether we want to face them or not. The development of schemes for the creation of images with computers is an investigation into the structure and fabric of the world we observe and participate in. Spend time with a video camera and you will confront some of the primary issues: What is this fleeting image called life? Why are we here sharing the living moment, a moment that is past yet present? And why are the essential elements of life change, movement, and transformation, but not stability, immobility, and constancy? Faced with the content of the direct images and sounds of life in one's daily practice as an artist, questions of form, visual appearance, and the "how" of image-making drop away. You realize that the real work for this time is not abstract, theoretical, and speculative—it is urgent, moral, and practical.

Responding in an adequate way to the questions of "why" demands a new balance between the emotions and the intellect, and a reinteg-ration of the emotions, along with the very human qualities of compassion and empathy, into the science of knowledge. Our work today as artists is not about describing the arrival at and possession of a goal, but instead it is about illuminating the pathway. It is not about a system of proofs and declarations, but a process of Being and Becoming.

Media art, in its possession of new technologies of time and image, maintains a special possibility of speaking directly in the language of our time, but in its capacity as art, it has an even greater potential to address the deeper questions and mysteries of the human condition. This is the challenge to the media arts at the turning point of the century and the passage into the millennium that lies just before us.

Pneuma 1994

"Pneuma" is an ancient Greek word that has no equivalent in contemporary terms. Commonly translated as soul or spirit, it refers as well to breath, and was conceived as an underlying essence or life-force that runs through all things of nature and animates or illuminates them with

Mind. In the installation, images alternately emerge and submerge into a field of shimmering visual noise, the ground of all images, and often hover at the threshold of recognition and ambiguity. Indistinct, shifting, and shadowy, the projections become more like memories or internal sensations

rather than recorded images of actual
places and events as the viewer
becomes surrounded by and submerged in their essence.

—1994

Pneuma, 1994, video/sound installation   259

Seeing and Being. My work as an effort to unify perception and ontology.

Seeing *is* Being. Aspects of this approach can be observed in the experience of being in the desert. Standing in the vastness, two things happen. First, you feel insignificant—a tiny black speck on the surface of the earth that can be wiped off at any instant. But secondly, a part of you travels out along with that line of sight extending for 50 miles or more and becomes part of that landscape, perception as touching, as contact, becoming a perception.

—Note, January 24, 1992

Déserts 1994

2 SEPT 1992

WATER SHEET .

1. LAMP, OBJECTS - Fall onto underwater rocks | Fixed Camera

2 objects fall in first
MUG + SOUP BOWL
Then Lamp enters .

LIGHTING: 3 options

1. DARK - Falling lamp
   appears to be sole
   source of light
2. SOME FILL - Falling objects
   first visible - "luminous"
3. WITH OUT OF WATER ABOVE
   LIGHT TO GIVE LIGHT RIPPLES

2.

Ⓐ OBJECTS BREAK SURFACE, | Fixed Camera
  PLUNGE UNDER

Ⓑ OBJECTS BREAK SURFACE | - Move Camera

Dif takes - INDIV. OBJECTS - Closer, Medium.
         SUCCESSION of OBJECTS · Farther

3.

HAND HELD (?) - CAMERA PERPENDICULAR TO
              OBJECT — CLOSE
      Breaks surface, sinks —
      camera follows down,
      remaining perpendicular

Window
Glass

(OBJECT BREAKS SURFACE — CAMERA FOLLOWS DOWN)
Multiple takes w/ different objects

261

The desert has occupied a central place in my work for the past 20 years. A recurring theme and motif, the desert is an essential crossover point and meeting place of the inner and outer worlds of human beings, and I have approached its terrain not only as the raw material of landscape but of the human psyche as well. I have used desert imagery as a basis of investigation into the following interwoven themes:

—notions of wilderness and the untouched natural world

—the "eternal landscape," the presence of an ancient, prehistoric and post-future time and place

—desolate physical existence as an evocation of the "other world" of death, mortality, and non-being

—the vast distances, extremes in scale, and severe minimalism as the basis of perceptual reorientation and reintegration

—a physical description of the extremes of the human condition: loneliness, isolation, and solitude

—contemporary sites for the ancient and traditional role of the desert as the locale of vision and revelation

In his notes and writings, Edgard Varèse (1883–1965) described a similar approach to the desert landscape, calling for a work that expresses not only the physical aspects of the American desert, but the concept of the desert as extended in scale and space into congruent terrestrial locations and beyond into the cosmos, as well as its psychological dimension in the interior of the individual:

"For me, 'deserts' is a highly evocative word. It suggests space, solitude, detachment. To me it means not only deserts of sand, sea, mountains, and snow, of outer space, of deserted city streets, not only those stripped aspects of nature that suggest bareness and aloofness but also the remote inner space of the mind no telescope can reach, a world of mystery and essential loneliness."[1]

For this project, I propose to create a visual composition that arises from the sound landscape of Varèse's music and yet is endowed with a life of its own as an expressive vision and personal work of moving-image art. The plan is not, as Varèse himself stated, to illustrate the music, nor is it to realize Varèse's specific vision regarding the theme of "deserts." I intend to create a complex mosaic of evocative, subjective imagery composed and itself structured along the lines of a musical composition and designed to complement, provoke, and generally interact with the music score. The work will be constructed with the presence of the score in mind, yet the images themselves will be selected and developed unconsciously and intuitively, without a specific plan or predetermined outline, more as a form of visual poetry, a method I have long been exploring.

The basic model of the work is that of thoughts and images as they well up and subside of their own accord on the surface of the mind,

1. Olivia Mattis, "Edgard Varèse and the Visual Arts". (Ph.D. diss., Stanford University, 1992).

viewed from a place somewhere between sleep and wakefulness, a border zone between the conscious and the unconscious, where normal distinctions and safe boundaries are allowed to dissolve and the lines between reality and imagination, between object and association, blur. The flow of images can be seen as a portrait of a mind absorbed in itself that has perhaps had some experience with or relation to the desert landscape, the embodiment of which, however, is never observed. It is a view solely from within.

The images will be composed into a dense, richly interwoven stream-of-consciousness flow, comparable to the temporal complexity and sonic textures of the music, and organized like cascading, flowing water, with its areas of rapid motion, smooth flows, frenetic turbulence, disorganized chaos, undisturbed tranquillity, repetitive swirling eddies, cyclical whirlpools, and backwater respites of stagnation, immobility, and reflection. In this project, I am proposing to continue my explorations of the aspects and themes of the desert as outlined above. Technically, the images will embody a wide range of qualities and textures, from older, lower format black-and-white video surveillance systems to state-of-the-art high-resolution color 35mm film or High Definition video. They will be comprised of material from my personal archive, as well as sequences shot especially for this project.

Unpublished proposal, *Varèse—Déserts*, a project with the Ensemble Modern, Frankfurt am Main, and ZDF/ARTE, Mainz, October 25, 1993.

Putting the Whole Back Together
In conversation with Otto Neumaier and Alexander Pühringer

Alexander Pühringer: In the most recent years there has been more talk about the human body in art. This is also shown by the last "documenta" of Jan Hoet. He said in an interview that when going through the "documenta" he got the impression that he had mainly invited artists whose topic is the body. It seems to me that the body, or more precisely, the physical experience of art, also plays a very important role in your work, but I think that's not what Jan Hoet meant.

When we talk about art the first thing most people think about today is the visual. Painting and sculpture are called the *visual* arts. This idea of the visual as an autonomous eye is recent historically, and not only does it negate some central aspects of art history (almost the entire body of classical Oriental, Islamic, and Indian art, for example, as well as much of Western medieval art, where the visual was only the apparent surface and symbolic language of an underlying, more real, divine order), but it also does not accurately acknowledge our present situation. Art has always been a whole-body, physical experience. This sensuality is the basis of its true conceptual and intellectual nature, and is inseparable from it. If the current discussion tells us that art now is about the body, then the danger is that you are unable to recognize that those images of bodies in works of art are more than just visual images—just as the essence of a person is always much more than what we can see. I am not talking about symbolic representation here— I mean a direct, physical, palpable language, a form of Being. We must free ourselves from the common idea of "visual" art. For me, when I think of the work that I am doing as related to the body, I don't necessarily think that there should be an image of a body in it, but that the persons who come in to experience the work have to receive it with

This text contains the main part of a conversation that took place in a hotel room in Düsseldorf on December 20, 1992, two days after the opening of Bill Viola's exhibition, "Unseen Images." The text was rewritten by the artist for publication in the exhibition catalogue *Bill Viola*, ed. Alexander Pühringer (Salzburg: Ritter Klagenfurt/Salzburger Kunstverein, 1994), 112–156 (German and English).

their whole body, not just with their intellect, or not just with their eyes, and that they will do so whether they are conscious about it or not.

Otto Neumaier: A similar thought can be found in philosophy. Amongst others already, Aristotle said that not the eye sees but the person sees. Yes, that is beautiful.

O.N.: And it is true. But maybe you would like to go further and say "I not only see something but I experience it as a whole." Yes, and this is also shown by language. When you understand something, a common response in English is to say "I *see*." There is such a deep connection between seeing and knowing that it is odd to think how the two could have been considered separate. There has been much discussion about the result of the famous dualism of Descartes, and it is obvious that today we do view body and mind as separate from each other, and we consider the intellect, senses, emotions, and so on, as separate parts of the mind. If we take a broader view of world culture, past and present, surveying the most advanced and sophisticated to the more fundamental and tribal, it becomes apparent that the present division that we in the industrialized West have developed is a kind of distortion. Going back to ancient times, the body was always a necessary part of the process of learning and in many cultures it was even considered to be a key instrument of knowledge. Today we have the situation in the classroom where if the children are asked to solve, let's say, a mathematical problem, and if one of the kids starts moving his or her body around, the teacher then reprimands the child saying "Sit still and do your work." That's completely crazy because the kid *is* doing the work. Baby ducklings do not learn imprinting if they are carried in a basket and not allowed to walk and stumble after their mother. You learn something so much more deeply when you move, when you move through it—in fact, thinking *is* a form of movement.

O.N.: That's the reason why children learn much more during the first period of their life when they are interacting *with their parents. They do not learn language so much by using their intellect but, rather, by hearing and feeling, by acting and reacting.* Exactly. I fully agree with that.

O.N.: Has it to do with your own development as an artist that you

emphasize the role of the whole person? As far as I know, it's really
exceptional that you did not "grow up" with visual arts, but that you come
from experimental music. You worked with David Tudor ...
Nam June Paik had a similar development.

 O.N.: OK, but you also did some research with acoustics ...
... which is the experience of space ...

 O.N.: ... and you worked in the dome of Florence.
I did sound recordings there. I was working in a local video-art studio
at the time.

 O.N.: Were you also influenced by those classical people such as
Dufay, in particular by his motet for the dome which is very close to the
proportions of the dome?
Not specifically, although the connections between music, sound, architecture, and visual proportion were important for me. Things like the
Golden Section, and other schemes such as the Neo-platonic influences
on Gothic cathedrals like Chartres, were of great interest to me—
anything that sought to unify the senses with intellectual knowledge.
Coming out of music certainly was important, but I would say that the
larger phenomenon of sound had the deepest effect on my work as an
artist. However, when I think back and try to pinpoint a specific
influence, I can't—it's all like a big bowl of Minestrone soup, which is
maybe the most accurate model of a human being. You just never
know what's going to be an influence—the time you got sick on a long
car trip, or reading a book on the history of religion. I guess I have
always been unconsciously aware of this phenomenon, because I
remember that from when I was quite young I always kept very active
notebooks. Not notebooks like sketchbooks, which I have never kept,
but notebooks like a journal or a kind of travelogue, mapping a
personal course through various readings, quotations, associations,
observations, experiments, and ideas for pieces, all jumbled into one.
There was an occasional picture but for the most part it was all written
down in words, even the visual things. Everything I have ever published or created as an artist has come from these books. I should call
them the Minestrone recipe books. It's an interesting thing, all the
words and so few pictures. It was like I've been trying to arrive at the
visual by skirting around it. I guess I do have a mistrust of only

working something out in pictures, a fear that it's possible to make something that looks good (that is, is successful) but doesn't *think* well (that is, have depth). For me, the visual has always been the end, the last step, so that the final point of making a work is to plunge, to dive right into the image, totally, suddenly, from all the work before. In my work, the visual is always subservient to the *field*, the total system of perception/cognition at work. The five senses are not individual things but, integrated with the mind, they form a total system and create this *field*, an experiential field which is the basis of conscious awareness. This is the only true whole *image*.

A.P.: When you emphasize that we experience art and the world as whole *persons and that we experience a* total, *this seems to be rooted in your knowledge of spiritual traditions that see human experience differently from our Western "scientific world view," and assume that "knowledge" has not only to do with intellectual activity, but is also the result of the totality of our sensual perception.*

Yes, that's true. But this kind of thinking has a presence in American thought, too—take Walt Whitman, for example. There is a kind of a tradition in America, going back to the idea of the *New* World, a mistrust of the intellectual, of the "learned professor" at the university who talks astronomy theory but never looks up at the night sky. There is a kind of *naive* view present in the intellectual history of America.

O.N.: This raises two questions: on the one hand, what are the reasons for the mistrust of the learned and, on the other, is there a trust in what you see and what you experience? Is it true that you don't go the longer way through intellectual analysis and argument, but that you trust your senses?

Yes, I do, but I trust my senses only to the point of knowing them well enough to know when not to trust them. It's very intuitive for me, part of my nature from when I was very young. I realized later that what I was trying to do was not necessarily to disregard the intellect, because that would be a mistake, a tremendous mistake. Human beings tend so much to think in extremes—good or bad, right or wrong. Our whole culture is based on a dualistic, exclusive, adversarial approach. Some say the intellect is the superior human function, others say we are emotional beings. For me, however, the point is to try to connect these two essential elements so that they are put in balance, so that one doesn't dominate the other.

A.P.: But what is the role that is played by the intellectual and the emotional sides of our self, and what are their limits?

I don't think there is much dispute that the emotional and intuitive sides of our beings have become atrophied, or at the least lack some formal acknowledgement or functional representation in contemporary societies of the developed world. Where the intellectual work is correct is in saying that the danger of the senses, the danger of the emotions, the danger of the so-called intuitive side, is that if you only do something that feels good, you never get anywhere. If left unattended, a child will always want to eat sweets because they taste good, but he or she will not get the proper nutrition for his or her body. Where the intellect comes in, and this is very important for me in my work, is to break habits, because habits will form when you just keep doing the same thing, even an unpleasant thing (which can be pleasurable in a way), and after a while it doesn't necessarily feel good or stimulating any more, it just feels normal. Then the intellect says, "*No*, I'm not going to do that," and you have this force of mind stopping the body from doing something that feels natural to do. Mind over matter. Many times in my work over the years I've stopped to analyze what I'm doing and said, "You are just going to do this other thing," without thinking about why. For example, "You're going to turn the camera on and you're going to hold it on something still for a long, long time, continuously recording," while all of my experience, training and the other people I was working with were telling me, "Don't hold the shot too long, that's bad technique." My mind told me to do that but my body told me not to do that. And there are other examples of the opposite situation. It is interesting that to the ancient Christian mystics, the spiritual work, something we tend to classify as intuitive, was called "the mortification of the appetites," an approach we consider to be intellectual. So, this relation between the intuition and the intellect is very important.

O.N.: Well, that's the point I wanted to come to with my question about music. Because it seems to me that you are an "integrative artist," you are integrating at different levels. You try to integrate the whole person, the sensual experience with the intellectual reflection, and so on. It also seems to me that you are integrating different artistic disciplines, and you are also integrating, let's say, different kinds of knowledge, or different intellectual experiences of humankind. In my opinion this is one of the reasons for the "power" of your work.

I was fortunate enough to go to an art school in a large liberal arts university. I soon developed very broad interests and was able to follow them. After I had finally figured out what studying and learning really were (that is, that they are motivated by desire and not to satisfy the professor's requirements), I started to read everything and sit in on as many classes as possible: Eastern philosophy, theories of perception, physics, electronics, religion and mysticism—art classes seemed the least interesting, at least as was the case at this rather conservative school. Art soon became a way to actualize, to synthesize or put into practice, all these general influences, and it was the only field traditionally broad enough to allow me to do it. This was also a very exciting time to be studying. It was the late 1960s and early seventies, a time of social change, and there was a genuine and exhilarating sense of discovery, of invention, of *seeing* things and putting the pieces back together. Coming out of the nineteenth century, we have been the inheritors of a scientific materialistic point of view that holds that the way to understand is to divide, to separate, to isolate, to categorize, to specialize. This was not only in the content of the classes I was taking, but was inherent in the very structure of institutions like the university. There was a feeling in the air (and in some ways it is still a dominant theme) that, although we've reached a high point of understanding through this approach of dividing and analyzing, we now have to put the whole back together. This is evidenced in developments as diverse as chaos theory in mathematics, the management of natural resources, nutrition and psychology entering into clinical medicine, as well as in the emergence of areas such as conceptual, performance, and installation art of the late twentieth century.

O.N.: This separation and differentiation of smaller and smaller fields of knowledge has a very long tradition. This process is even typical for European culture. And I agree with you that it is necessary to reintegrate. How, do you think, does this work on the individual level?

The basic models of human beings come from nature, because we are a part of nature. And if we look at the essence of what the natural world is about, we see that it's about *change* and *process*. So you find that in a human being, as he or she goes through life, there is a kind of a process we call in geological terms "sedimentation," where the layers of human experience become like sedimentary layers in the earth. As these layers build up they move from the levels of the "conscious" and reason at the visible surface, to the deeper layers of the unconscious and intuition below. As the years go by, things become submerged and covered over, but they don't go away. It all continues to exist, forming the base that supports the whole structure. So, all of the experiences you've ever had stay with you in life, and these all become what we define as being a person. The invisible is always so much more present than the visible. There is a fundamental direction in life which moves from the conscious to the unconscious. To master an instrument, the musician must make that instrument unconscious, even though when he or she first began every individual note was painstakingly pecked out in a highly conscious way. We learn something in order to forget it, to get the conscious mind out of the way, and this is true for musicians as well as for lecturers who effortlessly recall the relevant contents of their unconscious memory in a kind of controlled improvisation. The awe one feels witnessing the work of a master is contained in the common expression "they did it effortlessly, without thinking." Even though our education system places the conscious mind at the highest point, I have found that it is the destination of all the work, whether in practice or in appreciation, to reach the unconscious, the deepest submerged layers of the self, to "become nameless, as glance and gesture," as Rainer Maria Rilke put it. So, there is this process that creates a deeper structure, where all is not gone but exists to support the whole, and this structure is in itself the architecture of inspiration.

    O.N.: This is certainly an important point. My previous remark refers, however, not only to the process and structure of experience, to the role of our natural capacities, of our environment, and so on. What I wanted to say is, rather, that at least in Europe we have those esoteric schools who tell people that they should go back to intuition, which, they say, is the starting point of our experience. What you told us is, however, that intuition is something which is "learned" or "trained" by experience (for lack of a better expression).

What is intuitive for me now was conscious when I was 21 years old.

I first started using a video camera when I was 21. I had to think about where I was pointing it, how I was using it, what the light was, and so on. And this process was not only technical, it had a direct effect on the content of the work. Then I used that camera for 20 years, and that 21-year-old part of me who was struggling with composition and lighting is now somewhere deeper, and has migrated out to my *hand*. So that the center of consciousness has moved from my conscious mind to my hand. My hand now "knows" where to put the camera, which I do quite naturally, when I encounter a new location.

O.N.: ... like the pianist who has to "think" with his or her hands ...
Yes, and my hand would not know where to put the camera if I didn't spend the time when I was 21 years old struggling with my whole conscious mind, with everything I had, to try and master this object. It's a wonderful process.

O.N.: Now we have maybe reached a more important point: would you say that it is possible to deal with "life experience" in that way so that we "train" our abilities, the whole of our personal abilities, to deal with, let's say, the "essential questions" of our life? And what is the role of art in such a process? I wouldn't say that art is like an "eco-niche" where the "real life" is "shown" but I can imagine that art is at least one possibility to see more, or to experience more.
Art represents one side of the human being. If you think of the whole culture as a human being, you have a multiple personality that has a very precise side which is represented by science and a more open-ended side represented by art. I don't necessarily consider art to be in any kind of privileged position, because a lot of what science is for us today, in ancient times and certainly in prehistoric times, was a practice which today we would define as artistic. The great seminal triad of science, religion, and art was once a unified whole in the Paleolithic Age. They have now branched off, and today we find that science is ascendant and art is recedent. I think art still has a very important function. I consider art to be a branch of knowledge, not of aesthetics. The purpose of the creative act changes to fulfill the needs of the times. Today I think there is a requirement, a need for reintegration, for connecting us back to the fundamental questions and issues which have been passed by as active, imperative issues because of the "progress" of

ideas. In our daily life, in our society, we have come so far from these very fundamental kinds of things, from the so-called "big" questions, from the origins of religion and philosophy: birth, death, existence, and so on. The intellect can give you the misconception that you understand something simply by thinking about it analytically, so that we forget that these are not questions to be answered through discursive logic, not problems to be solved but, rather, arenas to be *inhabited*, to be encountered through Being. We can see the primary roots of this mode of scientific materialism in the work of Isaac Newton. Up until Newton's breakthrough work on gravitation, the main question was not *how* the apple falls but *why* the apple falls. The ancient Greeks said basically that the apple falls because it needs to be at its natural resting place, drawn there out of a kind of desire. But Newton, instead of solving that problem just ignored it. He rendered the question irrelevant by shifting the viewpoint over to another track and answered the question *how* the apple falls (that is, by this force called "gravity"). This is the measure of Newton's genius and accomplishment, but it still left the fundamental question of *why* unanswered. If you read his writings, Newton was aware of this problem, even troubled by it, and a lot of other people were too (people such as Pascal, Goethe, and especially William Blake, who called it "Newton's Sleep"). So here we have the basis of the illusion that we have understood something simply by rationally describing and analyzing its operation. Therefore, by the late twentieth century, issues such as birth and death no longer command our attention after they have been physically explained.

A.P.: Can you talk a little bit more about your ideas of the relation between art and so-called "fundamental questions?"
There is a concept in recent Western European history of the *progress of ideas*. The idea that we are making discoveries, adding building blocks to building blocks, and that this is all leading somewhere. The past therefore becomes subservient, an inferior, naive, or less developed version of the present, and the future becomes a potential ideal state. Old ideas have value primarily as the currency of our present position. The danger point in all of this is to assume that all questions are *answerable* first of all, and then that once they are answered, the answers are to be used as the basis for the next question. We are rather

far along now on this path, so that when we do encounter some of the elemental questions which gave the original impetus or push to philosophy and religion, we just assume that, because all the other things that came later were answerable, these are supposed to be treated in the same way. They are not. Ancient people call them "the Mysteries." These are not to be answered. There is no answer to birth or death. They are meant to be *experienced*, they can be approached and studied, but not finally answered. In the same way, the question of why the apple falls wasn't really a question to be solved. So, I've found that as a contemporary artist in the late twentieth century, going into these things connects me back to traditional art and some of the directions which the avant-garde broke with in France some 150 years ago.

O.N.: You have now differentiated between meaningful and meaningless questions. This means in this context that to ask why *we are born or* why *we die would not be a meaningful question, but it would be meaningful to ask* why we have to include death in our life.
That's a good point, although I don't know if any questions are really meaningless. The "Why" questions, which as applied to the material, objective world that intellectual speculation has mostly eschewed, lead us into the subjective personal domain of the emotions and feelings; whereas the "How" questions speak to mechanisms and structures. I think that the ideas of why we are born and why we die are valid questions for the individual today and were some of the original questions that led to philosophical speculation to begin with. Anyway, the question is usually more important than the answer. It's a very natural thing for me to say: "Why isn't my mother here right now? Where did she go?" Even though science tells me the reasons why the body stops functioning physically, I still have those questions. The question is the spark, the provocation that exists to push you to *discover*, to *learn*.

O.N.: It's like a Kôan, where you don't get a literal answer.
Exactly, there is not one answer. It's not like in mathematics.

O.N.: In mathematics, too, you can become aware that there is no answer to a mathematical question, and that is also a solution. Think of Gödel, for instance, or of some of Hilbert's problems. But you raised so many points that we have to concentrate on one of them. You said that art is not a separated part of intellectual history or, let's say, of spiritual history. It seems to me, however, that at least in our time art is to some degree separated from our life. It doesn't play a role as a part of knowledge or experience, although, on the other hand, art has indeed a common tradition with the other intellectual efforts to understand the world, to understand life, and so on. But what do you mean by saying that art is a branch of knowledge, *not of* aesthetics? *What do you mean by aesthetics?* Well, I use "aesthetics" in the sense of the classical Greek term pertaining to sense perception, particularly the visual, and having to do with beauty and visual form and the principles or judgements of artistic practice. Some of the tools of conventional aesthetics, and some of the theories I learned in art school, are certainly important and have been of use in my work. But I became more interested in the *phenomena* of sense perception as a language of the body and avenue to self-knowledge, and not in the ordering or analysis of sensory experience as a means to more successfully create, discuss, or appreciate pictures and objects. The term "aesthetic" in our society serves to keep the object under discussion away from the central life issues. As it has been at times in the past, art for me is a means to arrive at the point of knowing more, not of creating something that is merely beautiful, interesting to look at, or provides a new step in the discourse of contemporary art and art history.

 O.N.: At this point I would like to come back to Aristotle. He differentiated between three kinds of knowledge, namely theory, practice, *and* poiesis. *For him,* poiesis *(that is to say, in somewhat simplified terms, the artistic creation of some work) is an equally justified kind of approach to the world, of trying to understand it as theory, although Aristotle himself decided for theory. In the nineteenth century Nietzsche criticized the scientific prejudice that all kinds of knowledge which are not theory have to justify themselves, and are not accepted as "natural" kinds of knowledge. Art can thus be a branch of knowledge but, on the other hand, it is not necessarily something beautiful. And aesthetics is, in some sense, a theory on the meta-level, a theory which tries to explain some aspects of art (even if they have nothing to do with beauty). This is one part of aesthetics; on the other hand, aesthetics is also a theory of, let's say, a certain kind of dealing with the world, with bodily experiences, with sensual experiences. But, to come back, if you associate aesthetics with beauty only, then it seems that in this case your own work is indeed not a part of aesthetics, but something else. Is it correct to say that your work is in the tradition of* sublime *art (where "sublime" has to be understood in its original sense of representing something which goes to the limits of what is possible to experience for human beings)? One reason for that assumption is the topics of your work (birth and death, for instance), another one is the fact that it needs great efforts from the side of the spectator to grasp your works in their spatial and temporal dimensions.*

Yes, it's true that the forces behind and beyond our life play an important role in my work, those powers that are beyond what human beings are able to name and control.

O.N.: Another aspect of this kind of sublime art is that it provides us with experiences which many people do not like to have and which they try to taboo.

Well, this gets into the area of the effects of culture on behavior and individual consciousness. What is taboo for one is acceptable for another. In today's world, we need to transcend our cultural biases and limitations, or at least be aware of them. Let me try to weave this point together with some of the things we have been discussing: creativity and individual expression, aesthetics, over-specialization, and so on. I think it is apparent that the points I am making here are reflective of a larger process occurring in our lives where previously invisible contexts, such as social group, style of art, the laws of physics, and so on, are increasingly seen as participants in a larger, expanding whole. Through the circumstances of our position at the close of the century, with its historical perspective and increased knowledge, we are being given the broader view where no one system has dominance, autonomy, or privilege. To fully accept the challenge of this larger view is the courage and responsibility demanded of us at this historical moment. Now, if you apply this broader view to contemporary art, to see it as one part of other art practices, historical and geographical, you see that although there is evidence of a great range of styles and approaches co-existing today, there is also a major essential element lacking, an element which is present in many other situations, past and present. This is the fact that most of today's art bears no functional relationship to the communities it is being presented in, at least not in any formal or generally recognized way. The larger society does not consider that art serves any central function, not in the way science and technology are perceived to do. There is a real practical connection between the work of the scientist and the daily life of the people. And it is true that we need better bridges and cars, fax machines, laser surgery, more Velcro, and all the rest. But it is no coincidence that the two fields that speak directly to the individual's inner life, art and religion, share the same problems in this regard. This is a very big problem in America, where we have been disconnected from a continuous history and unified cultural tradition, and where most people consider art-making essentially a kind of hobby or lesser activity, not essential to the lives of human beings. This is really tragic.

O.N.: It may be the case that most people would say that science is important for their own lives and that they can see the results of science in technology. But on the other hand they also see the negative effects of the specific development of the sciences. There is now a great sceptical attitude towards science which has as a result or as a side-effect that art and aesthetics are now "re-discovered," but only as a place where "beauty" is. In so doing, art is disconnected from the rest of our life: in daily life you have a lot of problems, but then you go home and relax with art, you think of art as something that helps you to feel good.

Yes, that's true. We sometimes think that we have art only to feel good. And everybody wants to feel good. But that's human nature too. The King wanted only the stuff on the wall that was nice. He wouldn't want some jerk to come in and paint a scene of him losing the battle.

A.P.: At this point I would like to interrupt the present discussion and go back to a related question which we discussed before. When walking through the "documenta" I asked myself why it was in the first place that the video installations, in particular by Bill Viola, Gary Hill, and Bruce Nauman, made the greatest impression upon me. It seems to me that these artists working with video (including Marie-Jo Lafontaine, who was participating in the "documenta"), that all of you are dealing with conditio humana, *the conditions of human life. You go back to the basic questions of existence. Do you think that one reason which can be given to explain why especially video art has made this effect is the "technical" aspect? Video art can tell stories, there is a narrative element,* time *plays an important role in video unlike in other kinds of art such as painting and sculpture.*

More than the camera, the monitor, the video recorder, and so on,
I would say that time is the fundamental basis, the actual raw material
of my work. Human beings, as all living things, are essentially creatures
of time. However, it is human beings through their higher consciousness
who have been given the knowledge of time, the ability to extend the
self into time with the capacity to anticipate and to recall. For the
individual, the two finalities at either end of these extensions are the
great subjective poles of birth and death. Most important, it is the
awareness of our own mortality which defines the nature of human
beings and is in essence the *conditio humana* that you referred to.
As instruments of time, the materials of video, and by extension the
moving image, have as a part of their nature this fragility of temporal
existence. Images are born, they are created, they exist, and, in the flick
of a switch, they die. Paintings in the halls of the museum in the
middle of the night are still there, a form of sleep, but in the room of
the video projections there is nothing. The images are thoroughly non-
existent, gone into some other dimension. From the perspective of art
history, I personally feel that the late twentieth century will prove to be
an important turning point in visual art when images moved into
another dimension, the fourth dimension of time. I say the late
twentieth century because even though cinema has been around since
the nineteenth century, it was the electronic image and its expanding
uses that have made a more direct connection with the practice of
contemporary art. I think that this development will be potentially as
significant as Brunelleschi's and Alberti's "invention" of perspective in
the late fifteenth century. In the coming century, it will become increasingly difficult for people to think of images as *not* being related to time.
I wrote an article a few years ago entitled "Video Black—The Mortality
of the Image" where I tried to show that an image now is mortal, it has
been given a birth and a death, and therefore has a finite existence.
It even has behavior. So maybe for the aestheticians of the next century,
the field of visual aesthetics will be a kind of science of behavior.

    *A.P.: So you agree that artists working with video use this medium
because of its characteristics intentionally to deal with the human condition?*
If artists are drawn to these themes in their life and work then, yes,
they will find that video is very well suited to expressing these

concerns. But these issues go beyond a specific medium and become a reflection of our times. People such as Jenny Holzer and Christian Boltanski, whom I feel an affinity with, don't work necessarily with video. On the other hand, I don't feel that this work needs to be absolute, even though it is so necessary, urgent, and vital for our contemporary life. I accept and respect many forms of creative expression. As frustrating as it is that someone may only want from art to have something they think is nice to look at on their wall, this is still a valid impulse and a lot better than many other responses and actions. I can even feel a connection to the "Sunday painters" who show their works in the park. Creativity and the transformation of inspiration into action is a universal and fundamental part of humanity.

A.P.: Another characteristic of yours and of the artists mentioned before is maybe the use of video as the right instrument to give certain images life—such as those by Marie-Jo Lafontaine, who in her latest video installation deals with fire; you work with water, too. These are not the right images to be expressed by painting, because painting is not modern any more in this sense, with regard to the age of multi-media and television today.

Yes, each medium has affinities with certain things and connections to specific times and places. Painting, for example, was an essential part of the Renaissance, with its suitability to be integrated with architecture, allowing it to achieve the role of a dominant mass medium. But you can also think of the present situation where the video or television medium has a very high accepted truth factor in our society. In other words, most people who look at an image on the TV box think of it not necessarily as "truthful" in terms of context, but accept it unquestionably as something real, something that actually happened. I am not speaking only of the political aspects here, which have been much discussed, but of this phenomenon as a fundamental condition of the medium. For example, if you see an image of a stranger's face, someone you have never seen before, you know it was shot with a video camera and therefore you know that this person must exist. This "ontological confirmation" aspect of the medium is in the process of changing, as computer images become more and more indistinguishable from camera images, and it will be interesting to see what happens. In terms of my own work, in the large triptych piece, the *Nantes Triptych*, you have a classical form from the history of art that is represented in the medium of video. For today's viewer, if these images of birth and death, which have been depicted many times in history, were presented as painted images, they would be seen as subjective views, personal interpretations of these events.

O.N.: Painting and video are just different languages …
They have different values at different times in history.

O.N.: When you as an artist work with video, you are confronted with at least two problems. The first is this very attitude towards the "real" image, because it is a mediated *image, it is not what you see; the other is that we who are familiar with TV expect a* narrative, *we expect that there is a story. But you do not tell stories. It seems to me that your work is, for you as well as for the spectator, a* spiritual *practice. Do you think this is a misunderstanding, or do you use exactly this medium to develop the experience of the medium, of what it mediates?*
You are absolutely right in saying that I am making my work for myself. I think that all art, to be honest, must be a form of individual practice as you say, and not a form of address to an audience. However, the danger here is that private things can easily be incomprehensible or irrelevant to others. Put this together with the model we are using right now of the 150-year-old French idea of the avant-garde, the individual artist outside of the academy and tradition, and so on, and you can see the risk of creating a field of individuals just doing their own separate things. But to come back: yes, my works are first and foremost made for myself. They come from questions that arise from my own experience, sometimes in such a direct and simple way that it astounds me that people assume that they come from another kind of thinking or abstract speculation. It is thoroughly concrete for me. You know, our baby was born and it was one of the most profound experiences of my life, and so afterwards I felt the overwhelming desire, the *need* to show this, to share the knowledge of this experience. I guess in the end what's important for me is that experiences then get *shared*. The sharing is essential: it imparts life to the work. This is the gift side of art, as Lewis Hyde so eloquently talks about in his important book *The Gift*. If you look at the function of art historically,

its essence is this, the sharing of gifts. The notion of art as commodity, on the other hand, is relatively new. And it is this, I think, that is an underlying source of disorientation for artists today, even if many don't acknowledge or recognize it. If someone is creative, let's say, they play the piano or whatever, in English we say that they have a *gift*, a creative *gift*. Any artist knows that you must give something of yourself to each work. Something, large or small, gets burned up, used up, like a raw material consumed to give energy. When you put money into this system, it can be so arbitrary. I mean, how can you take this inspiration you have been given and put a price on it, and then compare it economically to other inspirations? Now, I am not here arguing to disengage art from the economic market system. This is a dominant language of today's culture. And I am not saying that there shouldn't be a price on art. I see no reason why a great work of art shouldn't cost more than, say, a small plane. But understanding the essential gift nature of art can put us back in touch with the inner reasons for doing this work and wanting to be close to it in the first place. And remember the most important aspect of gifts: that a gift is only a gift if the person who receives it can use it. This is the essence of the whole equation. It is the reason why all artworks, to be art, must be functional. In this sense I don't really care or expect that people will like all the works in my show. As cultural professionals, you or I should study all the things, regardless of whether they speak to us on a deep personal level. But generally speaking, you only need a couple of paintings, a couple of poems, a couple of pieces of music to last a whole lifetime. I have succeeded if a person walks away with one image, one thought, one realization, one feeling that they can use in their life, even if they can't remember my name, the names of the pieces, or how many they saw.

    O.N.: I see a problem in what you said, in so far as when people speak of a "function" of art many of them think that this means that art should function as this or that. And that's not what you mean.

Yes, that's not what I am saying. Or they confuse it with the William Morris thing—you know, the Arts and Crafts Movement in the late nineteenth century: a cup has to be beautifully made by an artist, but you also have to use it to drink coffee.

O.N.: What you mean with "function" is that art has to have a place in our life ...

Yes, it is a function in the original sense of art, in the sense of *ritual*. You can use it to learn something in your life, to go deeper. I showed my work *Science of the Heart* at an art fair in France, and a woman came in whose father had just died from a heart attack. In my piece there is an image of a human heart beating slower and slower until it stops. Then it comes to life and starts again. It's a difficult image to watch, but it is not negative or pessimistic. It contains both sides of life. A circle is not negative or positive, it's a circulation. So, what's down becomes up, and it all comes around. When she saw that piece, it really touched her and made sense for her in her life at the time, and she wrote me a letter saying that although her father was dead she felt him coming back to life through the piece. Things have become so backwards in the world of contemporary art. *These* are the essential things about art, and it is the critical analytical practices that dominate our lives as art professionals which are the secondary functions.

O.N.: So what connects the medium of video with life is time. That is, video is a medium that uses time in two senses of the word. Life also has to do with time, and it stops at some time. You have the idea of the cycle in your video work which is very different from our experience of life—at least before the background of European culture. If you believe in a cycle of different lives you have even more connections between video cycles and spiritual experiences. But in any case you see your own life as a part of something else. So it is some kind of religion, you see yourself bound to something which is greater than you.

Yes, there is a kind of religion there in the original sense of "religion," as opposed to, let's say, Christianity today.

A.P.: I read in the catalogue of your exhibition in Düsseldorf that at some moment in your life you made a cut with the Christian religion with which you had grown up, but at another place you say that you are religious. And when I told that to Otto, he said "Yes, but in the original sense of 'religion.'"

Yes, but then even that comes around. After moving away from my Christian upbringing, I got interested in Eastern culture, and I went to Japan, and I was practicing Zen meditation, and so. Then when I came back from Japan, I studied more intensively people such as the great Japanese lay Zen scholar Daisetz Suzuki, and another very important person for me, Ananda Coomaraswamy, the Sri Lankan art historian and scholar who redefined how Asian art was discussed and analyzed. Both Suzuki and Coomaraswamy were raised in the East in direct contact with ancient unbroken traditions, and spent their later years in the West, specifically America. Then, when Suzuki, Coomaraswamy, and a number of other Asian intellectuals got to the West, they began to study Western history looking for the same connections, which they knew to be there. They began writing about people I was not familiar with, such as Meister Eckhart, St. John of the Cross, Hildegard von Bingen, and Plotinus, as well as Plato and Aristotle. They recognized these people not as individuals, but as part of the other side of the Western tradition, a tradition that was carried on in the East and developed well beyond the advent of rational positivistic thinking (which took over in the West) and right up into the twentieth century. Then I started reading about very early Christianity, about the desert fathers in the Nile valley and Syria, staying out in the wilderness like Zen monks on retreat, studying with their spiritual masters. It was a revelation for me to find these roots in my own religion's history.

A.P.: But that is not practiced now under the present pope.
No, it's not practiced. This is religion in the negative view, the *via negativa* as it is called, as opposed to the accepted *via positiva.*

O.N.: The aspect of "the way" that is not based upon dogmas you have to believe but that emphasizes, rather, a certain conduct of life and is open for any human being can be found in other religions also, for instance in the Jewish tradition with its "halachah" view.
It's about union with the Divine—that it's possible for the individual to directly connect his or her spirit to the Godhead and not have to go through the priest. Of course, this is politically dangerous to the established powers. The English poet and artist William Blake, one of the great visionary artists in recent Western history, never felt that his gifts of insight were unique. On more than one occasion, he affirmed that *all* people are capable of having visions and being in contact with the Divine Imagination.

Distance and nearness are attributes of bodies,
The journeyings of spirits are after another sort.
You journeyed from the embryo state to rationality
    without footsteps or stages or change of place,
The journey of the soul involves not time and place.
And my body learnt from the soul its mode of journeying,
Now my body has renounced the bodily mode of journeying.
It journeys secretly and without form, though under a form.

—Jallaludin Rumi (1207–1273), *The Masnavi*

Previous page: Tiny Deaths, 1993, video/sound installation

Chronology

1951 Born in New York.

1960–73 Captain of the "TV Squad," P.S.20 Queens, New York. In 1964 makes first experiments with parents' 8mm movie camera and audiotape recorder.

1969–73 Studies art at Syracuse University, New York, and graduates from the Experimental Studios at the College of Visual and Performing Arts. In 1970, becomes founding member of Synapse, a group that installs a cable TV system and early color studio at Syracuse University. In 1972 makes an installation and his first three videotapes. During 1973 and 1974 produces 12 videotapes, five sound installations and ten video installations. First exhibitions, with Nam June Paik, Peter Campus, and Bruce Nauman.

1972–74 Technical advisor for video at the Everson Museum of Art. Works as an exhibition assistant to Peter Campus, Frank Gillette, Nam June Paik, and other artists. In 1973 meets David Tudor, performing in his Rainforest project and beginning a long-term relationship with him initiated by the formation in 1974 of Composers Inside Electronics (Tudor, Viola, and five other musicians). In 1974, first solo exhibition, four video and sound installations at The Kitchen, New York.

1974–76 Works as technical director and head of production at Art/Tapes/22 Video Studio, Florence. For *Red Tape*, 1975, uses the new portable color video camera for the first time. In Florence, shows the video/sound installation *Il Vapore*, 1975, first installation shown in Europe. Creates *Four Songs*, 1976, one of the first videotapes by an artist using computer editing techniques. Travels to the Solomon Islands in the South Pacific to record traditional music and dance, and to document the Moro cult movement. First visits Japan in 1976.

1976–81 Artist-in-residence at WNET/Thirteen Television Laboratory, New York.

1977–80 Travels to Java and Bali, Indonesia, to record traditional music and performing arts. Completes *The Reflecting Pool*, a collection of five videotapes. In 1977, is invited to Australia by Kira Perov (future wife and collaborator), director of cultural activities, La Trobe University, Melbourne. In 1978 they begin to work and travel together.

In "documenta 6," Kassel, exhibits *He Weeps for You*, 1976, which is then shown in 1979 at The Museum of Modern Art, New York. In 1978, receives Visual Artist Fellowship—Video, from the National Endowment for the Arts. In 1979, travels to the Tunisian Sahara Desert to videotape mirages, and produces *Chott el-Djerid (A Portrait in Light and Heat)*.

1980–81 Receives Japan/US Creative Arts Fellowship and lives in Japan with Kira Perov for 18 months to study traditional Japanese culture and advanced video technology. Practices Zen meditation with shiatsu master Shuya Abe and begins long-term relationship with Zen priest and painter Daien Tanaka. For *Chott el-Djerid*, receives Grand Prize at the Portopia International Video Art Festival, Kobe, Japan. In 1981 becomes the first artist-in-residence at Sony Corporation's Atsugi Research Laboratories. Produces *Hatsu Yume (First Dream)*. With Kira Perov, moves to Southern California.

1982 Travels to Ladakh in the Himalayas to observe religious art and ritual in Tibetan Buddhist monasteries. First comprehensive museum exhibition of videotapes, presented at the Whitney Museum of American Art, New York. Receives Video Artist Fellowship from the Rockefeller Foundation.

1983 Teaches advanced video at the California Institute for the Arts, Valencia. Becomes artist-in-residence at Memorial Medical Center, Long Beach, pursuing interest in imaging technologies of the human body. Produces the instalation *Science of the Heart* and the videotape *Anthem*. First one-person museum exhibition in Europe presented at ARC Museé d'Art Moderne de la Ville de Paris (two installations and videotapes). Produces *Room for St. John of the Cross*, an installation inspired by the 16th-century Spanish poet and mystic. *Hatsu Yume* is awarded Grand Prize at the US Film and Video Festival in Park City, Utah.

1984 Travels to the Fiji Islands to record Hindu firewalking ceremony. Begins long-term project on animal consciousness, and becomes artist-in-residence at San Diego Zoo. Spends three weeks with a herd of bison in Wind Cave National Park, South Dakota. Receives the inaugural Polaroid Video Art Award. *Anthem* wins Grand Prize for Video Art at Video Culture/Canada, Toronto, and First Prize for Video Art at the Athens Film/Video Festival, Ohio.

1985 Receives Fellowship in Video from the J. S. Guggenheim Memorial Foundation. Exhibits two installations and videotapes in "Summer 1985," Museum of Contemporary Art, Los Angeles, first major museum exhibition of installations in the United States.

1986 Completes *I Do Not Know What It Is I Am Like*, a feature-length videotape integrating work with natural landscape, animal consciousness, and religious ritual.

1987 Closes studio for six months to travel with wife Kira Perov throughout the southwestern United States to study ancient Native American archeological sites and rock art. Begins recording exclusively in black and white, including studies of nocturnal desert landscapes with low-light and infra-red video cameras. "Bill Viola: Installations and Videotapes," exhibition at the Museum of Modern Art, New York. Receives Maya Deren Award from the American Film Institute. *I Do Not Know What It Is I Am Like* is awarded First Prize for Video Art at the Festival International d'Art Vidéo et des Nouvelles Images Electroniques de Locarno, Lago Maggiore, Switzerland.

1988 First son, Blake, is born. "Bill Viola: Survey of a Decade," exhibition at the Contemporary Arts Museum, Houston, Texas. "Bill Viola: Installation and Videotapes," exhibition at Riverside Studios, London, first travelling show in Europe, to Dublin, Seville, Lisbon, and Basel.

1989 Records the childbirth process (to be incorporated into several works), initiating a renewed focus on the fundamental themes of the human condition. Premiers *The City of Man*, his first installation using video disc technology, altered aspect ratio, and first direct use of a classical art form, the triptych altarpiece, at the Brockton Art Museum/ Fuller Memorial, Brockton, Massachusetts. Receives a five-year Fellowship from the John D. and Catherine T. MacArthur Foundation. Largest exhibition to date (five installations) is held at Fukui Prefectural Museum of Art, Fukui City, Japan, as part of the Third Fukui International Video Biennial.

1991 Mother dies in February. Second son Andrei is born nine months later. After four years of production, completes *The Passing*, a meditation on birth, death, and the desert landscape in black and white. Creates first permanent installation, *The Stopping Mind*, commissioned by the Museum für Moderne Kunst, Frankfurt.

1992 Produces nine new installations, most of which focus on themes of sleep, death, birth, and mortality. Makes his first installation recorded with 35mm high-speed film, The *Arc of Ascent*, for "documenta 9," Kassel. First exhibition in a private gallery, Donald Young Gallery, Seattle. Creates a 24-hour-a-day continuous window projection, *To Pray Without Ceasing*. Exhibition of two installations at Anthony d'Offay Gallery, London, in September. "Unseen Images," an installation of seven new works from 1992, opens at Kunsthalle Düsseldorf in December, travelling for two years to museums in Europe and Israel. Receives a "Command Publique" a commission from the Centre National des Arts Plastiques, France, to produce *Nantes Triptych*, an installation to be shown in a 17th-century chapel, the Chapelle de l'Oratoire, Musée des Beaux-Arts de Nantes.

1993 Awarded the first Medienkunstpreis, presented jointly by Zentrum für Kunst und Medientechnologie, Karlsruhe, and Siemens Kulturprogramm. Receives the Skowhegan Award for video installation, New York. *The Passing* is awarded first prize at Festival International de Video, Cidade de Vigo, Spain. Exhibits six installations and videotapes, 1982–1992, at Musée d'art contemporain de Montréal. *An Instrument of Simple Sensation*, 1983, is restored and exhibited for the first time since 1983 at Anthony d'Offay Gallery, London.

1994 Invited by the Ensemble Modern to create his first work with music, *Déserts*, a film to be shown with the live performance of *Déserts* by Edgard Varèse (1883–1965), commissioned by ZDF/ARTE, Mainz, premiered in October at Wien Modern, Konzerthaus, Vienna, and broadcast on German Television in December; first production using full film crew, constructed set, and 35mm high-speed film in combination with video segments. Completes *Pneuma*, an installation based on the visual limits of an image and the limits of memory. Commissioned by the Bohen Foundation, New York, to produce *Stations*, a large-scale installation for five projections of the human figure submerged under water, first shown at the inaugural exhibition of the American Center, Paris.

1995 Receives degree of Doctor of Fine Arts, *honorus causa*, Syracuse University, New York. *Pneuma* is exhibited at the Anthony d'Offay Gallery, London. Represents the United States at the 46th Venice Biennale, where he presents "Buried Secrets," an exhibition of five new works created to function together as an integrated whole in the US Pavilion.

1996 Commissioned by The Chaplaincy to the Arts and Recreation in North East England to create an installation for the 900-year-old Durham Cathedral, the first video installation to be acquired by an institution of the Church of England, *The Messenger*.

1997 Receives honorary Doctor of Fine Arts degree from The School of The Art Institute of Chicago. The Whitney Museum of American Art organizes a 25-year survey exhibition of video installations and videotapes which opens at the Los Angeles County Museum of Art and travels in the next two years to The Whitney Museum, New York; Stedelijk Museum, Amsterdam; Museum für Moderne Kunst, Schirn Kunsthalle, and Karmaliterkloster, Frankfurt am Main; San Francisco Museum of Modern Art; and The Art Institute of Chicago.

Select Bibliography

Bélisle, Josée, ed. *Bill Viola*. Montreal: Musée d'art contemporain de Montréal, 1993 (French and English). Text by Josée Bélisle.

Bloch, Dany, ed. *Bill Viola*. Paris: ARC, Musée d'Art Moderne de la Ville de Paris, December 1983–January 1984 (French and English). Texts by Anne-Marie Duguet, Deirdre Boyle, John Hanhardt, Bill Viola.

Dantas, Marcello, coordinator. *Bill Viola Território do Invisível/Site of the Unseen*. Rio de Janeiro: Magnetoscópio, 1994 (Portuguese and English). Texts by Ivana Bentes, Kathy Rae Huffman; interview by Jörg Zutter.

de Loisy, Jean, ed. *Bill Viola: The Sleep of Reason*. Jouy-en-Josas, France: Le Fondation Cartier pour l'art contemporain, 1990.

Feldman, Melissa, and H. Ashley Kistler. *Bill Viola: Slowly Turning Narrative*. Philadelphia: Institute of Contemporary Art; Richmond: Virginia Museum of Fine Arts, 1992.

London, Barbara, ed. *Bill Viola: Installations and Videotapes*. New York: The Museum of Modern Art, 1987. Texts by J. Hoberman, Donald Kuspit, Barbara London; selected writings by Bill Viola.

Pühringer, Alexander, ed. *Bill Viola*. Salzburg: Verlag Ritter Klagenfurt/Salzburger Kunstverein, 1994 (German and English). Texts by Freideman Malsch, Celia Montolio, Otto Neumaier; conversation between Bill Viola, Otto Neumaier, and Alexander Pühringer.

Syring, Marie Luise, ed. *Bill Viola: Unseen Images*. Düsseldorf: Verlag R. Meyer, 1992 (German, English, and French). Texts by Marie Luise Syring, Rolf Lauter; interview by Jörg Zutter. Reprinted in expanded version: Basso, Carlota Alvarez, coord. *Bill Viola: Más allá de la mirada (imágenes no vistas)*. Madrid: Museo Nacional Centro de Arte Reina Sofía, 1993 (Spanish).

Valentini, Valentina, ed. *Bill Viola: Vedere con la mente e con il cuore*. Parco Duca di Cesarò, Italy: Taormina Arte, 1993 (Italian). Text by Valentina Valentini; selected writings by Bill Viola. Interviews: David A. Ross by Gianfranco Mantegna; Bill Viola by Jörg Zutter.

Yapelli, Tina with Toby Kamps, coords. *Bill Viola: Images and Spaces.* Madison, Wisconsin: Madison Art Center, 1994. Text by Tina Yapelli; selected writings by Bill Viola.

Zeitlin, Marilyn, ed. *Bill Viola: Survey of a Decade.* Houston: Contemporary Arts Museum, 1988. Texts by Deirdre Boyle, Kathy Rae Huffman, Christopher Knight, Michael Nash, Joan Seeman Robinson, Gene Youngblood, Marilyn Zeitlin.

Zeitlin, Marilyn, ed. *Bill Viola: Buried Secrets.* Tempe, Arizona: Arizona State University Art Museum, 1995 (English and Italian, for the United States Pavilion, 46th Venice Biennale).

Writings by Bill Viola

*Essays reprinted here have been revised by the artist.

'The European Scene and Other Observations." In *Video Art: An Anthology*, edited by Ira Schneider and Beryl Korot, 268–78. New York: Harcourt Brace Jovanovich, 1976.

*"The Porcupine and the Car." *Image Forum* (Tokyo), vol.2, no.3 (January 1981): 46–55 (Japanese).

*"Sight Unseen: Enlightened Squirrels and Fatal Experiments." *Video 80*, no.4 (Spring–Summer 1982): 31–3. Also published in *Bill Viola*, edited by Dany Bloch, 15–20 (French and English). Paris: ARC, Musée d'Art Moderne de la Ville de Paris, 1983. In *Bill Viola: Vedere con la mente e con il cuore*, edited by Valentina Valentini 31–6 (Italian). Rome: Gangemi Editore, 1993.

*"Will There be Condominiums in Data Space?" *Video 80*, no.5 (Fall 1982): 36–41. Also published in *Communications*, edited by Raymond Bellour and Anne-Marie Duguet, no.48 (1988): 61–74 (French). Also published in *Electrovisions: Japan '87 Television Festival*, 34–42. Tokyo: Video Gallery SCAN, 1987 (Japanese). As "Yaura-t-il copropriété dans l'espace de donnés," in *Communications* (Paris) 48, edited by Raymond Bellour and Anne-Marie Duguet, 48 (November 1988): 61–74 (French). In *Bill Viola: Vedere con la mente e con il cuore*, 37–45 (Italian).

"Video as Art." *Video Systems*, vol.8, no.7 (July 1982): 26–35. Also published as "An Aid to the Appreciation of Video Art." *1ère Semaine Internationale de Vidéo*, edited by Alan McCluskey, 14–19. Geneva: Maison des Jeunes et de la Culture, 1985.

"The Real Technological Revolution." *Cinema Canada*, no.114 (January 1985): 11. First presented as a paper for conference, Convergence, Montréal, 1984.

"Some Recommendations on Establishing Standards for the Exhibition and Distribution of Video Works." In *The Media Arts in Transition*, edited by Bill Horrigan, 50–7. Minneapolis: Walker Art Center, 1983.

*"History, 10 Years, and the Dreamtime." In *Video: A Retrospective, Long Beach Museum of Art 1974–1984*, edited by Kathy Rae Huffman, 18–23. Long Beach: Long Beach Museum of Art, 1984. Also published in *Bill Viola: Vedere con la mente e con il cuore*, 47–58 (Italian).

*"I Do Not Know What It Is I Am Like" (notes for laser disc, VHS). Los Angeles: Voyager Press; Boston: The Contemporary Art Television Fund, 1986. Also published in *Toyama Now '87 – New Art from Around the Pacific*, 29, 84, 99–102 (Japanese). Toyama: Toyama Museum of Modern Art, 1987. In *Genlock*, no.7 (French). Geneva: L'Association pour la Création Vidéo, 1987. In *Bill Viola: Installations and Videotapes*, edited by Barbara London, 59–62. New York: The Museum of Modern Art, 1987. In *Bill Viola: Vedere con la mente e con il cuore*, 136–8 (Italian). In *Bill Viola*, edited by Alexander Pühringer, 13–15 (German), 16–17 (English). Salzburg: Verlag Ritter Klagenfurt/Salzburger Kunstverein, 1994.

*"Bill Viola: Statements by the Artist." In *Summer 1985*, edited by Julia Brown. Los Angeles: Museum of Contemporary Art, 1985. Also published as "Pasajes y Tiempo," *Telos: Cuadernos de Comunicacion, Technologia y Sociedad* (Madrid) 9 (March–May 1987): 135–8.

*"The Sound of One Line Scanning." In *Sound by Artists*, edited by Dan Lander and Micah Lexier, 39–54. Banff: Walter Phillips Gallery; Toronto: Art Metropole, 1990. Extract first published in *1986 National Video Festival*, edited by Lynne Kirby, 40–4. Los Angeles: American Film Institute, 1986. Also published as "Le son d'une ligne de

balayage." *Chimères* (Paris) 11 (Spring 1991): 98–120. In *Bill Viola: Vedere con la mente e con il cuore*, 69–80 (Italian).

*"Video Black – The Mortality of the Image." In *Illuminating Video: An Essential Guide to Video Art*, edited by Doug Hall and Sally Jo Fifer, 476–86. San Francisco: Bay Area Video Coalition; New York: Aperture, 1990. In *Bill Viola: Vedere con la mente e con il cuore*, 59–68 (Italian).

*"Perception, Technology, Imagination, and the Landscape." *Enclitic* 11, no.3 (July 1992): 57–60. Also published as "Perception, tehnologie, imagination et paysage." *Trafic 3* (Summer 1992): 77–82 (French). A transcript of the original version, presented as part of a panel discussion at Spiral Hall, Tokyo (Japan 89: 2nd Video Television Festival at Spiral, August 5, 1989), was published under the title "The Visionary Landscape of Perception: The Earth is the ultimate HDTV" in *Delicate Technology*, edited by Video Gallery SCAN (Fujiko Nakaya) and I&S, 129–48 (Japanese and English). Tokyo: Video Television Festival Organizing Committee, SCAN, 1989.

*"Statement by Bill Viola." In *Japan 92: The 3rd Video Television Festival*, edited by Haruo Fukuzumi and Keiko Tamaki, 152–3. Tokyo: Video Gallery SCAN, 1992.

*"The Body Asleep." In *Pour la Suite du Monde: Cahier: Propos et Projets*, edited by Gilles Godmer and Réal Lussier, 56–7 (French), 80–1 (English). Montreal: Musée d'art contemporain de Montréal, 1992. In *Bill Viola: Vedere con la mente e con il cuore*, 81–4 (Italian).

"On Transcending the Water Glass." In *CyberArts: Exploring Art and Technology*, edited by Linda Jacobson, 3–5. San Francisco: Miller Freeman Inc., 1992.

Reasons for Knocking at an Empty House: Writings 1973–1994. Edited by Robert Violette in collaboration with the author. Introduction by Jean-Christophe Ammann. Cambridge, Massachusetts: The MIT Press; London: Thames & Hudson; in association with Anthony d'Offay Gallery, London, 1995.

Index

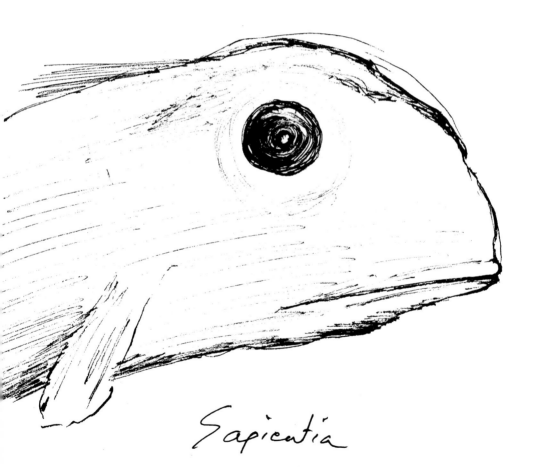

Sapientia

The Universe continues to be in the present tense.

—Ibn Arabi (1165–1240)